The Heritage of
MUSIC
VOLUME II

Essays by E. H. Fellowes, Philip Radcliffe,
Herbert Wiseman, W. H. Hadow, D. F. Tovey,
Dennis Arundell, Tom S. Wotton, Hubert
J. Foss, H. P. Morgan-Browne, Cecil Gray,
F. Bonavia, Walter Ford

Collected and Edited by
HUBERT J. FOSS

OXFORD UNIVERSITY PRESS
London : Humphrey Milford
1934

OXFORD
UNIVERSITY PRESS
AMEN HOUSE, E.C. 4
London Edinburgh Glasgow
Leipzig New York Toronto
Melbourne Capetown Bombay
Calcutta Madras Shanghai
HUMPHREY MILFORD
PUBLISHER TO THE
UNIVERSITY

FOREWORD

THE most promising characteristic of the musical scholarship or criticism of our own time is that it has ceased to be exclusive. It has amply realized the existence and also the importance of other composers than those who are generally termed 'great'. It knows that historical progress is not a journey from the lower to the higher planes, and that universality of appeal is not necessarily a sole criterion of musical merit or achievement. Indeed, more composers of the past have arisen through the new ideas of criticism into stellar prominence in our lifetime than have sunk into tired oblivion, and this very fact is sufficient to show that our celestial horizon has widened.

In the previous volume of *The Heritage of Music* I predicted an additional series of essays on composers if the public appeared, by its interest, to need them. The response has, I am glad to say, fully justified my hopes, and here is the second collection. It might seem to be a confession of the weakness of the first volume. Actually it is a token of the strength of the second, and a further sign that 'greatness' is not confined to the chosen few but resides in small places as well as big, in the obscurity of lesser achievement no less than in the popularity of the large.

For this second volume treats of not Bach but Handel: not Palestrina but Byrd. Mendelssohn takes the place of Schumann and Chopin that of Brahms. In opera Wagner and Purcell are supplanted by Gluck, Rameau, Weber, and Verdi. Schubert and Wolf are opposed in the tradition of the *lied*, and the two Scarlattis occupy the seat of Mozart at the keyboard.

Who shall say that any one of these composers is worse than the next, or better? Who, on the other hand, can truthfully say that each of them has not given us some

treasures without which every national collection of the
gems of art would be poorer? It may be invidious to
declare that this second volume is better than the first:
but it is true that it deals, equally authoritatively, with music
of equal value to that of the composers who were there
discussed. It is important that this volume should not be
considered as a secondary adjunct. Had there been no
first assembly, this one would have sufficiently represented
the title of the book.

To make the object of the series of essays clear, I venture
to repeat some of the words of the previous Foreword.
After an explanation that the models of Mr. Livingstone's
Legacy of Greece and Mr. Bailey's *Legacy of Rome* had been
followed, and that the link of subject is sufficient to draw
the book together into one unit, though the authors be
many, I added:

'It is an incidental matter, but one of considerable
interest and relevance, that the invitations to authors were
all made in precisely the same words, which requested "not
a biography or a criticism but a summing-up of the place
the composer holds in musical tradition and his present
and past influence".'

My debt of gratitude is obvious, to the authors and (as
I said before) to their patience, during the difficulties and
delays that beset any composite volume in its progress
from handwriting to manufactured book. I should like to
add an especial word of thanks to those of the musical public
whose practical interest in the first volume encouraged the
editor and contributors to make this second. Perhaps a
third will be asked for: there is still plenty of material.

H. J. F.

September 1933.

CONTENTS

I

WILLIAM BYRD
(1543–1623)
By E. H. FELLOWES

As we look back upon the history of English music we seem to see, beyond the almost barren plains of the eighteenth and nineteenth centuries, two distant ranges of mountains. The nearer of the two represents the Restoration school, in which the work of Purcell stands out as the most conspicuous peak; and in the farther distance we see that higher and wider range which we recognize as the Tudor school, and here the work of Byrd has the chief prominence. Purcell and Byrd are consequently two names in English music that stand for something more than individual achievement; for when our minds turn to Purcell we cannot allow ourselves to be wholly unmindful of the group of composers that included Blow and Pelham Humphrey, for example. As the greatest of them, he is their representative. Similarly Byrd is the outstanding and also representative name in the great group of sixteenth-century English musicians.

It follows, then, that if two English composers are to be selected for inclusion in a series of essays dealing with the leading composers of all nationalities, Byrd and Purcell have indisputable claim to be chosen. Purcell has already had a place in the former volume of *The Heritage of Music*, and Byrd duly follows in the present volume.

It is not our purpose in this short essay to discuss the school of Tudor composers in a general way, yet it is necessary, in view of its almost total neglect in the past, to stress its important position in the history of European music; and this is at last coming to be recognized by leading musicians on the Continent as well as in England. England has received all too little credit for the important contribution

B

which she made to modern music in its infancy. England led Europe in the thirteenth century with a school of musicians in advance of anything possessed by the Netherlands at this period. Again, in the fifteenth century, the English musicians, under the leadership of Dunstable, were given the pride of place on the authority of Johann Tinctoris, who also mentioned the encouragement given to music in the endowed church choirs in this country. If the supremacy passed for a short time early in the sixteenth century to the musicians of the Lowlands and Italy, it reverted once again to England in the latter years of that century. Fairfax, Taverner, Tallis, and Tye are among the names which form links in the chain that binds the school of Dunstable to that of the Elizabethans, and when we reach the year 1600 we find that there were as many as six Englishmen in the very highest rank of musical composition, living and working as contemporaries: albeit one was then a veteran and one a mere youth. Few countries can at any date have boasted such a sextet of contemporary musicians as Byrd, Morley, Wilbye, Weelkes, Dowland, and Gibbons.

And the greatest of these was Byrd. Born in 1543, or late in 1542, he had the good fortune to reach manhood not during, but just after, the most troubled times of the bitter controversy and harassing conditions that must have affected musicians so intimately during the latter part of the reign of Henry VIII, and the reign of Edward VI and Mary. The dissolution of the monasteries, which involved the disestablishment of numberless choirs, had occurred a decade before his birth; Byrd thus escaped the experience suffered by Tallis and a vast crowd of musicians of being turned out of house and home with occupation gone. Again, the substitution of the vernacular for the Latin tongue in the services of the Reformed Church had been effected while he was a mere child; and when, at the age of nineteen or twenty, he became organist of Lincoln Cathedral, the new problems of setting English words to music and performing them in the choir had to some extent already been solved. The time was in fact precisely ripe for the advent of a man of first-class genius such as Byrd possessed. The old traditions of the Latin rites had not yet passed away so far but that he still could follow them, building upon them, with modern invention and imagination, structures more beautiful than any yet devised by an English composer, in the form of the Mass and the Motet. And the new traditions of the English rites had not yet passed the experimental stages of development; it remained for Byrd to set a new and enduring standard of design and attainment for the English Service and Anthem.

Turning to secular fields, the working life of Byrd from the age of twenty to eighty saw big developments in the mechanical side of keyed instruments, and of string instruments too, and in both these departments Byrd worked with the hand of a finished master, though at the same time he was but a pioneer. Once again, in the department of the madrigal and solo song he seized upon these forms of art, as newly brought from Italy, and made them his own with a distinction and individuality of style of rare excellence and beauty. The versatility of Byrd's genius is in fact among the most remarkable features of his work; no other composer of the period, either English or continental, can compare with him in this matter. He not only excelled in every branch of musical composition known in his day, but ventured into new paths hitherto untrodden; and in every branch he met with success at least as conspicuous as that attained by any of his contemporaries. Like Palestrina and Orlando di Lasso he excelled in Latin Church music; like Tallis, Weelkes, and Gibbons in English Church music; like Marenzio, Monteverde, Morley, Wilbye, and Weelkes in madrigals; like Farnaby, Bull, and Gibbons in keyboard music; like Tomkins and Ward in chamber-music for strings; like Dowland in song.

We have little material to form any precise judgement of his personality and character, nor do we know much about his career. He was but a few years at Lincoln; and after his appointment to the Chapel Royal the remainder of his long life was spent either in London or its near neighbourhood, at one time at Harlington in Middlesex, and latterly at Stondon in Essex. It was there that he died on July 4th, 1623. A certain number of details about his later years at Stondon have recently come to light, chiefly owing to the researches of the late W. B. Squire. These reveal his character in a somewhat unpleasant light. We find him engaged in litigation with Mrs. Shelley, the former owner of his house, Stondon Place. We also find him quarrelling with his neighbours about a right of way on his farm; and his relations with the vicar of Stondon seem to have been the reverse of cordial. In his family, too, there was trouble with his eldest son, whom he eventually disinherited. Possibly these troubles are to be explained as the weaknesses of old age; and perhaps what is known as the 'musician's temperament' became more difficult to control in his years of retirement. On the other hand, there is evidence which points to a deep sincerity of mind and a breadth of sympathy of a sort that in those days of bitter controversy cannot have been too common. For example, it speaks volumes for his width of outlook that with his steadfast and lifelong adherence to the unreformed party of the Church he should have brought to the setting of the words of the new English Liturgy a zeal no less fervent and a skill no less brilliant than that which he displayed in his Latin settings. Byrd was pre-eminently a man of devout religious feeling; this is unmistakably evidenced in almost every page of his Church music; and the same spirit is breathed in his dedicatory addresses to his patrons and the prefatory statements in his printed volumes of works. Here are some phrases selected from these sources. In the dedication of *Gradualia*, Bk. I, Byrd attributes any merit or beauty in his music to the spontaneous suggestion of the sacred words themselves; thus:

'ita profecto, Sacris sententiis, quibus Dei ipsius, cælestiumque Civium, laudes decantantur, nulla nisi cælestis quaedam (quantum eniti possumus) harmonia conveniat. Porro, illis ipsis sententiis (ut experiendo didici) adeo abstrusa atque recondita vis inest, ut divina cogitanti, diligenterque ac serio pervolutanti, nescio quonam modo, aptissimi quique numeri, quas sponte accurrant sua, animoque minime ignavo atque inerti, liberaliter ipsi sese offerant.'[1]

The following (from *Psalmes, Sonets, and Songs*, 1588) is Byrd's eighth and last 'reason . . . to perswade every one to learne to sing': 'The better the voyce is, the meeter it is to honour and serve God therewith, and the voyce of man is chiefely to be imployed to that ende. *Omnis spiritus laudet Dominum*.' And in 'The Epistle to the Reader' (ibid.) 'If thou find any thing heere worthy of lykeing and commendation, give prayse unto God, from whome (as a most pure and plentiful fountaine) all good guifts of Scyence doe flow, whose name be glorified for ever.'

And apart from these quotations we must recall the feelings of universal admiration and veneration with which Byrd was regarded by the musicians of his own day. To them he was 'the musician never to be named without reverence'; he was 'homo mirabilis'; he was the subject of 'unfeigned affection'; he was 'Britannicae Musicae Parens' —the Parent of British Music. Without doubt he was a man of striking personality, an unquestioned leader of musical thought and expression in his time; he was ready and indeed eager to contend, even to the point of legal proceedings, for any cause which he conscientiously sup-

---

[1] 'For the purpose of expressing in music the words in which the praises of God or of the citizens of heaven are to be sung, heavenly harmony, as far as we can devise it, is alone suitable. Moreover, there is present in the words themselves, as I learnt by experience, such an abstruse and hidden power, that to one who will diligently and earnestly ponder and meditate upon the sacred subjects, the most suitable musical phrases (I cannot explain how) will spontaneously suggest themselves.'

ported in temporal affairs; but in spiritual affairs, although steadfast in his convictions, he was free from those feelings of bigotry, and stood aloof from the strife which was so terribly prevalent in his day.

In order to form any idea of Byrd's position in the history of music there seems to be no means of avoiding the conventional course of reviewing the various branches of his work separately. First and foremost among these is his Latin Church music. It is this department of composition with which his name is most commonly associated; and rightly so, for it is that in which he most excelled; and the largeness of his output, even apart from its exceptional merit, gives it a degree of importance which cannot pass unnoticed. There are no more than three Masses, and one set of Lamentations, but in addition to the five published volumes of motets there are some forty or more compositions surviving in manuscript, making a total exceeding 250 motets. Byrd's first published volume was one which he shared with Tallis in 1575; his two volumes of *Cantiones Sacrae* were issued in 1589 and 1591; and the two sets of *Gradualia* in 1605 and 1607. The date of the publication of the Masses is conjectural; that for five voices may have been issued about 1590, and the other two about 1610.

To review so large a store of Church music in detail would not be possible with the limits of space at our disposal here, but a few typical examples may be selected for comment. To take the Masses first: the features that perhaps assert themselves most strongly are the melodic beauty of the phrases and the concise method of their treatment. These features are all the more noticeable if we glance back to the work of Tallis and Tye, and still more, a generation earlier, to that of Taverner. It is a common error to speak and think of Tudor Church music as if it all belonged to the same category, and was entirely covered by a uniformity of style. It must be remembered that the Tudor period extends from the year 1585 to 1603, while the term is commonly allowed, by a sort of convenient licence both in literary and musical circles, to include the reign of James I. It will be recognized, therefore, that the progress made in this period was almost as great as that made in the century that followed it. Thus the riper work of Byrd is as far removed in style from that of Taverner, or even the earlier work of Tallis, as Purcell's is from Byrd's; while the more experimental work of Orlando Gibbons, for example, his anthem 'This is the record of John', very closely foreshadows the design and style of the 'verse' anthem of Purcell's day; and Gibbons died but two years after Byrd. The truth of this statement will be the more readily appreciated if we contrast the *Sanctus* of the five-part Mass of Byrd with the *Sanctus* of Taverner's *Sine nomine* Mass. This comparison is particularly interesting, because there is a certain similarity of design in the two works. Both are for five voices; both begin with the two top voices alone; both have a homophonic phrase for all the voices at the words *Domine Deus*. The second section *Pleni sunt coeli* shows less similarity, but the phrase set in imitative counterpoint, for the words *Gloria tua,* has an amazing resemblance in the two settings:

Yet in spite of this similarity of material, its respective treatment by the two composers dates the work of each of them with absolute certainty. Byrd's setting is ripe and rich, imbued with the feeling of the closing decade of the century and the era of the madrigalists. Taverner's is stern and dignified, and by no means devoid of beauty, but clearly influenced by the atmosphere of monastic reticence. And, passing to the lovely *Agnus Dei* of Byrd's five-part Mass, it is inconceivable that Taverner, or any other composer in the days that preceded the dissolution of the monasteries, could have been inspired, as Byrd was, with the tender feeling of emotion and pathos that is expressed with such subtlety, yet without a vestige of sentimentality, in the closing passage, *dona nobis pacem*. This is perhaps the high-water mark of loveliness in all Byrd's music, surpassing even his *Ave verum* and his *Justorum animae*.

It is impossible to examine the contents of the five volumes of motets printed in Byrd's lifetime without realizing that he was a supreme master of this particular type of composition. There is an immense wealth of material contained in these books, the level of excellence is maintained at a wonderfully high standard with scarcely a dull number; every phase of religious sentiment is expressed, whether penitential, meditative, supplicatory, or laudatory; a great variety of style and treatment is also shown in the musical setting of the words, though of course the unaccompanied, or *a capella*, principle is uniformly observed.

In the 1575 volume of *Cantiones Sacrae* Byrd seems to show something more of an academic influence than in his later work. *Libera me*, set to a plain-chant melody in the Cantus part, is an example of this; and another is to be found in *Diliges Dominum*. This last motet affords an astonishing exhibition of academic skill in musical composition; it is written for eight voices in a form technically known as 'eight in four cancrizans', that is to say: designed for double choir, each of four voices; the music

for both these choirs is identical, but whereas the first
choir begins in the normal way and thus proceeds to the
concluding chord, the second choir begins on the concluding chord and sings the music backwards, ending
with the opening chord; the words are, of course, arranged
to proceed normally for both choirs so that no confusion
arises, and the extreme ingenuity of the construction is
in no way apparent to the listener.

Diliges Dominum is a fine piece of music judged solely
on aesthetic principles quite apart from the ingenuity of its
construction, yet it does betray a slightly academic flavour
as compared with Byrd's other work, and we may be
thankful that having placed on record this astonishing
example of his skill he did not give way, as so many
virtuosi have been tempted to do, to the mere display of
this remarkable aspect of his genius. Byrd's subsequent
work is singularly free from the various types of strict
canon such as we are accustomed to find in the compositions of the Polyphonic school, and which often proved
a source of danger to the main interest and beauty of the
music.

And from a similar point of view, though as a slight
digression, we may consider Byrd's subtle use of realistic
devices for the purpose of suggestion in setting words to
music. This too is matter which, in the hands of any but
an artist of the first rank, may lead to mere display and so
to banality and failure, but here again his larger ideas in
clothing phrases with music are never obscured by the
smaller details of picturesque suggestion. As an example
of this we may quote his treatment of the phrase *Terra
tremuit* (*Gradualia*, Bk. II, No. 23):

Ter - ra   tre - - - - - - - mu - it,

We may content ourselves here with mentioning a few typical examples showing the variety of subject which Byrd treated, ranging from the most elaborate designs to the simple form that is little more than a hymn tune. As an instance of the latter, we have the setting of the Compline hymn *Christe qui lux*, which curiously enough is not found in the printed volumes, though it fortunately has survived in manuscript. Another beautiful but simple number printed among the *Cantiones* published in 1575 is *Siderum Rector*, the soprano melody of the first stanza being repeated by the tenor voice in the second.

The setting of the *Lamentations* has already been mentioned; it has survived in manuscripts in the British Museum, St. Michael's College, Tenbury, and Christ Church, Oxford, but it was not printed in Byrd's own time. No Latin setting by Byrd of the *Te Deum* or *Magnificat* is known to exist, but a fine *Nunc Dimittis* for five voices appeared in the first book of *Gradualia*. One noteworthy number in this same book is entitled *Turbarum voces in passione Domini secundum Joannem*. This belongs to the type of Passion Music much in vogue in Germany in the sixteenth century, and designed for performance in conjunction with the traditional plain chant for the Evangelist's part. Similar settings by Orlando di Lasso and other contemporaries of Byrd's are known, but Byrd alone among Englishmen attempted such a thing. It has been rightly said that these short 'Turba' choruses of Byrd anticipate those of Schütz in concise dramatic intention, and it was Schütz who in the following generation paved the way for the 'Oratorio Passion' which reached its fullest development in the hands of J. S. Bach.

It has been held that the two books of *Gradualia* contain Byrd's finest and most mature work. It is true, to enumerate only a few of the gems, that they contain *Justorum animae*, *Ave verum*, *Gaudeamus omnes*, *Hodie Beata Virgo*, *O magnum misterium*, *Surge illuminare*, *Psallite Domino*, *Tu es Petrus*, and many more splendid numbers;

yet it is difficult to say that the two books of *Cantiones Sacrae* are in any way inferior to these, for in the first book are such fine motets, to select a few, as *Tristitia et anxietas*, *Vide Domine*, *Deus venerunt gentes*, *Domine tu iurasti*, *In resurrectione tua*, with its brilliant short Alleluia, *Ne irascaris*, *Vigilate*, and *Laetentur coeli*, and in the second book are *Laudibus in sanctis*, with its vital rhythmic strength at the words *resonent resonantia tympana*, and its sparkling and joyous *Halleluia canat*; other glorious pieces are *Tribulatio proxima est*, with its lovely ending, *Haec dicit Dominus*, a very expressive number with its subject Rachael weeping for her children, *Salve Regina*, *Exsurge Domine*, *Cantate Domino*, *Haec Dies*, and *Domine non sum dignus*, in which is a syncopated passage curiously resembling one in the Brahms *Requiem*:

Among the works surviving only in manuscript we may mention, among many other fine examples, *Petrus beatus*, and three massive motets: *Ad Dominum cum tribularer* and *Quomodo cantabimus*, both of which are for eight voices, and *Domine quis habitabit*, which is for nine voices.

Byrd's achievement in writing music for the English religious rites is the more remarkable when we realize the conditions under which he worked. It is not easy in the twentieth century to appreciate the magnitude of the task with which the musicians were confronted at the first appearance of the Book of Common Prayer, when the Latin rites were completely superseded. Not only was there nothing available for immediate use, but there was no tradition as to the form or method of setting the canticles. Further than this, a new principle had been enunciated by Cranmer, namely, that as far as possible no single syllable of the words should be set to more than one note of music. Though composers undoubtedly accepted this principle in a general way, it is an error to state, as is frequently done, that this was an injunction issued to them by Cranmer's authority; it was no more than a personal expression of opinion contained in a private letter from the Archbishop to King Henry VIII. The service of Tallis 'in the Dorian mode' is probably the earliest example we have of a setting that conformed to the new conditions, and as such it is no mean achievement. The service known as Tye 'in G minor', though more probably to be attributed to Osbert Persley of Norwich, is possibly an even earlier example than that of Tallis. It was left to Byrd (at what exact date is unknown) to compose the first English 'Service' that can be said to reach high excellence. The more we study this so-called 'Short Service' of Byrd, the more we appreciate his outstanding genius; the melodic beauty and moulding of each phrase, the perfection of treatment as regards verbal accentuation, and the well-balanced schemes of modulation by which the interest is sustained, call for the highest admiration. As a model for the more concise type of English 'Service' this little work is nearly perfect, and in its own line it has never yet been surpassed.

It is curious that it has so often and so definitely been enunciated that modulation was practically non-existent before the close of the sixteenth century. A very striking example of Byrd's feeling for key variety is to be found in the *Magnificat* of his second 'Service'. Beginning in G minor a close in D major is reached at the words 'his hand-maiden'. Then Byrd proceeds through F major thus to C major.

After this he passes successively through F major, B flat, D major, D minor, F major, and D major to G major.

The sequential treatment of the phrase 'and ever shall be' in the Gloria of this same *Magnificat* shows a lightness of touch that is almost unbelievable in the work of an Elizabethan composer:

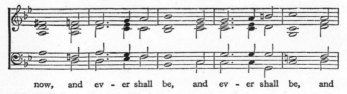

ev - er shall be, world with - out . . . . end.

This feature of the Byrd services has been somewhat fully touched upon here because variety of modulation is not found to quite the same extent in his other work; and indeed the 'Great Service' is far less freely treated than these shorter works in the matter of modulation; but in saying this we must not overlook the wonderful effect produced by means of key contrast at the words 'And was crucified' in the *Credo* of the 'Great Service'.

Byrd's English anthems are on the whole of less interest than his Latin motets, yet a very high level is reached in *This day Christ was born*, *Sing joyfully*, and *Praise our Lord, ye Gentiles*, among other *a capella* anthems. Byrd also essayed the solo, or verse, anthem, and in this style his *Have mercy upon me* is a lovely work, while the Christmas song *From Virgin's womb* has a refrain set to the words 'Rejoice, rejoice' for two soprano and two contralto voices *a capella* that surpasses in its brilliance anything that either Byrd or any other composer of the period wrote. We cannot leave the subject of Byrd's English Church music without just a mention of the sublime *Lullaby*, a carol of the Holy Child, the exquisite chorus of which is sometimes isolated from the carol and performed as a secular madrigal.

As a madrigal writer Byrd developed a style wholly dissimilar from that of the rest of the Elizabethans. His earlier work was built directly upon song form, and many of his madrigals were composed in the first instance as songs with an accompaniment of viols; the style of the string parts was vocal rather than instrumental; it was thus a simple task for the composer to adapt them for voices and to set words to them; the songs were thus converted into madrigals. When he published them in this new form Byrd described the original solo part as 'The first singing-part', and it will be seen that in this voice part there is rarely any repetition of the verbal phrases, and that it has on the whole a melodic continuity, although each line or phrase is usually separated by a bar or two of rests. The constructive principle being of this description, it will be recognized at once how fundamentally Byrd's madrigals differ from those of Morley or Wilbye for instance. Yet Byrd did on occasion introduce elaborate contrapuntal imitations of the more conventional kind into his madrigals, and he sometimes wrote with considerable complexity of rhythmic device. *Though Amaryllis dance in green* affords an example of such complexity, yet this was one of those madrigals which he originally constructed on the song plan, and the top voice part is labelled 'The First singing part'.

Byrd was a man of austere disposition, and he was at his best in treating subjects of a serious or contemplative character. Among his best pieces is the setting of Henry Walpole's *Why do I use my paper, ink, and pen?* and another good one is *Come, woeful Orpheus*. But it is a mistake to suppose that Byrd had not also a lighter side to his imaginative gifts. *I thought that Love had been a boy* is in the best vein of light lyrical setting; *In winter cold* is treated with subtle touches of satire; and in *Who made thee, Hob, forsake the plough?* Byrd has exactly caught the spirit of the blunt rustic humour of the words.

In the department of secular solo song Byrd did little; like Wilbye, Weelkes, Gibbons, and other leading madrigal writers, he seems to have stood aloof from the great group of lutenist song-writers. Why so hard and fast a line was drawn between these two classes of composers is a point that cannot readily be explained, though the fact remains. Morley and Pilkington are the only two composers of importance who produced work in both styles. But Byrd has left us at least one song which by itself sets him in the front rank of art-song composers: *My little sweet darling* was written for solo voice with the accompaniment of a quartet of viols. This song is an example of that perfect balance of interest between the voice part and the accompaniment which distinguishes the highest class of song. It has often been claimed for Schubert that he was the first composer to raise the accompanist to the level of a duettist in equal partnership with the singer, yet we find that in Dowland's work this principle was fully recognized two centuries before Schubert's day; and even earlier than Dowland, *My little sweet darling*, composed at least as early as 1583, shows us that Byrd could write the perfect art-song in which he provided an accompaniment of independent interest and importance, though at the same time it never hampers or detracts from the supremacy of the singer as the senior partner in the joint enterprise.

We have still to consider Byrd's instrumental compositions. It is impossible to over-estimate his influence and importance in the history of keyboard music. It is not too much to say that he is the father of it. Himself a brilliant executant, he could write with a masterly appreciation of technical effect. The keyboard music available when Byrd was a boy was restricted almost entirely to dance-tunes and adaptations of polyphonic vocal music. Byrd was one of the first composers, if not actually the first, to exploit the idea of writing variations on a theme. In the first instances well-known melodies of songs or dance-tunes were used for this purpose. Out of this grew the practice of composing original melodies to be treated in variation-form. Fortunately a large number of Byrd's keyboard works are in existence and in themselves they provide a profoundly interesting subject for study and research, but the quality of his work marks him off very clearly as standing on a higher plane than the best of his contemporaries, among whom Farnaby, Bull, and Gibbons were conspicuous, and he did more than any of them to develop the scope and design of this class of composition, as well as to create a keyboard technique.

But interesting as this is from a historical point of view, it is eclipsed in this direction by his chamber music for strings. In his handling of the String Fantasy of his time Byrd laid the foundations of what is technically known as form in composition. One of the clearest examples of this is to be found in the string sextet, published in his 1611 volume. Here we practically have a work planned in three independent sections or movements, contrasted in style, and the scheme of modulation in the middle section foreshadows to an amazing degree the ideas of the eighteenth-century musicians on form. One of Byrd's string quintets, styled a 'Prelude' in the manuscript in which it survives, is written on a ground-bass—a very early example of this form, possibly the earliest that is known. But the composition known as *Browning* is somewhat similar in design; it is constructed upon a single popular snatch of melody to the words 'The leaves be green, the nuts be brown'. This melody, eight bars long, is repeated in the several parts consecutively, and without variation except as regards key, twenty times, while the remaining instruments vary their thematic material in conjunction with it.

There are several examples of the *In Nomine* form among Byrd's instrumental compositions. This form was essentially academic, and it is a little difficult for us to-day to conjecture why it should have found such wide popularity as it did with the sixteenth-century composers; but it is evident that the greater freedom of the fantasy-form caused it to be superseded at the close of the century, and where Byrd led in the closing years of the sixteenth century he was followed early in the seventeenth by Gibbons, Tomkins, Ward, and Dering, among others, and shortly afterwards by Martin Peerson, Jenkins, Young, and Matthew Locke, paving the way ultimately to Purcell.

A word must be said about the part that Byrd seems to have played in evolving a distinctive instrumental, as opposed to a vocal, technique. Up to a certain period viol players were content to perform the voice parts of any *a capella* music, either sacred or secular; and even as late as the beginning of the seventeenth century composers described their madrigals as 'apt for voices or viols'. From the view-point of a string player this must have been a comparatively dull business, but the idea of chamber music, as embodied in the 'consort of viols', was as yet primitive. We owe it largely to Byrd that a technique more interesting and more suitable to the instruments should have been evolved. In order to understand fully what Byrd actually accomplished in this all-important detail it is necessary to explain that the eyes of modern string players have become accustomed to the crotchet as the standard unit of beat, and it is difficult nowadays to visualize a phrase chiefly consisting of minims and crotchets with the necessary quickness, whereas the same phrase expressed in notes of half the value can be apprehended at a glance. The music of Byrd's day was written with the minim as the standard unit where we should now use the crotchet, and when the instrumental works of that period are set out in terms of the shorter values, as in the following examples, it will immediately be seen that the figures and phrases are pre-eminently instrumental in character. These examples are taken from Byrd's Fantasia for String Quintet (Brit. Mus. Add. MSS. 17786–91). The bowing marks are added by the present writer:

and

Two further examples may be quoted from the five-part Prelude (Brit. Mus. Add. MSS. 17792–6).

The above passages are given at the original pitch; but with modern instruments these compositions may be played with better effect transposed up about a fourth.

In conclusion, it would be a grave mistake to suggest that Byrd's chamber music has a very high artistic value in the light of all that has been written since. At his death chamber music was still in its infancy; it did not reach manhood until the eighteenth century. Yet in the history of chamber music Byrd occupies a very important place; this fact has never yet been recognized as it deserves to be; for he certainly was the greatest of the early pioneers who led to the discovery of that most perfect art-form, the string quartet. But after all, much as we must dwell upon his versatility and admire it, Byrd's claim to greatness rests ultimately upon his Church music. In the music of the polyphonic school he ranks with Palestrina, and to say this is to place him unhesitatingly in the first flight of the world's composers.

2

THE SCARLATTIS

By PHILIP RADCLIFFE

(i)

ALESSANDRO SCARLATTI

(1659–1725)

THE Scarlatti family enjoys the rather unusual distinction of having produced a father and son who were both composers of great merit. A similar record belongs to the English families of Tomkins and Wesley. Both of these, especially the Wesleys, were responsible for some admirable music, but in neither case were the results as important to the musical world in general as those produced by the two Scarlattis. Of Alessandro Scarlatti's work much is beautiful and all is historically important. The work of his son Domenico, if less important as a historical landmark, is intrinsically even more striking.

Alessandro Scarlatti was born at Palermo in 1658 or 1659. His family migrated to Italy in 1672, and the rest of his life was spent mostly in Rome and Naples. He is said to have studied under Carissimi at Rome, but this cannot have continued long, for Alessandro was only fifteen years old when Carissimi died. He was appointed maestro di capella to the Viceroy at Naples in 1684. In the year 1702, wearied by the necessity of writing in the style popular at the royal palace, he left Naples and undertook the less remunerative post of assistant maestro di capella at the church of Santa Maria Maggiore in Rome. In 1713 he returned to his old work at Naples, and there he remained—except for the period 1719–23, spent at Rome —until his death in 1725.

In order to appreciate the importance of Alessandro Scarlatti's work, it is necessary to look back some way into the previous stages of Italian music. Until the latter half of the sixteenth century, music was based on 'white note' modal scales; it was conceived melodically and the ideas of 'key-feeling' or tonality on which classical music was founded had not yet come into existence. It would never have occurred to a composer of the fifteenth and sixteenth century to emphasize the tonality of a motet or madrigal by opening with a theme built upon the notes of the common chord, such as the first subjects of Beethoven's Ninth Symphony, or Brahms's Violin Concerto. Nor would he have regarded accidentals as a means of modulation, in the classical sense; they were introduced solely for harmonic colour, and were usually contradicted shortly after their appearance. Most important of all, any kind of aggressively marked rhythm is not found in serious music. This does not mean that serious composers had no feeling at all for measured rhythm, produced by regularly recurring accents; they felt it, perhaps subconsciously, and systematically went against it, and one of the chief charms of their rhythm is the conflict of the two principles. The absence of aggressively marked rhythms was intensified by the polyphonic character of all serious music of the time: the long phrases of the individual parts began and ended at different moments, each having its own rhythm, and when cadences occurred in the course of a movement, they did not merely mark the end of a section, as in a dance-tune, but served as a kind of junction between the preceding and following phrases. Consequently, in music of strictly polyphonic texture, a cadence occurring in the middle of a movement has less rhythmic force than in a homophonic dance-tune; if it occurs on a note other than the final of the mode in which the movement is written, it will not give the effect of a definite modulation to another key. It follows, therefore, that the power of modulating in such a way as to give the impression of being temporarily, but quite definitely, in a new key could not come before the establishment of a musical style in which the cadences had more rhythmic prominence.

It was a long time before this was established: the increasingly chromatic style of Marenzio and the impassioned declamation of Gesualdo and Monteverdi broke through the limits of the modal system, but these composers, especially the last two, were occupied with dramatic expression rather than purely musical development. However, in Monteverdi's last opera, *L'Incoronazione di Poppea*, the music is more coherent and symmetrical, and the tonality more firmly felt. The work of Carissimi, who was born in 1604, is typical of the period of transition. His melodies are flowing and amiable, composed largely of carefully balanced periods; he is particularly fond of writing a four-bar phrase ending with a cadence, and repeating it in some nearly related key, such as the dominant. This device gives a very definite 'key-feeling', but is employed so frequently as to become monotonous.

However, although Carissimi's melodies are often lacking in breadth, his sense of tonality was, for his time, remarkably sure. Already in his work we find a strong predilection for the so-called 'Neapolitan cadence', which is common in the music of Alessandro Scarlatti, and in the final chorus of his oratorio *Jephtha* he uses poignant and expressive dissonances which are in some ways reminiscent of the later madrigalists, but have no modal flavour.

Italian composers after Carissimi tended to modulate less frequently and to think in longer melodic sweeps, which meant that their modulations, when they did occur, had a more definite significance. This is well exemplified in the work of Carissimi's pupil Cesti, who was born in 1620. Cesti's music has not the depth of feeling that we find in Carissimi's best work, but he had in a considerable degree the gift of lyrical grace and neatness. The solos in his opera *Il Pomo d'Oro* show a clear sense of tonality.

Most of them contain a modulation to some nearly related key—usually the dominant if the music is in a major key, and the relative major or the dominant minor if it is in a minor key. The modulation is emphasized by a fairly well-marked cadence, after which the music returns to its original key. Often, in order to give unity of form, the final cadence is approached by the phrase—now, of course, transposed to the tonic—which led to the previous cadence. This is an important point, for recapitulation, in the tonic, of previous material is a nucleus of the classical sonata form.

The earliest works of Alessandro Scarlatti show considerable traces of Cesti's influence. They have, however, a more elegant melodic style, which Scarlatti learned from Alessandro Stradella, a composer who had considerable melodic gift, but rather a weak sense of form. Scarlatti's arias are constructed on the same lines as Cesti's, but they usually have an independent second section ending in some key that has not previously been used, after which the first section is repeated. This was known as the *Da Capo* form, and was so frequently used by Alessandro Scarlatti that he has been credited with the invention of it—untruly, for it appears even in the music of Cavalli, who died in 1676. The musical material of Scarlatti's early work is neat and pleasing rather than emotional, and of the three earliest of his surviving operas, *Pompeo*, which deals with the most serious subject, is far less successful than the other two, *Gli Equivoci nel Sembiante* and *L'Honesta negli Amori*. He does not as yet show his wonderful power of writing long sweeps of melody, but a definite foretaste of that power is found in an early cantata *Ben folle è che non parte*, especially in the final arioso quoted by Professor Dent in his life of Scarlatti. The cantatas, of which five hundred have survived, show in some ways the most intimate side of Scarlatti's work. He continued to write cantatas throughout his life, and their relation to his operas has been aptly compared with the relation of Beethoven's sonatas and

chamber music to his symphonies. The cantatas, though
the harmonies are necessarily filled in from the figured
bass, are in fact chamber music; the bass itself is always
conceived as a singing part and is often more closely
related to the vocal part than it is in the more massive
style of the operas. We often find that the first phrase of
the bass, in the preliminary instrumental ritornello, anticipates that of the voice.

Scarlatti's operatic output increased after his settling at
Naples in 1684, and in the operas *La Statira* and *Pirro e
Demetrio* the full individuality of his style appears. The
Da Capo form of the aria has now become a normal feature,
and in the first repeated section of the arias Scarlatti shows
more strongly than Cesti a feeling for the balance of
cadences. In the shortest of Cesti's arias there is room
only for one cadence in a foreign key; in the longer specimens there are often two, the second occurring not long
before the end. In this case it is the second cadence that is
recapitulated in the tonic, with the same music and words,
and sometimes the recapitulation follows the original
modulation too closely to produce a satisfactory balance
of tonality. Scarlatti, on the other hand, always allows
plenty of time for the tonic to establish itself, even if there
is more than one cadence in a foreign key. Sometimes he
has a full cadence in the tonic a little before the end and
another actually at the end. An exact recapitulation, in the
tonic, of a foreign cadence is by no means a regular feature
in Scarlatti's arias; it occurs only in cases where the words
set at the two cadences are identical, and not always
even then.

From 1697 to 1702 Scarlatti, doubtless hampered by
the limitations of the Viceroy's taste, produced operas of
rather inferior quality. In his cantatas, however, his style
showed no decline. A good example is the beautiful *Sarei
troppo felice* analysed in Professor Dent's biography. Incidentally this contains an aria 'Tal se premo sentiero
odorato' with a particularly well-marked recapitulation,

in the tonic, of the central cadence, which has the additional interest of being not in the dominant, as is customary, but in the mediant minor. Here also we see how, after the recapitulation, Scarlatti ends with a kind of coda containing an additional cadence to emphasize the tonality. It is, however, not surprising that he thought it unnecessary for this exact recapitulation to appear in all his arias. After all, the first part would be heard again in entirety after the second. In some of Scarlatti's work of this period there are strong traces of Corelli's influence, particularly in the use of the rhythm of the 'gigue', as in the delightful duet from the Assumption oratorio quoted by Professor Dent, and in the equally attractive aria sung by Daniel in the Christmas oratorio.

Of the operas that Scarlatti wrote at Florence, where he spent about a year before settling at Rome in 1703, none have survived. In the *Mitridate Eupatore*, which appeared in 1707, he rises to a remarkably high level. Here is found in the aria 'Cara Tomba' a marvellous combination of smooth and flowing vocal writing with poignant harmonies, produced mainly by suspensions. This aria is essentially operatic in that there are none of the intimate contrapuntal relations between the voice and the bass which we find in the arias of the cantatas; when the voice is singing, it stands out—except for a few bars of violin solo—against a background of strings, and when it is silent the strings develop an arpeggio figure of their own which barely occurs in the vocal part. To the year 1707 also belongs the fine cantata for two voices, *Questo silenzio ombroso*. In this work, and particularly in the final section beginning with the words 'Sia più sonno di morte', an almost equally high emotional level is reached through the expressive contrapuntal interweaving of the two vocal parts.

His feeling for harmonic colour was now strongly developed. In 1712 he and Francesco Gasparini made an exchange of cantatas, Gasparini sending his setting of *Andate o miei sospiri* to Scarlatti, who replied with two

settings of his own. Of these two the former, though very
chromatic in places, is the simpler; the second, written in
a deliberately abstruse style, contains surprising enharmonic modulations which, though quite convincing in
themselves, rather detract from the significance of the
melodic line.

Scarlatti's operas of this period show an increasing
interest in the instrumental writing. The violin parts are
often brilliant and important. *Il Ciro*, produced in 1712,
contains interesting and attractive ballet music. In 1715
appeared *Tigrane* which, thanks to its massive and impos-
ing brilliance, won greater fame than any other of Scarlatti's operas. A more sympathetic aspect of his genius is
shown in the oratorio *San Filippo Neri*. Here the recitative
'Con moribundo ciglio' and the following aria 'Mio Gesù'
are worthy of Bach in their deep pathos, while in the aria
we see once again the emotional use of dissonance. It is
by these means that Scarlatti produces his most moving
effects. When, as in the second 'Andate o miei sospiri', he
employs abstruse enharmonic modulations, the results are
interesting intellectually rather than emotionally. His
latest operas are mellower in style than the group that
culminated in *Tigrane*. *La Griselda*, the last of all, contains
an aria 'Figlio! Tiranno!' of superb dramatic power.

Scarlatti's instrumental music consists of four 'Sonate
a quattro' for strings, twelve symphonies, capable rather
than inspired, for small orchestra, and some harpsichord
music which shows a feeling for the instrument, but does
not contain much material of interest. In the sphere of
Church music he was most successful in some of the unaccompanied motets, such as *O magnum mysterium* and
Tu es Petrus; his masses do not, on the whole, represent
him at his best.

What would be the attitude of the musical world to
Alessandro Scarlatti, were more of his work accessible?
Almost certainly he would make a greater appeal to-day
than he could have made in the nineteenth century. Then

the tendency was to underrate the emotional effect produced purely by expressive melodic lines, a tendency well
illustrated in the *Oxford History of Music* by Parry, who
expresses a doubt whether Scarlatti 'ever wrote a single
passage that really stirs the depths of human feeling'. This
would surely be questionable even if melody had been
Scarlatti's only gift, which it was not.

In musical form he was not a pioneer. He made no
attempt to alter the conventions of the cantata, and he left
opera the same odd mixture of tragic and comic elements
that he found. What he did realize more than any of
his predecessors was the significance of classical tonality,
and his power of combining, when at his best, beauty of
melody with expressive harmony may well have exercised
some inspiring influence even upon Bach and Mozart.

DOMENICO SCARLATTI

(1685–1757)

DOMENICO SCARLATTI, the eldest son of Alessandro, was born at Naples in 1685. Of his life little is known, except that he travelled much. In 1708 he was at Venice, studying under Gasparini; from 1709 to 1719 he was at Rome. In 1719 he went to London, in 1721 to Lisbon. From there he returned to Naples, but in 1729 he was invited to the Spanish Court, and there he remained till 1754. He then returned to Naples, where he died in 1757.

His importance in musical history is due to his instrumental work; he wrote operas and cantatas, but they are comparatively insignificant. His harpsichord music is of the highest interest and shows an astonishingly bold and adventurous outlook. Some of it, owing to its brilliant character, has been much played, but only since the appearance of Alessandro Longo's complete edition in eleven volumes has it become accessible in its entirety. It marks an important stage in the history of the instrumental sonata form.

Attention has already been called, in connexion with the arias of Alessandro Scarlatti, to a practice of recapitulating in the key of the tonic, at the end of a movement, material that had previously been given out in some other key, usually the dominant. In Domenico Scarlatti's harpsichord sonatas we find this practice more definitely established than in any contemporary instrumental music. It occurs in some of Couperin's pieces, *Le Réveille-Matin* for instance, and oftener in Bach, as in the first two movements of the Fifth French Suite and in some of the preludes from the second book of the Forty-Eight. In Domenico Scarlatti's harpsichord music it occurs almost without exception, but a consequent monotony which might have been expected is avoided by a remarkable variety of treatment.

His texture—and the same is true of Couperin—is often not polyphonic. Some fugues he did write, including the fine and exhilarating *Cat's Fugue* in G minor, but in most cases they succeeded, as Parry wrote in Grove's *Dictionary*, less because they were good fugues than because they were Scarlatti's. In some other cases his sonatas begin with a brief fugal exposition, but the subjects are not developed fugally at any length. Sometimes, indeed, he does not even write a counter-subject, but having given out the subject he repeats it unaccompanied in a different register. His style, however, is not purely lyric, like that of Couperin, but often dramatic in a manner that anticipates some of Beethoven's characteristics, and those who know his music merely from having heard one or two pieces, probably in a 'modernized' edition played by virtuosi, can have only an incomplete idea of the vitality of his inspiration.

His variety of resource in handling the sonata form is extraordinary and is particularly conspicuous in his treatment of opening subjects. Sometimes the opening subject dominates the whole movement, as in the Sonatas in F (No. 188,[1] in which there is an odd anticipation of the Scherzo of Beethoven's Seventh Symphony) and in F sharp minor (No. 481), where it has several exceptionally distinct sections. Sometimes it is completely laid aside after its first presentation, as in the Sonata in D (No. 365) and the exciting Sonata in C (No. 205). In these cases it merely has the effect of asserting the tonality, and has no thematic importance. Usually, however, it appears at the beginning of the second half of a movement, often in the key in which the first half ended, and in one or two cases, for example the very beautiful Sonata in F minor (No. 187), it is actually recapitulated in the tonic before the reappearance of

[1] The numbers quoted are those of Longo's edition, which is not arranged chronologically.

the second subject. In the character of the first subjects themselves there is considerable variety. Sometimes, as in the F minor Sonata just mentioned, they are flowing and lyrical. More frequently they are rhythmic rather than melodic. Sometimes, to emphasize the tonality, they have the nature of a trumpet fanfare.

As a rule it is to the second subjects of his sonatas that Scarlatti devotes most attention. The term 'second subject' is rather unsatisfactory as applied to passages which vary enormously in character and design. Some of them, as in the brilliant and fairly well-known Sonata in D (No. 461), open with a quiet lyrical phrase standing out in obvious contrast with its surroundings, a feature which recurs in the work of later composers. In this sonata—and the same is true of many others—the second subject as it proceeds shows considerable elaboration of design. The quiet lyrical phrase is followed by rapid and brilliant passages; it is then resumed, and leads to further rapid passages, after which the first half of the movement closes with a kind of 'codetta'. Where the second subject is of such length, the development section is usually shortened in proportion; in this sonata it occupies only five bars and a half. Scarlatti had a strong feeling for key contrast; even where there is no contrast of mood, it is common to find sonatas in a major key whose second subjects begin unexpectedly in the dominant minor. Sometimes he chooses a still more unusual key, such as the relative minor or submediant minor. Frequently in Scarlatti's sonatas is found a second subject which consists of a fairly long paragraph built upon a single short phrase and leading to an emphatic cadence. Often in these cases the harmonies are mainly tonic and dominant, as in the well-known *Tempo di ballo* Sonata in D (No. 463). Sometimes, on the other hand, he emphasizes the tonality of the second subject in a more subtle way, by laying stress on its dominant and subdominant, and postponing any emphatic expression of its tonic until the cadence is reached. This occurs most often when the second subject is in a minor key. It produces an effect of singular pathos, suggestive of the Phrygian mode, and lends colour to the interesting theory that Scarlatti was influenced by music heard during his sojourn in Spain. The Phrygian mode during the sixteenth century was favoured by composers in Spain more than elsewhere on the Continent, and it recurs in modern Spanish works such as de Falla's *Andaluza* and *Fantasia Betica*. Of course, in Scarlatti, there is no question of the tonality of such movements being modal as opposed to major or minor; the tonic, temporarily avoided by him, is made to sound all the more emphatic when it reappears at the cadence. Two very beautiful instances occur in the second subjects of the Sonatas in F minor (No. 382) and F major (No. 474); in the latter the second subject is entirely in the dominant minor.

Scarlatti's methods of modulating from the key of his first subject to that of his second are often delightfully roundabout and inconsequent. Sometimes in their unexpectedness they are suggestive of Schubert. A good instance occurs in the Sonata in E (No. 44). Here the first subject, in E major, is followed by a sudden modulation to E minor, after which the music passes rapidly through G, D, B minor, D again, A, E, B, F sharp, and finally settles down in B, all within a very short space. The development section of the same sonata contains a modulation to the remote key of E flat. It is not only the inconsequence of some of Scarlatti's modulations that anticipates Schubert, but also their clarity. Even in a chain of rapid transitions, such as the passage described above, the tonality is never for a moment obscured. In this respect the harmonic effects of Domenico differ from those of his father, in whose later cantatas, such as the second *Andate o miei sospiri* and *Nel centro oscuro*, we often feel that he is intentionally producing an impression of vagueness. It may almost be said that, while the methods of Domenico forestall Schubert, those of Alessandro look ahead to Chopin and Wagner. The son lays stress, as it were, upon the end of the journey, the father delights in the process of travel. Another interesting feature of Domenico Scarlatti's harmonic style is his fondness for internal pedal notes, often leading to most surprising dissonances, which many editors of the last century discreetly expunged. Such passages are probably the result of Scarlatti's acquaintance with the Spanish guitar. Some interesting specimens are quoted in Mr. J. B. Trend's book on Manuel de Falla. Another striking instance, almost barbaric in its intensity, occurs in the Sonata in D (No. 415). The harpsichord can suggest vividly the twanging effects of the guitar, and these sounds were probably as stimulating to Scarlatti as was the ripple of the modern piano to Chopin. This probability is in a degree confirmed by the fact that some sonatas written by Scarlatti for violin and figured bass are not only more archaic in form than his works for harpsichord solo, but show no sign of his individuality. These sonatas may, of course, be early works, although they appear in a late volume of the Venice manuscript.

The emotional range of his music has, on the whole, been underrated, mainly because comparatively few of his works are familiar to the public. As a rule pianists confine their attention to the rapid and brilliant sonatas, and neglect the slower pieces, of which many are remarkably beautiful. These may be divided into two classes. The works belonging to the first and larger group show traces of operatic influence; they are mainly homophonic in texture and usually in a major key. Some of them are dull, but the Sonata in E (No. 257) is interesting and original, and those in A (No. 238) and D (No. 183) have great charm, showing an almost Mozart-like tenderness of style. The Sonata in F minor (No. 187), though emotionally it has much in common with the second group, may on account of its texture be placed in the first. Of the second group the characteristics are a more contrapuntal texture and movements expressive throughout of a deeply pathetic emotion, for which Scarlatti has seldom been given due credit. Outstanding instances are the Sonatas in B minor (No. 33), D minor (No. 267), F minor (No. 382), and D minor (No. 362). Nor must it be supposed that the quick sonatas are purely light-hearted; indeed one of Scarlatti's characteristics is abrupt change from gaiety to pathos. Numerous examples might be quoted; as good as any is the second subject, already mentioned, of the Sonata in D (No. 461). It is important that such passages should be played sympathetically and imaginatively, yet with no suspicion of a change of pace. Often it happens that the harmonies move more slowly in these passages than in their surroundings. This produces an illusion of slower motion, which is unduly exaggerated if the actual pace is retarded.

Domenico Scarlatti's music, as well as his father's, is suggestive of some modern developments. He was obviously much interested in problems of musical form, and the relish with which he uses dissonances, not merely as a result of contrapuntal clashings but also for the exhilaration of the sound, is most remarkable. So far as form is concerned, he was more of a pioneer than his father, and he gave to instrumental music a vitality and a feeling of adventure which was quite new in his time and keeps its freshness to-day. Although we do not find in his music the long melodic lines which were his father's delight, he was far from being deficient in feeling for melodic beauty. Most characteristic, and also prophetic of later composers, is his way of using a short phrase as the foundation either of a string of modulations or of a longish passage in one key, rising usually to a melodic climax followed by a full cadence. This method of thematic treatment is quite unlike the fugal polyphony of Bach and looks ahead to the music of later composers, particularly Haydn and Beethoven. Domenico Scarlatti's work may not appeal equally to all temperaments, and the fact that some of his most emotional passages are interrupted, as Mr. J. B. Trend says, 'by a dry cackle of laughter' may be a real stumbling-block to some, while others may find in it an additional charm of style. So also the thin, clear texture of his work may not be sympathetic to all. Yet even those to whose temperaments the style does not appeal cannot but admire its great vitality and the distinctive gifts which inspire it. Domenico Scarlatti was certainly among the greatest musicians of his day, and one from whom much can still be learned.

The writer gratefully acknowledges his debt to sundry published books, especially Professor Dent's *Alessandro Scarlatti*. Above all, he was helped by a generous loan from Professor Dent of valuable unpublished material.

3

LES CLAVECINISTES

COUPERIN (1668–1733)
RAMEAU (1683–1764)

By HERBERT WISEMAN

WAS there ever in the history of the world such a contrast between two succeeding reigns as there was in France between those of Louis XIV and of Louis XV?

Louis XIV, the 'Grand Monarch', had had a long and splendid reign. Music, literature, and painting had flourished at his court in a really grand manner. Lully, the Italian, the court composer and leader of the King's band of 'Petits Violons', by skilfully adapting himself, as a courtier should, to the circumstances, had exercised a powerful influence on French music. Racine and Corneille were the grand monarchs in the realm of drama. Painting, architecture, and the decorative arts were all inspired by pretentiousness and pomposity.

On the death of the King in 1715, Louis, the well-beloved, then a child of five years of age, succeeded to the throne, and during the next eight years while Philip, Duke of Orleans, was regent, there was a natural reaction. 'Across the land, from high and low, came a mighty sigh of relief; light airs fanned the faces of the people; the starch melted out of the stiff and demigoddish pose; all France, weary to scant tolerance of the pomposities of the sixteen-hundreds, flung off the solemnities and followed the Regent and his Abbé in the dance and riot' (Haldane Macfall in *The French Genius*).

The change of attitude is manifest in the paintings, the houses, and the furniture of the new régime. It was the age of elegance and daintiness, and the new spirit of France found its perfect expression in the pictures of Watteau and in the music of Couperin.

François Couperin is, like Chopin, one of the lone figures in the world of music. There had been, it is true, clavecinists before Couperin, as there had been composers for the piano before Chopin. Jacques Champion de Chambonnières, who was appointed clavecinist to Louis XIV in 1643, had done much to explore the possibilities of the instrument, and as Chopin followed John Field in writing nocturnes for the piano, so Couperin was indebted to those who went before him for suggestions not only for the music which he wrote but also for the titles which he gave to his compositions. Chopin and Couperin alike, however, brought such an originality of outlook, such a genius for their instruments, to bear on their work that each in his own particular sphere stands alone, without a rival and without even a companion.

The French school of clavecinists (clavecin being, of course, the French name for the harpsichord) can trace its descent from a flourishing school of organists. Indeed, most of its members were organists as well as clavecinists, and many wrote compositions for both instruments.

While Lully was writing the first French operas and composing music for the ballets and court dances, Jacques Champion de Chambonnières was stringing together little dances for the clavecin in the manner of the suites which had been fashionable for the lute. The lute suite was of a very definite and formal type, and consisted of three dances in the same key arranged in the following order: Allemande, Courante, Sarabande. In order to extend the suites, sometimes a Prelude was inserted before the Allemande, and a Gigue after the Sarabande. Other dances, such as a Gavotte, a Passacaglia, a Bourrée, a Rigaudon, a Chaconne, or a Minuet, were often added between the Sarabande and the Gigue. Lionel de la Laurencie in the *Encyclopédie de la musique et dictionnaire du Conservatoire* gives the following diagrams which show very clearly two schemes which

might be followed in building up a suite. In these, the
main movements which have been mentioned are represented by their initial letters, the Allemande (A), Courante
(C), and Sarabande (S) being designated the Head (Tête)
of the suite, and the dances which follow them the Tail
(Queue). (The Gigue is represented by 'G'.)

(1) P.   A. C. S.   Danses intercelées   G.
             (Tête)   (Queue)

(2) P.   A. C. S. G.   Danses ajoutées
             (Tête)   (Queue)

From time to time other modifications were made. Just
before the time of Couperin, for instance, some of the
Allemandes were more lively than others, and certain
composers had substituted for a slow Allemande a
Tombeau, in which tribute was paid to some friend who
had died.

It is hardly necessary to point out that the dances of the
suite, like the waltzes and mazurkas of Chopin, were not
intended to accompany dancers and so differed from the
majority of the dances of Lully, which were written for the
court ballets in which the King himself took part. The
dances of the suite were more intimate things, beautiful
little cameos, made for the joy of the performer and of the
listener.

The local organist at Chaumes, one Charles Couperin,
had three sons, Louis, François, and Charles, and as
Chaumes was near the family estate of Chambonnières,
and as the Couperins, like the Bachs, were a musical family,
it was natural that the three boys should become pupils of
the great player and composer.

Louis (1626–64), the eldest brother, became a composer
of clavecin music, little, if in any way, inferior to that of
his teacher. Lionel de la Laurencie quotes a beautiful and
touching *Tombeau de M. Blanc-Rocher*—'un véritable
petit poème symphonique'—which begins thus:

François, the second brother, became organist of Saint-Gervais in Paris on the death of his elder brother, and composed several songs and some organ music.

Charles, the youngest (1638–79), who was also organist of Saint-Gervais, married in 1662 Marie Guerrin, and of this marriage, François Couperin, 'le grand', was born, on November 10th, 1668.

In due course he became the pupil of Jacques Denis Thomelin, the organist of Saint-Jacques de la Boucherie. The post of organist at Saint-Gervais seems to have been almost the prerogative of the Couperin family, and it is stated that during the time that 'le grand' held the post, he attracted a crowd of admirers. In 1693 he was appointed organist to the King, and in 1717 he was given the title of 'ordinaire de la musique de la chambre du roi'.

The first of his sets of *Pièces pour Clavecin* was published in 1713, two years before the death of Louis XIV. It consists of five 'Ordres' which follow to a certain extent the normal plan of the suite. The first, second, third, and fifth start in quite orthodox fashion with an Allemande, two Courantes, and a Sarabande, though it should be noted that the Allemandes and the Sarabandes are given descriptive tags and sub-titles, to indicate their character. The first Allemande' is L'Auguste', the second 'La Laborieuse', the third 'La Ténébreuse', and the fourth 'La Logivière'.

From these we can gather that even in the first book Couperin is showing a mind of his own, refusing to bow to convention and endeavouring to find words to designate his moods.

In these four Ordres, the 'galanteries', or 'danses intercelées' or 'ajoutées', are numerous. Couperin is not content merely to interpolate a Gavotte or a Minuet or any of the usual dances, he releases his imagination and gives us any number of beautiful poetic things of which even the titles have a fascinating sound. In the first Ordre we have Rondeaus—a favourite diversion of the composer—'Les Sylvains', 'Les Abeilles', 'L'Enchanteresse', 'La Bourbonnoise', and several other fanciful trifles.

In the fourth Ordre, Couperin breaks away entirely from tradition. Here there is no Allemande or Courante. The first movement is 'La Marche des Gris-Vêtus' and then, in vivid contrast to the drab clothing of this, the second is 'Les Bacchanales'. This is in three parts: (1) 'Enjoüemens Bachiques', (2) 'Tendresses Bachiques', and (3) 'Fureurs Bachiques'—a complete drama. The third movement is 'La Pateline', and this smirking, wheedling lass may have no relation to 'Les Bacchanales', but she is sufficiently attractive in herself to get as many admirers as she can wish.

'La Pateline'.

&c.

The last movement is 'Le Réveille-matin', and, as it is full of vigour and out-jigs many orthodox 'gigues', we may take it that the composer's philosophy is that so long as there is no headache in the morning, and one is fit to skip about like this, very little harm has been done.

This is far removed from the usually accepted idea of a suite, but even here 'La Marche des Gris-Vêtus' bears some faint resemblance to an Allemande, and 'Le Réveille-matin' to a Gigue, and there is continuity of key, F major alternating with F minor.

The separate numbers in the other Ordres in this set are, in similar fashion, linked by revolving round one key-centre. In the first, the key is G minor or G major, in the second D minor or D major, in the third C minor or C major, and in the fifth A minor or A major.

In the preface to this book Couperin gives us a glimpse of the thoughts and ideas which are at the back of his mind when composing:

'J'ay toujours eu un objet en composant toutes ces pièces; des occasions différentes me l'ont fourni; ainsi, les titres répondent aux idées que j'ay eues; on me dispensera d'en rendre compte; cependant, comme, parmi ces titres, il y en a qui semblent me flatter, il est bon d'avertir que les pièces qui les portent sont des espèces de portraits qu'on a trouvés quelquefois assez ressemblants sous mes doigts, et que la plupart de ces titres avantageux sont plutôt donnés aux aimables originaux que j'ay voulu représenter qu'aux copies que j'en ay tirées.'

The titles are therefore not merely appended to the pieces in a haphazard way. Couperin is by his own statement a writer of music which owes its inspiration to something outside of itself. He has, as he says in the above quotation, always tried to represent something external, suggested by various events or by ideas which have occurred to him. It is delightful to find him apologizing for his presumption in daring to use certain titles and explaining these as 'the type of portraits of which one has sometimes found a fairly good likeness under my fingers'. His favourite form is the rondeau, and this simple form is the medium through which he expresses many varied moods and sentiments, and paints many portraits.

He is at all times careful to leave no doubt in the mind of the performer as to his intentions. His book—*L'Art de toucher le Clavecin*—was written to explain his methods. He uses different kinds of ornaments: les pincés, les ports de voix, les coulés, les tremblements, les tierces coulées, les cadences, and les arpèges. Each of these has several variants, and Couperin pleads that they should be studied with care. The ornaments are essential, and a slovenly performance, to quote his own words, is unpardonable. In many modern editions of his works the original notation of the ornaments has, unfortunately, been replaced by modern substitutes. The better way is, as is done in the Brahms-Chrysander edition, to print the original signs and along with these, Couperin's own explanatory table.

The second book of *Pièces pour Clavecin* was published in 1717 and contained seven Ordres. In it Couperin almost completely breaks away from the old dance titles. There is an Allemande à deux clavecins in the ninth Ordre, an Allemande, two Courantes, and a Sarabande in the eighth, an odd Gavotte, and a Minuet. All the other movements are miniatures in which the music depicts the subject suggested by the title. We have 'Les Moissonneurs', 'Les Langueurs tendres', 'Les Bergeries', 'La Raphaèle', 'La Rafraîchissante', 'L'Olimpique', 'La Fringante', 'Les Juméles', and many others. These are mentioned merely to show the wide range of his subjects.

In the eleventh Ordre there is one of Couperin's most brilliant efforts, 'Les fastes de la grande et ancienne M–n–str–nd–s–' (Ménestrandise), a little suite within a suite, in which he pokes fun at what we might call the incorporated society of fiddlers who were then at daggers drawn with the organists and the clavecinists. The first act of this satiric comedy is the pompous march of 'Les

Notables et Jurés—M–n–str–nd–s–'. (Dare one compare it
to the Procession of the Master-singers, or does this savour
too much of sacrilege? They are, at any rate, both in C
major!) The second act is that of the hurdy-gurdy players
and the beggars, and is built on a delicious hurdy-gurdy
drone. The third is an episode of jugglers, acrobats, and
mountebanks, complete with bears and monkeys, and is
built, like the former, on a drone bass. The fourth presents
the invalids, or the folks who have been crippled in the
service of the great M–n–str–nd–s–. Here the right hand
in a series of dotted-note jerks suggests the disjointed ones,
and the left hand those who are painfully limping along.
The last act shows the disorder and the rout of the whole
troup caused by the drunkards, the monkeys, and the bears.
It is good to know that this piece of satiric comedy was not
wasted and that the fiddlers did not win!

In this book there are many charming things, such as
'Les Bergeries' in the sixth Ordre, and in the seventh 'Les
petits âges'—a regular *coin des enfants*, to borrow a phrase
from Debussy with whom Couperin has much in common.
The tenth Ordre contains a spirited battle-piece with
sounds of war and the rejoicings of the victors, and in
conclusion a fanfare in which the right hand plays in a
different rhythm from the left.

This Ordre finishes with 'Les Bagatelles', of which the
opening is quoted:

'Les Bagatelles'.

This is called by Couperin a *Pièce croisée*, and he explains
that the hands must play on separate keyboards of the
clavecin. He shows, however, that the medium through
which the work is presented is not of supreme importance

to him by also remarking that this piece can be played on two viols or two violins or even two flutes if the second makes one or two slight changes of notes to bring them into its range.

There are several others like 'Les Bagatelles' designed for two claviers. Of these the most generally known and played is 'Le Tic-Toc-Choc' in the eighteenth Ordre. In the preface to the Brahms-Chrysander edition it is suggested that if these movements are to be played on one keyboard, either the right hand must play an octave higher, or the bass an octave lower, but there is much to be said for a judicious rearrangement, and the version of 'Le Tic-Toc-Choc' which is given by Louis Diémer in the third volume of *Les Clavecinistes Français* (Durand) sounds probably nearer to the effect intended by Couperin than anything which could be produced by mere transposition of one of the parts.

In the third book, which was published in 1722, there are still fewer movements which are definitely called Allemande, Courante, or Sarabande. There are seven Ordres in it, and here, as in fact right through the Ordres, the only link between the movements is the link of tonality. In every case the separate numbers have the same tonic; the tonality may be major or minor; there may be all sorts of modulations, but the tonic is the same throughout. In many cases the minor keys appear with one flat less in the signature than we are accustomed to in modern times, and though this may upset many players, it does not alter the key.

There are many beautiful and fanciful things in the third book, including the well-known 'Sœur Monique' and 'Le Rossignol en amour'. Couperin, of course, was not the first to give titles to his musical efforts. His predecessors in France had done so, and the virginal music of our own Elizabethans abounds in such inscriptions. Is it possible that Couperin knew 'Mr. Byrd's Battle' from Lady Neville's virginal book, 'Le Rossignol' of Peter Phillipps,

'The Ghost' of William Byrd, or such things as 'His Rest', 'His Humour', or 'Pawles Wharfe' by Giles Farnaby?

The most amusing thing in this third book is 'Les Folies françoises, ou les Dominos' in the thirteenth suite. This is, academically speaking, in the form of a Passacaglia, and consists of free variations on a ground bass. If, however, we can shut our ears to the formal aspect, and look upon these variations as a revelation of the frailties of human nature, we shall without doubt hail this as a masterpiece of musical delineation. I make no apology for not translating the titles—there are no equivalents in our language. The first presentation of the subject in the cold key of B minor is headed 'La Virginité sous le Domino couleur d'invisible' (typical Couperinesque humour). This in its fresh innocence is very beautiful and attractive. It is followed by 'La Pudeur sous le Domino couleur de rose'. The choice of colours is superb. 'La Pudeur' is succeeded by 'L'Ardeur sous le Domino incarnat', the warmth of passion here being expressed by the urgency of the dotted notes. 'L'Espérance sous le Domino vert' is marked 'gaiëment', and is a light-hearted gigue in 9/8 rhythm. 'La Fidélité sous le Domino bleu' is a very tender variation written in notes of twice the length of the others—the signature is 3/2. 'La Persévérance sous le Domino gris de lin' (grey linen is a lovely touch!) is marked 'tenderly: without tardiness'. 'La Langueur sous le Domino violet' marked by the composer 'également' and written with the time signature 1/2 which I feel should be 1/1 as the measure of the bar is in the bass, which is expressed in equal semibreves for the most part.

The next variation is headed 'La Coquéterie, sous diférens Dominos'. This is a perfect little picture. The time alternates between 6/8, 3/8, and 2/4, and the directions to the performer are 'gaiëment', 'modéré', and 'légèrement'. Couperin, in this, has anticipated some of the rhythmical devices of the modern composer. Then we have 'Les Vieux Galans (Galants) et les trésorières suranées, sous des Dominos pourpres et feuilles mortes'. It is marked appropriately 'gravement', and in it one can hear the gossiping tongues wagging. The significance of the changes in the bass part should not be missed.

This is followed by 'Les Coucous bénévoles, sous des Dominos jaunes' (again a fine colour). It is headed 'Coucou, coucou'. The top part is merely a variation of the cuckoo call which, on Shakespeare's authority, 'mocks married men', and the import of the episode can hardly be missed. 'La jalousie taciturne' appears 'sous le Domino gris de maure', and the last couplet is 'La Frénésie ou le Désespoir, sous le Domino noir'.

Perhaps the finest stroke of this arch-humorist, Couperin, is that he follows 'Les Folies françoises' by a short poignant movement called 'L'Âme en peine'.

The succeeding suite begins with the fascinating 'Le Rossignol en amour', to which Couperin has added a note to say that the nightingale can be made to sound effective on the flute 'when it is well played', and in the same note he seems to make a plea for tempo rubato: 'It is not necessary to adhere too strictly to the measure in the following variation. Everything must be sacrificed to the feeling of neatness in the passages and to attention to the accents as shown by the *pincés*.'

Later in this Ordre there is 'La Julliet' which, as will be seen from the following quotation:

'La Julliet'.

would seem to present an insoluble problem to any clavecinist even though he had a double row of keys; but a note from Couperin makes it plain that it is designed for two clavecins—the first to play the top stave with the bass, and the other the second stave and the bass. There are several other pieces in the third and fourth books which may be treated in the same way.

Incidentally, I wonder how many musicians have discovered how jolly it is to play the Bach Organ Sonatas on two pianos, the first player taking the top part and the bass as written, and the second taking the second part and playing the bass an octave lower.

There is little to be said about the fourth book, which was published in 1730. It contains eight Ordres in which we have the same gifts of fancy and humour; the same evidence that Couperin, even though he was working in a limited sphere, was the possessor of a poetic all-round mind. The last suite of all—No. 27 in B minor—reverts to a formal opening with an Allemande. This is called 'L'Exquise', and it is truly exquisite! The succeeding numbers, 'Les Pavots', 'Les Chinois' (was Couperin thinking of any connexion between Chinamen and poppies and an exquisite lady?), and 'Saillie', are all equally characteristic, and one is left wondering whether Couperin meant the title of the last to bear its usual prosaic meaning, or whether he was thinking of it as meaning a witticism, in which case one feels that it might well be applied to nearly everything which he wrote.

The works of the other clavecinist-organists of this period are seldom heard now. It is almost incredible that the numerous pianists who have played *Le Coucou* of Daquin have not had enough curiosity to look up some of his other compositions, and that the students of music who have read of the contest in improvisation between Marchand and Bach have never wished to see for themselves what manner of composer this was who would even think of challenging the great man. In view of the fact that the knowledge of even Couperin and Rameau which many people have is confined to one or two selected pieces, it is perhaps too much to expect that anything should be known of the works of d'Anglebert, Dandrieu, Clérambault, Dagincourt, and others. A very good general impression of the group may be gained from the volumes of *Les Clavecinistes Français* (edited by Louis Diémer and published by Durand). Their compositions are well worthy of study, though they have neither the brilliancy and wit of Couperin nor the more solid excellencies of Rameau.

Jean Philippe Rameau was born at Dijon in 1683 and died at Paris in 1764. He was a man who took his art very seriously, and by his studies in harmony and by his compositions made a far greater mark on the general trend of music than Couperin. His activities in the earlier years of his life were not altogether crowned with success, and it was not until he was about fifty years of age that he became recognized as a master who is but little removed from the very first rank.

The harpsichord works can be most easily studied in the volume published by Durand and edited by Saint-Saëns, who was also responsible for the general supervision of the complete edition of Rameau's works. In this volume there is an interesting preface by the editor, who claims that the music is faithfully presented without 'ce luxe parasite d'interpolations—indication de mouvements, de nuance, de doigtés'. He makes some general remarks about the tempi which should be adopted in playing the music of this period and calls attention to one interesting direction of the composer which, if read in conjunction with the remark of Couperin which has been quoted above, seems to prove that the device of tempo rubato was well known in these times. In Rameau's case it is a negative direction. In *L'Enharmonique* he asks that a certain section be played 'sans altérer la mesure', and this surely indicates that the practice of varying the tempo was fairly common, if not universal.

Rameau's own table of ornaments and their proper interpretation is more extended than Couperin's, and it is printed in the Saint-Saëns edition along with a corresponding modern notation which is used throughout the volume.

The first book was published in 1706, and consists of a single suite. It begins with a Prelude of which the opening section is free and unbarred. This is followed by two Allemandes, a Courante, with the characteristic alternation of bars of 3/2 and 6/4, and, reversing the usual order, a Gigue and two Sarabandes. Then came, as pièces ajoutées, a Vénétienne, a Gavotte, and a Minuet. These early pieces do not show much of the mastery of the later Rameau. They were inspired mainly by Marchand and are rather stiff and stilted with the exception of the two Sarabandes which are graceful and expressive.

The next set, published in 1724 and revised for a new edition in 1731, shows a great advance. It opens with a Minuet, followed by an Allemande, a Courante, and two Gigues, of which the second is 'En rondeau' (Rameau was almost as fond as Couperin of the simple rondo form). The next piece is 'Le Rappel des Oiseaux', a charmingly poetic fancy. There are two Rigaudons with a variation of the second, a 'muséte en rondeau'; the well-known jolly 'Tambourin'; another rondeau 'La Villageoise', quite a delightful bit of painting; still another rondeau, 'Les Tendres Plaintes', a very sensitive movement, and 'Les Niais de Sologne' which demands a little more than a mere passing mention, for these 'simpletons' are not so simple as they look. The main theme is stated with naivety in a way which rather reminds one of a Scarlatti sonata. The composer then gives two variations, the first of which is a fine study of three against two—the right hand playing in triplets against the steadier throb of the left. The second has the original tune against a running bass in semiquavers, and is worked up to a fine climax.

The other pieces in this group are mainly rondos under various titles. Rameau, like Couperin, prided himself on being an accurate delineator of his subjects. Here, 'Les Tourbillons' (Pirro remarks, 'That is to say, the swirls of dust driven by strong winds') is quite a graphic picture. It starts quite innocently and works up at the end to a real whirlwind. 'Les Cyclopes' is mainly noteworthy on account of what may be called its pianistic effects, the broken chords and the crossed hands.

The *Nouvelles Suites de Pièces de Clavecin* which follows has even more claim to our attention. The opening Allemande is on a bigger scale than the previous Allemandes. So is the Courante. The Sarabande is a thing of rare beauty. The next piece, 'Les Trois Mains', is a most ingenious effort in which the hands cross and re-cross in a manner which puts even Scarlatti's best attempts in the shade, and which produces an effect as if a third hand was really being used. One of the most interesting things in this suite is a Gavotte in A minor with six variations. These variations are full of striking devices; the broken chords and repeated notes for alternate hands of the fourth, and the broken octaves of the fifth and sixth variations, distinctly anticipate later developments of keyboard technique.

Included also in this book is the well-known 'La Poule', an effective representation of an excited clucking hen, in which the clucking is suggested by very simple means—a little rising arpeggio. 'Les Triolets' and 'Les Sauvages' follow, and then we have 'L'Enharmonique', a more than usually poetic trifle which owes its title to a phrase like the following:

'L'Enharmonique'.

Rameau apologizes for the effect that this modulation may

have on the ears that may hear it for the first time, but he
assures his listeners that they will get accustomed to it, and
will even find it beautiful—'l'on en sent même toute la
beauté quand on a surmonté la première répugnance que
le défaut d'habitude peut occasionner en ce cas'. He gives
specific directions about the performance of this passage.
He asks the player to lighten his touch and to make a
rallentando as he approaches the critical point of the change,
where the pause mark should be carefully observed. He
adds that the effect comes from the difference of a quarter-
tone which is found between C♯ and D♭.

The note, from which I have quoted the above, sounds
curiously modern, and might have been written as an
analytical note on a composition by one of our experi-
mentalists of to-day.

The suite closes with the jolly 'L'Égyptienne' and the
proud 'La Dauphine'.

The remaining pieces in the Saint-Saëns edition are five
extracts from the *Pièces en Concert* transcribed by the
composer. They were originally written as Trios for a
harpsichord with a violin or flute and a 'cello, and are
interesting in their original form as marking a stage in the
development of chamber music. Each instrument is
treated on equal terms. The clavecin is no mere accompanying instrument, but has a definite part of its own. In
their transcribed form they are not so full of interest, and
they hardly fall within the scope of this essay, which concerns Rameau, not as a student of harmony, nor as a
composer of operas and chamber music, but as a writer for
the clavecin. His works show him to have been a virtuoso
with a fine and prophetic knowledge of the possibilities
of keyboard technique, with a real musical message to
deliver, but without the intimacy and daintiness of touch,
without the humour, the 'savoir faire', or the wit of
Couperin, who will always be, to me, the true poet of the
clavecin, and the real portrayer of the genius of his time.

It is not unfair, I think, to suggest that the relationship

of Rameau to Couperin is comparable, *mutatis mutandis*, to the relationship of Schumann to Chopin. Schumann was the more versatile, all-round composer who, among other activities, wrote a large number of fine works for the piano; but the piano was to Chopin the sole medium for the expression of his inmost thoughts. In similar fashion, Rameau was a composer of operas, ballets, and other works, and his harpsichord writing, though full of interest and of fine musicianship, does not show the subtlety and intimacy which characterize the compositions of Couperin.

4

GEORGE FREDERICK HANDEL
(1685-1759)
By W. H. HADOW

WHEN, at the age of twenty-five, Handel paid his first visit to England, he had no intention of settling here or even of making a prolonged stay. He had recently been appointed Kapellmeister to the Hanoverian Court and had entered upon the duties of his office. After a few months of routine work he readily obtained leave of absence and came over, on a private invitation, with no formal commission, no knowledge of our country, and no understanding of our language. He little thought that this voyage of discovery was to lead to the most momentous crisis of his career.

During the Restoration our music was still predominantly English: not only our Church compositions which naturally centred round the Anglican rite, but in all secular fields as well. Opera meant *Dido* and *King Arthur* and the *Fairy Queen*: choral work was typified by *St. Cecilia* and the *Welcome Odes* and the *Yorkshire Feast Song*: chamber music, though partly influenced by Corelli, was essentially national in melody and idiom. But in 1695 the whole tradition was broken by the death of Purcell. There was, indeed, no one to carry on the succession. Blow, a true genius, was too modest and self-effacing for leadership; Croft wrote little outside the precincts of the Church; Tudway, who actually became composer in ordinary to Queen Anne, is now known solely as a collector and antiquarian. Meanwhile the vacant boards were increasingly occupied by Italian musicians: Tosi and Gasparini at the end of the seventeenth century, Margharita de l'Épine at the beginning of the eighteenth; in 1707 the failure of Addison's *Rosamond*, incompetently set by

Clayton, only gave encouragement to the invaders; in 1708 Nicolini, the greatest singer of his time, was 'attracted to London by the English passion for foreign operas'. The libretti at first presented in 'lame hobbling translation' became gradually bilingual, and the climax was reached in the enthusiastic reception of an anonymous opera called *Almahide*, 'the first opera', says Burney, 'performed in England wholly in Italian and by Italian singers'. *Almahide* was produced in January 1710 and repeated fourteen times during the summer. At the end of 1710 Handel arrived in London.

His reputation as a composer of Italian opera had already preceded him, established and consolidated by the success of *Agrippina* which he had produced at Venice in the winter of 1709. On his arrival he was introduced to Aaron Hill, the astute and versatile manager of the Haymarket Theatre, who carved for him a libretto out of Tasso's *Jerusalem*, had it retranslated into Italian, engaged Nicolini to sing, and prepared to stage the work on a scale of unprecedented magnificence. Handel wrote the music in eleven days; by the middle of February the scheme was completed; on February 24th *Rinaldo* made its appearance and at once took the town by storm. Addison gently satirized the profusion of its display—the birds in Armida's garden, the fire-breathing dragons which drew her chariot —and congratulated our nation on its presumed acquaintance with a foreign language. His voice was drowned in the stream of public applause: night after night the theatre was crowded; the melodies of 'Il tricerbero' and 'Lascia ch'io pianga' spread far and wide beyond its doors; at one stroke Handel had achieved his conquest and set himself in a position of acknowledged supremacy.

In June 1711 Handel returned to his duties at Hanover, where for the next year he resided and wrote much chamber music for the use of the court. But England had still for him a powerful attraction. In Hanover there was then no provision for opera—even *Rinaldo* could not be given—while in London there was the Earl of Burlington for patron, and the Haymarket for opportunity, and the memory of a past triumph to reawaken. By the end of 1712 the temptation had become irresistible; he once more obtained leave of absence, left Germany, and thenceforward made England his home. He began badly with a weak *pasticcio* called *Il Pastor Fido*, some of the music of which he used after his manner in later compositions. A few weeks later he made ample amends with *Teseo*, the most moving and dramatic of his operas, containing among other treasures Medea's passionate scena 'Morirò ma vendicata morirò' and the golden melody of 'Vieni torna', assigned in the third Act to Agilea. The success of this work not only restored him to full popular favour but attracted the attention of no less a patroness than Queen Anne, who accepted from him a birthday ode, conferred on him a pension of £200 a year, and commissioned him to write a *Te Deum* for the Peace of Utrecht. A year later she died and was succeeded by the Elector of Hanover, from whose services Handel had so long been playing truant; but this contretemps, which might easily have been disastrous to him, appears to have had no appreciable effect upon his fortunes. George I, whose love of music was his most amiable quality, magnanimously forgave the runaway, confirmed and doubled his pension, attended in his honour the revival of *Rinaldo* and the new opera of *Amadigi*, appointed him clavier-master to the two princesses, and remained to the end of life one of the firmest and most constant of his supporters.

After *Amadigi* the course of Handel's operatic writing was checked, first by a visit to Hanover in the King's train, and after his return by a temporary appointment in the household at Cannons where he wrote the Chandos Anthems, and laid in them the foundations of that massive choral counterpoint for which opera afforded no scope and for which his oratorios were, some twenty years later, to be so notably distinguished. It is significant that the masque of *Haman and Mordecai* which he composed at this time assigns an unusually prominent part to the chorus and suffered in this respect little change when he remodelled it later on into the oratorio of *Esther*.

But the claims of opera were silenced only for a time, and in 1719 arose a new occasion for calling Handel back to their allegiance. This was the re-establishment of the Haymarket Theatre under the title of the Royal Academy of Music with the King as patron, the Duke of Newcastle and Lord Burlington as directors, Heidegger as impresario, and Handel, Ariosti, and Giovanni Bononcini in control of the music. The King gave £1,000, another £50,000 were rapidly subscribed, the best available singers and players were summoned from the Continent: Senesino was annexed from an Italian company at Dresden, Durastanti came as prima donna to be succeeded in turn by Cuzzoni and Faustina, every device of pageantry and splendour was adopted, and the whole venture set sail under a Favonian wind of good augury.

From the first year the clouds began to gather. Ariosti dropped out of the triumvirate, Handel and Bononcini were left in joint command, and when in 1720 the one produced *Radamisto* and the other *Astarto*, both with overwhelming success, the town was divided by a bitter feud between their respective partisans. Two years later the balance was inclined by Handel's *Ottone*, which is said to have been the most popular of his operas, partly from its flow of attractive melody, partly because in it Cuzzoni made her début; but Bononcini had great influence with the nobility, especially with the powerful house of Marlborough, and his polished manners and gift of intrigue made him a dangerous antagonist. Up to 1727 they wrote opera in almost annual competition, while John Byrom watched with sardonic amusement these 'differences of Tweedledum and Tweedledee'. Then Bononcini fell into merited disgrace and left Handel master of the field.

But he was also master of a very turbulent household.

Senesino was beyond reasonable human measure vain, irritable, and arrogant: Cuzzoni and Faustina, commonly known as 'the two fighting cats', filled the theatre with interminable bickerings which were echoed and re-echoed by their respective partisans: finally the quarrel extended to the court itself, and while the King's party remained faithful to the Haymarket, that of the Prince of Wales set up an opposition at Lincoln's Inn Fields with Porpora for composer and his pupil Farinelli for chief soprano. Against these obstacles Handel maintained a heroic struggle, producing opera after opera amid scenes of nightly riot and disturbance: *Giulio Cesare* in 1723, *Tamerlano* in 1724, next year *Rodelinda*, next year *Admeto* with two others. Then in 1728 Gay and Pepusch captured popular taste with the *Beggar's Opera*, and the Academy closed its doors.

Even this disaster left Handel unconquered. He shook off Bononcini, joined partnership with Heidegger, ransacked Italy and Germany for singers, and reopened at the Haymarket on his own account. Between 1728 and 1740 he wrote no fewer than nineteen new operas, besides a complete revision of *Rinaldo*, and gave them successively, some at the Haymarket, some after his transference to Lincoln's Inn Fields, which he exchanged with the victorious forces of the opposition. Many of these operas were successful, particularly *Orlando*, *Arianna*, *Ariodante*, *Giustino*, and *Berenice*; many were attended by the King and the more loyal of the nobility; but the fashionable public was increasingly drawn away to the new entertainment of the Masquerade, and to this more than any other cause must be ascribed the close of Handel's operatic career. The expenses were enormous, the takings gradually diminished; in 1740 Handel presented his last opera, *Deidamia*, and retired once more into bankruptcy.

In estimating the quality of Handel's composition it is therefore appropriate to begin with the operatic writing to which his first fifty-five years were mainly devoted. He began his career, on leaving the University, as violinist

in the Hamburg Theatre, where he played in the operas
of Keiser and wrote three of his own—*Almira*, *Nero*, and
the diptych *Floridante* and *Dafne*; indeed we are told that
one of his reasons for leaving Hamburg was that the last
of these was mutilated in performance by a clownish
director. During his Italian period, from 1705 to 1710, he
made his name chiefly with *Roderigo* at Florence and
Agrippina at Venice. The so-called oratorios composed at
Rome, when the theatre was closed by Papal edict, are
operas in the thinnest disguise: the whole plan of the
Resurrection, for example, is essentially dramatic, and
Lucifer's song 'O voi del Erebo' might equally serve for
any powerful and determined rebel. It is not surprising
that he made his English début in opera. He had been
trained for the stage, he had won there his most conspicuous triumphs, he had come to regard it as the most
fertile and congenial field for his abilities.

He accepted in the main the customary conventions of
his time: a plot derived from classical history or romance,
a cast of few characters, a large predominance of solo
music, a chorus rarely taking part in the action and usually
restricted to a short passage of comment or jubilation at
the end. But he breathed into these conventions a life
which they had never known. In *Teseo*, for instance, the
character of Medea is well and consistently drawn throughout: in *Tamerlano* the songs are as expressive and passionate as those of Gluck, though they admit the *fiorituri*
which Gluck was afterwards to condemn: *Rinaldo* is full
of chivalry, *Radamisto* of adventure, *Orlando* of enchantment; in almost all cases the music is fitted with entire
appropriateness not to the words, which are often poor
enough, but to the ideas which they are intended to convey.
A technical point worth noting is the boldness of harmonic
invention with which, on occasion, Handel can illustrate
and enforce his theme. Ordinarily he 'wrought in the
primary colours', satisfied with few keys and diatonic structure; when the situation demanded it he would venture

into unknown regions which no dramatic work of the time had ever approached. In *Giulio Cesare*, for example, there is a scene of unaccompanied recitative which centres round the urn containing Pompey's ashes. The accompaniment begins, without key signature, in G sharp minor, modulates almost round the gamut, and ends enharmonically on the minor of A flat. In the days when we knew nothing of equal temperament the effect must have been astonishing, and we can well understand Burney's comment that this opera gained more reputation from its recitatives than even from its airs. The same opera is also distinguished by one of Handel's most audacious experiments in instrumental colour—the landscape-picture at the slopes of Parnassus, which is scored for oboe, harp, viola da gamba, and theorbo, with accompaniment for strings and bassoon. He was fond of trying new combinations of sound, using horns sometimes to replace trumpets, sometimes in combination with them, adding a piccolo to the flutes in Armida's bird-song, giving special prominence to bassoon and oboe, anticipating by half a century some of the effects of tone and contrast which are often attributed to the later development of orchestration. His method is different from that of Bach, whose obbligati, always beautiful and appropriate, are determined less by the delight of pure sound than by the weaving of contrapuntal parts. Handel is more concerned with the quality of the *timbre* as such, and he places it on his canvas with an unerring hand.

But chief of all his operas are a storehouse of lovely and expressive melodies, of 'Lascia ch'io pianga', and 'Verdi prati', and 'Ombra mai fu', and the delightful 'sicilianos' that tread a measure for which he had special predilection. They touch every range of their art, simple or recondite, gay or pathetic, quiet or passionate; they gather in fragrant clusters like the blossoms in a garden of roses. It may be that the fashion of the stage has turned away from Handel, that we are following other aims and other pursuits: no change of fashion can touch the beauty of his songs; their infinite variety is beyond the despoiling hand of age or custom.

We have seen that Handel, when he was at Cannons, wrote a masque on *Haman and Mordecai* for the use of the Duke's private theatre. It was entirely a domestic affair, the entertainment of a house-party. Pope and Arbuthnot are said to have collaborated on the text; the music was a *pièce d'occasion* such as half a century later Haydn composed for Prince Esterhazy. It is notable for the amount of its choral writing—the final chorus alone occupies forty pages in Chrysander—which reflected both the personal tastes of the Duke and the influence of the Chandos Anthems. Some twelve years later, in 1732, Handel recalled it and proposed to include it among his operas at the Haymarket: it was censored by the Bishop of London, on the ground that a Biblical subject was unsuited for dramatic presentation: whereupon he remodelled it and gave it, as Burney says, 'in still life', without the support of action or pageantry. The term oratorio had long been current in Italy: this was, so far as we know, the first example of its employment in England, and its adaptation so hit the popular taste that two more sacred representations, *Deborah* and *Athalia*, were added in the next couple of years. We have a curious sidelight on its growing prevalence. Hogarth's plate called 'The Chorus', printed in 1733, represents a group of musicians rehearsing the oratorio of *Judith*, composed by William Defesch who was then leading the orchestra at the Marylebone Gardens: a sure sign that the novelty was coming into vogue, and was spreading through other places of public entertainment. These oratorios differed from opera *proprio nomine* in that they were recited, not acted, that they were marked by greater dignity and gravity of treatment, and that they assigned an increasingly large part to the choruses—those of *Deborah* being particularly fine. But the Biblical subjects were adapted with great freedom and the libretti written in the current rhetorical verse of the time: they stood in fact almost as near to the secular theatre as Racine's *Esther* and *Athalie* do to *Phèdre* or *Andromaque* or *Britannicus*. The same is true of Handel's next oratorio *Saul* (1738), which is essentially dramatic in feeling, and in which certain of the scenes almost demand the movement and circumstance of the stage. There is a significant story that he wished to end it with a 'Hallelujah' and was dissuaded by his librettist Charles Jennens on the ground that this would be an incongruous close to a tragedy.

We can thus measure the change wrought by *Israel in Egypt* which he compiled, adapted, and partly wrote a few weeks after the appearance of *Saul*. It is beyond question that much of the music is borrowed from other composers; the claims of Erba and Urio, of Kerl and Stradella, are indisputable, and have given rise in our own time to endless controversies about quotation and plagiarism. But far more important than all these is the daring novelty of the general scheme. In it Handel, for the first time, discarded the dramatic fable and the artificial libretto, selected his own words unaltered from Holy Writ, made the chorus his protagonist, and raised the whole structure from the compromises of sacred opera to a level of epic grandeur and sublimity. It is interesting to see how the conception grew under his hand. In the second part, which was first in order of composition, he assigns some portions of the text to soloists, though the chorus largely preponderates: in the earlier, which narrates the plagues of Egypt and the beginning of the Exodus, there is but one aria and that the weakest of its numbers; all the rest is a succession of choral narrative.

This innovation was too sheer to be acceptable. The general public, then as always preoccupied with the pleasures of the solo voice, resented the disappointment of its hopes and heard with undissembled weariness music which was as unintelligible to it as *Paradise Lost* had been to the wits of the Restoration. Handel endeavoured to meet it by intercalating a few airs and recitatives from his operas, but even this mutilation of his work did not restore it to popular favour. *Israel* was given a few times to rapidly dwindling houses and then withdrawn into a retirement from which it did not emerge for a period of nineteen years. Precisely the same fate attended the only other oratorio of Handel's on which the methods of the theatre have left no trace. The *Messiah*, produced at Dublin in 1741, met on its transference to London with entire and disastrous failure. It was censured as dull, it was condemned as irreligious, it was withdrawn after three performances amid a chorus of disapprobation. Not until 1750 did it win any hold on our affections: not until 1767 was it published. We, who are building Handel's sepulchre with so much assiduity, may do well to remember the stones with which our fathers greeted him, and to realize that on the *Messiah* and on *Israel in Egypt* their heaviest volleys were directed.

There is little wonder that Handel reverted to that adaptation of the operatic method for which alone, it appeared, was any audience available. *Samson* in 1743 had a success which was due as much to the politics of George II as to the intelligence of the public, and thereby earned a few lines of banter from Horace Walpole (letter to Sir Horace Mann, February 24th, 1743). Thenceforward to the end of his life he produced a series of works which bear the title of oratorio, but show a good deal of variety in its interpretation. Some of them are frankly on secular subjects—*Semele* for instance is not only opera but light opera. *Hercules* is an adaptation from a Greek tragedy, *Alexander Balus* from the story of Cleopatra; *Theodora* is virtually an opera in three acts on the same theme as Massinger's *Virgin Martyr* and almost as dramatic; the Occasional Oratorio is a hymn of thanksgiving for the victory at Culloden. Others include *Joseph* (1743), *Judas Maccabaeus* (1746), *Solomon* (1748), *Susanna* (1748), and *Jephtha* (1752) which are of the same family as *Saul* and *Samson* and maintain the same tradition. Of these *Judas Macca-baeus* came in on a wave of patriotism and won instant recognition and applause, *Solomon* and *Susanna*, those treasure-houses of melody, were received with the customary neglect, *Jephtha*, the swan-song of his old age, made some real amends, and enabled his declining years to be spent in comfort.

When therefore we compare the general style of Handel's oratorios with that of his operas we shall find that, apart from one important respect, the differences are less of kind than of degree. Indeed, M. Rolland has ingeniously conjectured that Handel's principal reason for turning to oratorios was that the British public was better acquainted with the Bible than with Tasso or Apollonius Rhodius. In both forms alike Handel shows great power of characterization, but, as we should naturally expect, 'it is in the oratorios comparatively restrained and simplified'. They afford less scope for passion—those at any rate on sacred subjects, for Handel is nowhere more passionate than in *Hercules*. Only once, and that in *Susanna*, does comedy intrude her audacious face; a certain dignity and decorum are prescribed by the presence of a great theme. We have not the analogues of *Medea* or *Tamerlano* or *Radamisto*, but we have the contrast of the king and the two mothers in the second part of *Solomon*, the insulting challenge of Harapha in *Samson*, the exquisite discrimination of the two chief songs in *Theodora*; the portraits are drawn in fewer and broader lines but they are not more unmistakable. And this finds its analogue when the emotion is not indicative of any particular speaker. Pathos has never been more fitly expressed than in 'He was despised', or jubilation than in 'Rejoice greatly'. Again, as oratorio affords more scope for narrative so it gives Handel more opportunity for those gifts of picturesque effect in which he excelled: the Carillon in *Saul*, the sun standing still in *Joshua*, the triumph in *Judas Maccabaeus*, and many others. Of these some are childlike and even trivial: the flies in Egypt ap-

proach the furthest bound of reason, the frogs overleap it;
but these are the marks of an unsophisticated age and may
be paralleled by the realistic effects of Kuhnau and Tele-
mann and the descriptive choruses in the *Creation*. It is
a far higher gift by which Handel can suggest the very
atmosphere and significance of a scene sometimes by
special effects of theme or harmony, sometimes by the
timbre of particular instruments. *Israel*, which is throughout a model of mid-century orchestration, is full of examples: the twofold use of the trombones for solemnity
and vigour, the flutes in 'But as for His people', the bassoons deepening the string-tone in 'He sent a thick darkness'. The *Messiah* would supply an equally striking
instance in 'The people that walked' if we were ever
allowed to hear it in its original form, as it was before
Mozart laid editorial hands upon it and turned its darkness
into a golden twilight. We may remember that all Handel's
oratorios presuppose an organ accompaniment, for which
definite provision is made in the overture to *Saul* and which
the composer himself supplied by improvisation. When
we read of his reputation as an organ-player and see the
evidence of it in his organ concertos, we can well believe
that the original performances far outstripped the indications of the printed score.

For pure delight of melody the oratorios are in no way
inferior to the operas: witness 'He shall feed his flock'
and 'Sound an alarm' and 'Waft her, angels' and scores
of others which come crowding into the memory, bringing us, in Dryden's phrase, as much pleasure as we can
bear. But the chief glory of all his sacred music lies in the
massive and epic splendour of its choral writing. He can
manifest this as well in the more restricted as in the ampler
ranges of polyphony, in the three-part texture of the early
Chandos Anthems as in the eight-part texture of *Israel*;
he can attain it through complexity of treatment, as in
'They loathed to drink of the river' and in 'Hear us, O Lord,
on Thee we call', or as in *Zadok the Priest* and in the last

chorus of *Deborah* through an elemental simplicity of means which has no need of ornament or device. Two of the most famous choruses of the *Messiah* are enlarged from chamber-duets and are as appropriate in the latter form as are Bach's adaptation to overture and concerto of movements from his violin sonatas. One of his great sources of strength is the foundation of his chorus on a theme of plain diatonic phrase—sometimes the reiteration of a single note, sometimes the constituents of the common chord—and its subsequent elaboration with running figures and counter-subjects. And always, when the suitable climax demands, he can check the moving surge of the music and with a few simple harmonies interpret and drive home the innermost meaning of his text.

It is impossible, within the limits of this essay, to do more than indicate the main point of comparison between Handel's choral writing and that of Bach. As a rule Handel's melody is the more direct, Bach's the more reflective: one more concerned with the immediate presentation of his theme, the other with meditation upon its content. Again, Handel thinks harmonically and uses his mastery of counterpoint to enhance and decorate a scheme conceived in harmonic terms; Bach thinks contrapuntally and his richness of harmonic colour arises in great measure from the interplay of the moving parts. At their furthest they stand as far removed as the Dagon chorus in *Samson* from the opening number of *Wär' Gott nicht mit uns* or that of the Ascension Oratorio. Such contrasts indeed are so salient as to be hardly comparable. A more significant illustration is given by two examples which appear to approach more nearly to one another—the closing choruses of the *Messiah* and of *Ich hatte viel Bekümmerniss*. They are on the same theme—the universal hymn of praise from the fifth chapter of Revelation—both begin with passages of ascription, in which the voices sing note against note, and develop into radiant fugues which rise and circle and re-echo to the very steps of the Throne. But though in their scheme and purpose they are one, in essence they are as different as the angels of Milton from those of Dante. Handel treats his ascriptive passages as a prelude: Bach sets the note of jubilation from the outset. Handel begins his fugue with a thundering unison of basses and tenors: Bach begins quietly with the solo voice and builds up his climaxes gradually to the soaring trumpet-call at the close. Handel appends an Amen in close canon, a monument of polyphonic skill which a little overweights the general structure: Bach preserves an exactitude of proportion to which even so noble an accessory would have seemed superfluous. It is idle to inquire which of the two types of genius is the greater; one might as well institute a comparison between Dante and Milton: they stand apart as twin peaks of the eighteenth century, different in character and career, alike in supremacy of achievement.

We have been so long accustomed, in this country, to associating Handel's name with vocal music that we have thrown out of perspective the greatness and abundance of his music for instruments. There are probably few English readers of M. Rolland's excellent monograph but have felt some shock of surprise at finding that more than half the chapter on technique is devoted to the instrumental works and learning from it that 'Handel's compositions for clavier are the most popular of any that he wrote and have achieved the greatest number of European editions'. Apart from the overtures his instrumental writing occupies no less than thirty-two volumes of the catalogue: they range from the Oboe Sonatas of 1696 to the Organ Concertos of 1753; some contain nine or twelve or fifteen separate compositions; they fill the measure of almost every form that was current in his day. It is true that he appears to have set little store by them: of some the parts only were printed, others were enforced by the piracies of a rascally publisher: none the less we may find in them some of his truest inspiration and of his unerring command of resource.

F

In his youth he was a proficient player on oboe and violin and grew to such a mastery of the clavier that he is said to have rivalled Bach in performance and surpassed him in improvisation. To this, and to his astonishing gift of spontaneous melody, we may attribute the precocious maturity of his style: his genius was born at full growth and never faltered in its appropriate means of expression. His first known sonatas were written when he was eleven, his first organ concerto when he was eighteen, and in these there is so little touch of the prentice hand that it would be impossible to date them from internal evidence. The *Suites pour le Clavecin* which he published in 1720, and the fifth of which contains the so-called 'Harmonious Blacksmith', represents the harvest of a score of years and is as uniform in style and conception as are any of the three collections which followed it.

For these and for the other sonate da camera he usually adopted the customary form inherited from Corelli and the Italians: a grave introduction, a vigorous contrapuntal allegro, and a brief adagio, often but a few bars in length, leading to a light-hearted and melodious finale. Occasionally he included actual dance-measures—Minuet or Gavotte or Bourrée—not with the system and regularity of Bach but interspersed among the other movements as fancy dictated. Two of the violin sonatas from 'Op. 1' are still famous in England, No. 3 in A major with its delightful Siciliana, and No. 13 in D, the second movement of which was afterwards adapted for a chorus in *Solomon*; the others are well worth rescuing from the unaccountable oblivion in which they have been surrounded.

In the Concerti Grossi he usually followed the Italian scheme: a concertino of two violins and a 'cello, a large force of strings and wood-wind for accompaniment. On occasion he varied or enlarged his plan. The collection published in 1736 as 'Op. 4' was popularly known as the Oboe Concertos from the prominent part assigned to that instrument. There is a double concerto for two concertini

of oboes and bassoons with ripieno strings, written anti-
phonally and marked 'a due cori', and another in which
the wood-wind is reinforced by horns, a close anticipation
of Haydn's orchestra. Still more notable are the organ
concertos: brilliant virtuoso pieces of which the solo part
is often marked 'ad lib', and which, we are told, gave
Handel a special opportunity for extemporization.

There remain the two most extensive of Handel's instrumental works, the two in which he most nearly rivalled
the symphonic scale and magnitude of later times. These
are the *Water Music*, which was chiefly written between
1715 and 1717 and revised in 1740, and the *Firework
Music*, which was written to celebrate the Peace of Aix-la-
Chapelle in 1748. The former is in twenty-one movements
and contains a stately overture, a vivid and tuneful horn-
pipe, and one of the loveliest arias that even he ever composed. The latter is a gorgeous piece of pageantry, eight
movements long, with a gigantic orchestra of 100 performers and, we are told, salvos of cannons at the moment
of special climax. Apart from this doubtful accessory the
score is of great historical interest, for it indicates the exact
numbers and proportions which Handel chose for his
most grandiose effects. Trumpets, horns, and drums are
each on three staves and each stave has three players to the
part; there are twelve first oboes, eight second and four
third, eight first and four second bassoons, and a full force
of strings doubling the wood-wind throughout. In a few
movements the brass is silent for reasons of contrast; in the
long and elaborate overture, the allegro called 'La Réjouis-
sance', and in the second minuet the entire forces are heard
in combination. No such splendour of sound had ever
acclaimed an outburst of national rejoicing.

The *Firework Music* has passed away with the ceremony
which gave it occasion, and a vast number of its contemporaries are either forgotten or antiquated. It is hardly an
exaggeration to say that no living person in this country
has heard one in ten of Handel's compositions; we have

trodden in narrow pathways and have left the greater part
of the field unvisited. Yet there is no musician whose
name is held, by our nation at large, in more widely spread
honour and affection. Some of his themes have become
household words, as familiar as a line of Shakespeare or
a text of Holy Writ: the march in *Saul*, the triumphal
chorus in *Judas Maccabaeus*, the 'Hallelujah' of the *Messiah*
which sets all Heaven before our eyes. It is our own loss
that we carry the quest so little farther. On every page
there await us marvels of skill and invention, of pathos and
sublimity, of grandeur which stands broad-based and
mountain-high, of melody which wells from the rock in
a perennial fountain of delight. The alleged unworthiness
of his collaborators is more often an excuse than a reason:
Pope wrote one of his libretti, Gay another, Congreve a
third, a fourth and a fifth are taken from Milton; and even
the formalities of our lesser eighteenth-century poets are
ennobled and enriched by the radiance with which he has
illuminated their verses. His music is simple, direct, universal, too sincere for artifice, too great for subtlety; it
speaks a language which all may understand who will, and
uses it as a garment for some of the noblest thoughts and
emotions of mankind.

5

CHRISTOPHER WILLIBALD GLUCK
(1714-1787)
AND THE MUSICAL REVOLUTION OF THE EIGHTEENTH CENTURY

By D. F. TOVEY

THERE are five great composers who have become the special property of the non-musician. This is not an unmixed advantage, either to the reputation and preservation of the music or to the non-musician's understanding of it. The layman's approach to other arts lies through many normal experiences which are much more closely related to these arts than to music. It is only in recent times that pictures have been held to be the worse for having subjects that are describable in literary terms; and poetry itself is not wholly unapproachable through literature. But there are notorious disadvantages in approaching music through literature: indeed, it is a pity that the disadvantages are not more notorious than they are. The non-musician's composer gains a large measure of his popularity at the expense of his musical qualities. The purely literary critic seldom knows anything about the literary side of the musician's work, and therefore sheds no expert light upon it. Histories of English literature are not thought defective if they omit all mention of Purcell and Handel, who gave new values, both classical and popular, to the poetry of Milton, Dryden, Pope, and the Authorized Version, besides immortalizing humbler writers from Nahum Tate downwards; while even in the case of Metastasio, every line of whose work was written for music, the orthodox encyclopedist is content to tell us that his works were too poetical for music and too musical for poetry. Meanwhile, the composers tend to become represented by such works and features of style as can be described without any commitments of musical judgement. Performances and editions of their works are undertaken by enthusiasts whose knowledge is weakest on the musical side; and isolated fragments obtain, by some accident of effective performance or popular fancy, an extraordinary vogue. Then comes the more expert musical showman, who dresses up these items or whole works in a tasty modern confection with selected quaint-nesses from the styles of several centuries; and the public and critics rejoice in the ever-fresh appeal of the grand old pioneer with his naïve sincerity.

The most famous sufferer from this fate is, of course, Handel; the most dangerous of all composers; the most industrious and unscrupulous in writing himself down; but, when he chose, exactly what Beethoven called him, the 'master of all masters, and capable as no one else of producing the greatest effects with the simplest means'. Less than one-twentieth of Handel's work is known to the public, and most of what is known is buried in a debris of modernization which the *Musikgelehrte* of the present day removes often to create worse confusion by failure to include common sense and general musicianship as elements of scholarship.

Berlioz is another non-musician's musician. His French prose is far less amateurish than his music, though few men of letters except W. E. Henley have taken notice of it. But his music is saved from its own amateurishness, and from amateurish production and interference, by the fact that he is a pioneer of the modern orchestra. Inextricably mixed with his curious ineptitudes, there is an astounding intuitive grasp of certain principles, not only of orchestra-tion, but of composition on a very large scale. He is a master of vast exordiums and perorations, and also of sky-vault heights and infernal depths. Neither in time nor in harmonic space has he any material for middle regions; but the very hollows reverberate impressively, and he is even less amenable to correction than Gluck.

At the opposite extreme we have Chopin, with vision strictly confined to the pianoforte, but with perceptions in form and harmony so deep as to transcend equally the comprehension of the admirers and the detractors of his fame as a writer of salon music. His music, again, is to some extent protected from misrepresentation by the fact that it is difficult enough for those who murder it to feel conscious of their barbarity.

The most fortunate of non-musician's composers is Wagner. Amateur productions of his works are obviously impracticable, and the mastery of his mature style is beyond the cavil of any musician who knows enough to have the slightest fear of giving himself away.

A defective technique is a grave disadvantage to the non-musician's great composer. To the interesting or charming historical figure it does not matter. No musician with a sense of humour nowadays wishes to correct Domenico Scarlatti. Bülow had a sense of humour, and did, nevertheless, correct Scarlatti; but Bülow's habits of tidying up were an anachronism even in his own eccentric personality. With composers of the calibre of Gluck or Berlioz a bad technique is a great bar to their intelligibility. It aggravates the controversies which must in any case arise between the musician and the non-musician. The musician's criticisms are not easily presented in a better light than that of pedantic objections irrelevant to the pioneer's or reformer's vast and noble aims; and the non-musician merely loses his temper at such cavils, helplessly, but with popular sympathy on his side. What the general reader is seldom told about the controversies is that for the most part the musician has the advantage of talking not only about music, but about this music in particular: whereas every word that the non-musical enthusiast has to say can be said, and has been said, of any number of other composers known only by name to readers of books on musical history. Performances of the works under discussion will not always help matters. The technical defects of the composer do, in fact, require some intervention on the part of the conductor or editor; and the minimum intervention is the thin end of a wedge which usually leads, as we have already noted, to the dispersal of the composer's style through the idioms of two and a half centuries. Then we have the purists and the modernizers at each other hammer and tongs, with amateur incompetence evenly divided between them, both in fact and in imputation.

Gluck is perhaps the most interesting of all composers who are in this predicament. The literature about him is enormous, and for the most part very readable. He is in touch with interesting people throughout his career, including the French *encyclopédistes*. By far the most readable essay that could be written about Gluck would consist mainly of extracts from the correspondence, private and journalistic, that raged around him throughout his life. I confess myself quite incompetent for such a task; but any temptation I might have for adding to the volumes of Gluck literature from this point of view would be annihilated by one simple reflection: it does not matter a brass farthing what contemporary musical name you substitute for Gluck in the whole of such literature, as far as the music is concerned. It would not be true to say that there was no trace of a musical judgement in the whole of that literature, but it is quite fair to say that it contains few statements, however many there be that seem shrewd and discriminating in form, that you can trust to retain a discoverable meaning when confronted with the music.

An eminent critic has recently quoted with approval a remark of Fétis, that in order to appreciate a symphony of Haydn you should listen to symphonies by Stamitz and Vanhal, so as to measure the immense progress that Haydn's work represents. It has been suggested that we should follow this advice in public concerts. But I am afraid that the result would convey nothing, except to musicians who could have attained it with much less time and trouble by a glance at the works of Stamitz and Vanhal

in a good musical library; and that the effect of a public
performance would only be to set going the usual outburst
of enthusiasm from people who have no sense of composition, who recognize styles merely by tags, if at all, and who
think that anything contemporary with Haydn and Mozart
must be worth reviving so long as it is not by either of
those masters. Where such enthusiasms are genuine the
enthusiasts are probably quite right about the qualities they
see in their hobbies. Their one mistake is that these are
the only qualities they can see in all art and life. That is
why we may at any moment find ourselves attacked by new
Piccinnists at the expense of Gluck. Their appreciation of
music quite possibly will not even go far enough to do
justice to Piccinni, who was himself an out-and-out
Gluckist. I have often envied the connoisseurship of a phil-
atelist, but nobody wants to know what it feels like to have
a mind that has never contemplated a larger field than that
of a postage-stamp. The brutal truth is that the great
masters and the Interesting Historical Figures differ in the
fact that the great masters can compose and the I.H.F.s
cannot. The general public has, if it is given a chance, some
feeling for composition, though it is easily taken in by patchwork. But most of the discussions that rage around the composers of what has, more by its misfortune than its fault,
become literary music are discussions that have nothing
to do with musical composition at all; and for the purpose
of such discussions the compiler of shreds, patches, and
clichés is quite as useful a topic as a real composer.

If the reader who has borne with me so far will bear with
me a considerable way farther, I hope to arrive in this
essay at some estimate of Gluck as a composer. But a large
dump of literary debris remains to be cleared away before
we can get an unobstructed view of his music.

The worst of musical history is that when the history is
interesting the music is often disappointing without it, and
when the music is great it often has no describable history.
But there are a few composers whose work has made

history and also become immortal on its own merits. In such cases we do not need the history to explain the music; on the contrary, we read the history in the light of the permanent value of the music, and produce an official legend that is much too good to be true. Such is the legend of Palestrina as a reformer of Church music; and such is the legend of Gluck as a reformer of opera. Palestrina did reform Church music, and Gluck did reform opera; but neither the corruptions nor the reforms were quite the obvious affairs which legend has made of them. In order to measure Gluck's achievement it is necessary to understand not merely the outward forms of opera in his day, but the whole nature of the change that was revolutionizing music, both instrumental and vocal, independently of the theatre.

Gluck was born in 1714 and was producing operas in London in 1745, five years before the death of Bach and fourteen before the death of Handel. Yet we rightly think of Gluck as belonging to a later period than the age of Bach and Handel. Our chief mistake is in thinking that the age of Bach and Handel regarded those composers as its representatives. Aesthetically, our estimate of that age is a fairly just verdict of history. If all the music of other composers contemporary with Bach and Handel were annihilated, we should miss the equivalent of museums full of china-ware, and should still have the musical equivalent of all the great sculpture and architecture of a Golden Age. But to the music-lovers of 1740 the annihilation of Bach and Handel would have meant the disappearance of Bononcini's successful rival and of an obscure scholar locally famous in Leipzig. The rhymester would still have sung:

> Strange that such difference there should be
> 'Twixt Tweedledum and Tweedledee.

For there were dozens of Tweedledums waiting to contend with Bononcini. When we associate the first half of the eighteenth century with the music of Bach and Handel, we naturally think that the period is one of classical polyphony; but it is no way to be compared with the 'Golden Age' of the sixteenth century. The contemporaries of Palestrina certainly thought that they were witnessing the culmination of pure polyphony; and we agree with them. The polyphony of Bach and Handel is the art of a musical renascence; its principles are not those of the pure vocal art of the sixteenth century, but are profoundly and organically modified by an equally classical sense of the properties of instruments in themselves and in their effect upon voices. This renascence art not only culminates in Bach and Handel, but reaches in those masters the only maturity which interests us. To their contemporaries, this renascence was old-fashioned. Latin could still be quoted in Parliament, and fugues could still be written in oratorios; but in the drawing-room Latin was hardly more out of place than fugues. It was still possible to adumbrate fugues after the fashion of a parliamentary quotation; and if the subject was lively and repeated itself with an echoing tag, a composer like Vanhal could, even in a later generation, write fugues that were amusing enough to be considered elegant. But the pages of Burney show again and again that he had witnessed in his youth the production of Handel's later works, enjoyed the personal acquaintance of Gluck and Philipp Emanuel Bach, watched with disapproval the prodigious career of the young Mozart, and brought his *History of Music* to a conclusion in 1789, all without the slightest idea that Handel's immortality lay in his choruses, that contemporary polyphony was anything but pedantry, and that any more important revolution had taken place in music beyond the 'new ways of taking appoggiaturas and notes of taste'.

In his contempt of polyphony Burney voiced the best opinion of his day. Handel himself, before he finally deserted the glories of Italian opera for the less fashionable 'good works' of oratorio, had made the texture of his later operas more and more like that of the works of his illustrious contemporary Hasse, whose wife, Faustina, he succeeded in getting to sing in the same opera with a rival prima donna, Cuzzoni. A contemporary writer of sonatas, Alberti, who died in 1744, ought to rank as one of the greatest composers in musical history, if the highest art were not to conceal but to avoid art. He invented the 'Alberti bass'; or, if he did not invent it, at all events made it his own, and, like the famous grimy writer of a testimonial to a famous soap, having used it in his first works, used no other for the rest of his life. Hasse's favourite texture consisted of chords repeated in quavers, a device which saves even more labour than the Alberti bass. It is not to be confused with the tremolo, which, limited to measured semiquavers, Handel uses often enough, but never without imagination. Neither it, nor any similar apparently worthless formula, is a resource to be despised by dramatic reformers. But we shall never understand Gluck's early environment until we realize that such resources were already in full use, and that the age of Bach and Handel was an age in which those masters stood (except for occasional freaks of art elsewhere) alone in all the qualities that we admire in Handel, and in every aspect of Bach's art. The age was one in which, to a contemporary, the renascence of polyphony had long spent its force. To a mind less complacent than Burney's it was an age of decadence; for there was little chance for the ordinary observer to guess that in a future century Johann Sebastian Bach would be discovered as a supreme master, and that Handel himself would join the ranks of the immortals on the strength of works written after he had twice become bankrupt as a producer of operas. The present-day worshippers of the later phases of Russian ballet are not more hostile to Brahms than the musical fashions of 1745 were to Bach.

In this period of Alberti basses and vocal acrobatics, Gluck began to make his mark in Italy as a fairly successful writer of Italian opera. We shall do his early works no injustice by inferring their character from collateral and subsequent events. They succeeded well enough in Italy to cause Gluck to be invited to London to compose for the Haymarket in 1745. Here he made little impression; the works were severely trounced by the critics; and Handel pronounced on Gluck his famous judgement that 'he knows no more counterpoint than my cook'. In this early visit to England Gluck made a better impression by his performances on the 'musical glasses', for which he wrote a concerto. The instrument was not the nerve-racking system of bowls revolving on a spindle and played by moistened finger-tips for which Mozart wrote, some thirty years afterwards. It was a more primitive affair struck with some kind of soft hammer; and the vogue of Gluck's performance on it is in all probability commemorated in the phrase 'Shakespeare and the musical glasses'. Indeed, unless the phrase can be discovered to be used before 1745, no other origin for it seems possible.

We are told that Gluck's first impulse towards reform of opera rose from the failure of a pasticcio which, in accordance with a common-sense custom of the day, had been made out of the most applauded numbers of his other operas. Let us take that legend at its face-value and note what it means. In the first place it implies that pasticcios did not often fail; in the second place the cause of this failure was ascribed to the fact that the music fitted the words in the original operas but did not fit those in the pasticcio. Now this is remarkable, for it implies that Gluck's music had become essentially dramatic long before he had any idea of reforming opera. Probably if we could get at the music and texts both of the originals and the pasticcio, we should find that the facts were not quite so simple; that, for example, when Handel made a pasticcio his librettist made a better job of the text than Gluck's librettist; or that Handel's arias are too effective to be ruined by literary causes to which nobody paid any attention, whereas the success of Gluck's early music was at best a trembling in the balance. Still, the legend is significant; and we must not too hastily assume the unimportance of Gluck's early music. Handel himself was not more reluctant than Gluck to write a new piece when an old one could serve; and the greatest of Gluck's works live as unscrupulously as Handel's, by taking in not only each other's washing, but the washing of operas which the historians tell us relapsed into the bad old style which Gluck so drastically reformed. In short, it is quite possible that the chief merit of the works which Gluck produced in London in 1745 was a new kind of dramatic fitness, and that when this disappeared in the adaptation to a new text the other merits proved insufficient.

If this new kind of dramatic fitness was anything like an adumbration of Gluck's mature style, we need inquire no further as to the nature of its importance. But we must not suppose it to have been the only kind of dramatic fitness that existed. Nowadays, great if sporadic efforts are made to revive Handel's operas; and the propagandists in such revivals always claim that Handel is a genuinely dramatic composer. In the performances less is spent on spectacle and costume while more attention is paid to stage-management and gesture than was perhaps usual in Handel's time; and the arias, especially those with much coloratura, are cut down, sometimes considerably below the limits of musical coherence. Enough beautiful music remains to entertain the listener; and as Handel is a consummate rhetorician whose music is connected with the words in a not wholly accidental fashion, the result is remarkably like an opera. But before we acquiesce in the enthusiastic opinion that Handelian opera should have made Gluck's reforms unnecessary, we should do well to realize that this result has been obtained by cutting out the elements on which Handel chiefly relied; and that if such a production of his operas had been offered him, he would have flung his wig at the producers, and good Princess

Caroline would have had to say, 'Hush! hush! Handel is angry'.

How much counterpoint did Handel's cook know? This is a fundamental point in the case for reform of opera. Handel's cook was Mr. Walz, a singer with an excellent bass voice, on whom Handel relied for small roles in his operas. It is quite possible that Mr. Walz could have written a tolerable thorough-bass to an air of his own composition. Clarissa Harlowe is supposed to have had this much accomplishment, and Richardson even contrived with the aid of a clerical friend to give the music of a song she wrote, figured bass and all. In a polite age the horror of pedantry is itself a scholarly instinct; and the object of contrapuntal skill was then, as always, not to display erudition, but to move easily and gracefully. The good contrapuntists, Handel, Hasse, Graun, and other masters of the time, all yielded more or less to the temptation to write flimsily; but the Alberti bass itself moves better under the guidance of a contrapuntist than under that of a writer who really knows no higher art of accompaniment. We need not impute to Handel the stupidity of complaining that Gluck did not write fugues. Handel himself seldom carries a fugue out to completion even in his most serious works; and the fugues in his opera-overtures coalesce into the diddle-diddle of the cat and the fiddle as soon as the third voice has entered with the theme. But the contrapuntist guides Handel's harmonies and basses as surely as a draughtsman may guide the scene-painter splashing his colours out of a pail. Handel was quite right in saying that Gluck lacked counterpoint. The criticism was relevant, and the difficulty contributed far more than dramatic immaturity to the failure of Gluck's early operas. It was never entirely repaired. In moments of inspiration all difficulties vanish; and in Gluck's greatest works inspiration is present almost throughout. But large and elaborate works cannot depend upon the highest and most impulsive inspirations from beginning to end. They need a considerable bulk of matter that may be characterized as 'business'; and the 'business' needs resources that can obviously be classed as technique. In the last resort the artist with a brilliant technique finds inspiration for the 'business' as well as for the supreme moments of his work. He attends to everything in its proper place; his brilliant handling of the 'business' does not interfere with the grand simplicities of the main inspirations, and the main inspirations are recorded by methods which do not make the adjustment of details impossible when their time comes. Gluck did not attain any such balance of power. His routine technique was and remained poor. It is interesting, by the way, to note that Verdi, also (as he himself admitted) an unlearned but a very experienced composer, never could quite understand why Gluck ranks so high in musical history. His dramatic merits Verdi took for granted; his imperfect musicianship offended, as showing the very difficulties from which Verdi had set himself free with mighty struggles. A lack of counterpoint is a very serious handicap to the designer of large musical works, even if he never wishes to combine his themes at all.

There are two ways, and two only, out of the difficulties resulting from this lack. The drastic and thorough way is Beethoven's. Finding polyphony as necessary to his music as air to his lungs, Beethoven forced himself to become a contrapuntist in spite of all obstacles. The natural contrapuntal styles of Bach, Handel, Haydn, and Mozart were beyond his reach. To him they were like ideal instruments; and he had to use the imperfect instrument of his own style. The only difference between it and other imperfect instruments, such as the pianoforte and the instruments of the orchestra, is that its imperfection is not that of a material object. Nevertheless, Beethoven transcends it exactly as great artists transcend the imperfections of material instruments; the difficulties are deliberately turned into qualities. Or we may compare the style with a language rather than with a material instrument. For no two artists use quite the same language; and genius may force an exquisite precision out of an uncouth language, thereby expressing subtleties beyond the reach of smoother tongues.

Gluck has another way out of the difficulties of his imperfect technique. It is an infallible way only under favourable circumstances; in other circumstances it is not available at all. It amounts simply to this; get your librettist to devise the simplest possible dramatic situations of sublime emotion, and become inspired by them yourself. In such situations a small technical apparatus in the hands of an inspired composer may achieve the same result that would have been achieved by a larger technical apparatus in the hands of a master who prunes away superfluities. Handel is a master with a large technical apparatus which he hardly ever puts into operation. When he is inspired there is no ready means of distinguishing his technique from that of his laziest work. It is his rhetoric, not his counterpoint, that you must study in order to see where the mastery lies; and then you will find that in essentials it is very like Gluck's. Such a masterpiece as Stanford's favourite illustration, the air 'Total eclipse' in Handel's *Samson*, is not a thing in which a note could conceivably be altered; and if Gluck had been given the task of expressing the situation of the blind and captive Samson, he would have been glad enough to achieve an air on exactly Handel's lines. To the inspired composer such problems solve themselves. A good school of melodic rhetoric comprises all that is needed for their technique.

Unfortunately, dramas cannot be constructed entirely on a sequence of beautiful emotions without a rational sequence of events to connect them. Two of Gluck's greatest operas, *Orfeo* and *Alceste*, were designed by their enthusiastic librettist Calzabigi to realize as nearly as possible this agreeable consummation. No account of Gluck's operatic reforms is honest unless it faces the fact that in the two works in which this reform was accomplished Gluck and his librettist simplified the dramatic problem almost out of existence. But here the word 'almost' is the key to the situation. There is drama both in *Orfeo* and in *Alceste*; and it demands an inveterately dramatic music. But in *Orfeo* there is practically no 'business'; and in *Alceste* the need for a certain amount of dramatic 'business' has wrecked the original Italian third act and caused such changes and interferences in the later Paris version that the supreme action of Alceste's return from the under-world is badly patched up by another hand. In his last works Gluck handles more complicated libretti; and we recognize more clearly in them where the composer finds no inspiration and the craftsman falls back upon doctrinaire mannerisms.

Before dealing with Gluck's greater works in detail, let us continue to investigate the legend. Accepting Handel's judgement that Gluck had never learnt counterpoint, let us ask what he had learnt. His master Sammartini (or San Martini) was an excellent contrapuntist. But his vogue was that of a writer of operas and concertos and chamber-music. Haydn was said to have come under his influence, but was by no means gratified by that report, which he indignantly denied, saying that Sammartini was a 'dauber'. Let us thank Haydn for this admirable word, which so exactly describes the essential quality of musical scene-painting from the point of view of a master of genuine chamber music. From Sammartini the non-contrapuntal Gluck could learn to daub, and to use with a sense of dramatic fitness the various forms of tremolo, including such as he could afterwards invent for himself or pick up in the theatre orchestras of Paris. Besides picking up these useful and splashy accomplishments, a pupil of Sammartini was in the position of an apprentice in a painter's atelier; he was allowed to complete the less important parts of his master's works. We hear much of the plagiarisms of Handel and of other masters of the eighteenth century; but it would be interesting to know whether an eighteenth-century composer was allowed during the lifetime of his master to claim his share in the works that went under the older master's name. Many charges of plagiarism were brought against Gluck in later years, sometimes interesting, sometimes merely comic; and, as has already been mentioned, all Gluck's works lived by taking in each other's washing. But it might be worth while to discover what early arias of Gluck's pass under the name of Sammartini. Not only the splashy theatrical texture, but also the larger aspects of Gluck's musical form owe much to Sammartini. The sonata-style of Haydn and Mozart is inveterately dramatic, to an extent of which its reputed pioneer Philipp Emanuel Bach had no conception. But it is not through the sonata-forms that Gluck arrived at his dramatic style. The instrumental forms of Sammartini are, like the textures associated with them, degenerated from the style of the concerto grosso. In the greatest examples of the genuine style, such as Bach's Third Brandenburg Concerto, we shall find large stretches in homophonic vibration, by way of relief, or even as a means of bringing more highly organized textures to a climax. Gluck's overtures to *Alceste* and *Iphigénie en Aulide* are as intimately connected with the operas as any Wagner Vorspiel; and their orchestration is wonderfully satisfactory to modern ears and was quite acceptable to Mozart. But such resemblance as they have to the sonata-style is rather deceptive: their material and contrasts are conceived far more on the lines of the concerto grosso. Strange to say, the classical symphony itself was an offshoot from operatic overtures in this style and did not immediately coalesce into the genuine sonata forms. Philipp Emanuel Bach is a lyric rhetorician whose style grew steadily more aloof from dramatic action; yet the first movements of his symphonies are not in line with his sonatas, but with Gluck's overtures.

But these are matters of musical form which belong to a later stage of the present discussion. It is futile to discuss the problem of opera as if it were primarily musical. At

least four-fifths of the problem are centred in the libretto.
An opera may be a concert on the stage; and this was, if
only for financial reasons, its main purpose and the main
cause of its vogue before Gluck. The performances of
great singers were ruinously expensive, and it was well to
provide some four hours' entertainment for the cost.
Expensive dresses and expensive scenery entertained the
eye, and so relieved what would otherwise have been a strain
on the attention of the ear. An opera with a simple plot
would not employ enough singers, nor could it give its few
characters enough material for the required thirty-odd
arias with which to fill out the four hours' entertainment.
When Handel deals with the subject of Alceste, the title of
the opera is *Admeto* and the story has a counterplot. What
the counterplot is, I frankly own I have forgotten, if I ever
knew; and those who know it know something that
Handel's audiences never thought about. To the best of
my recollection all the plots of Handel's operas are complicated. Seven characters are almost obligatory in normal
circumstances. In special circumstances, special measures
are needed. Thus when Handel induced the rival prima
donnas Cuzzoni and Faustina to sing in the same opera, it
was necessary to design two imperial roles, one that of the
tragedy-queen, the other that of the bride or bride-elect of
the conquering Alexander. The two queens first entered
together singing in thirds. In writing the score, it is
necessary to write one part under the other. Handel was
careful to put the higher notes on the lower stave at the
outset. In their second duet the queens exchanged relative
positions, both on the stave and in pitch; and probably
a more minute statistical examination than I have the
patience to undertake would show that neither of them had
a single quaver's cause for jealousy. Handel's diplomacy
was for several nights quite successful, and the two prima
donnas bristled with beautiful modesty. Unfortunately
the public began to take sides. If it is almost certain that
'Shakespeare and the musical glasses' dates from Gluck's

visit to England, we may perhaps conjecture that the phrase 'this beats cock-fighting' dates from the rivalry of Cuzzoni and Faustina. At all events the phrase became appropriate enough when the public had decided to spoil Handel's game.

Apart from its comic aspect the game is interesting for this reason, that it concerned the librettist quite as much as the composer. The revivers of Handel's operas tell us with enthusiasm that he was a bold innovator. The Cuzzoni-Faustina hen-fight was one of his innovations. The opera *Teseo* embodies two other innovations, inasmuch as it is in five acts instead of the customary three, and its arias are allotted to the characters in pairs. The dramatic value of these daring innovations is not obvious, and they must have been accomplished by the librettist before a note of the music was written. We can base a better case for Handel as a dramatic composer on the masterpieces of rhetoric which are perhaps as frequent in the operas as in the oratorios. But the operatic masterpieces are for the most part happier out of their context than in it. Perhaps the great scene of madness at the end of the second act of *Orlando* has something to gain from the drama that leads up to it; and there is much in the rest of *Orlando* that would have interested Gluck, who was only prevented by Piccinni from treating the same subject. But even here Handel would not have been able to write a *scena* of unprecedented range if his librettist had not laid out the text accordingly.

The problem of the libretto must be solved as to its general principles before the composer can even begin to theorize about operatic reform or operatic ideals. We may neglect the theories of the fact-proof egotist who would like to write the music first and get a libretto fitted to it afterwards. Hardly less negligible is the view of the professional hack-writer for music, and of the kind of composer for whom he caters. The ideal music-drama will not be based on a low estimate of the subtleties and resources of

music, and will contrive to move at the pace of the music
without sacrificing literary qualities. Weber, in the course
of nine revisions of the hopelessly tangled libretto of his
greatest work, *Euryanthe*, exclaimed, 'You don't suppose
a musician allows a libretto to be put into his hand like an
apple!' But he also said 'Give me all the strange rhythms
and inversions you can think of; nothing stimulates the
composer's invention more'. The composer of operas
cannot help sometimes wishing that he could take an extant
stage play more or less as it stands, and set it to music with
the minimum of alteration. Since Wagner achieved complete continuity in a music that moves at the same pace as
the drama, this ideal is no longer remote. Oscar Wilde's
Salome, Hofmannsthal's *Elektra*, and Maeterlinck's *Pelléas
et Mélisande* had made their mark as plays before they
became operas; but it is not too much to say that the
consummate art of Strauss's and Debussy's timing ensures
that they are better acted as operas than they have ever
been as plays. If the composer's traditions and musical
apparatus are simpler than Wagner's and the drama older,
more adjustment is needed; and Boïto had to go to great
lengths in simplifying Shakespeare before the *Otello* and
Falstaff of Verdi could come into being. One of the
most remarkable facts in Gluck's achievement is that
after effecting once for all the reform of opera in two works
with libretti purposely designed with extreme simplicity,
he was able to continue by setting the classical dramas
of French literature in fairly recognizable shapes.

If we neglect the views of the hack-writer of verse for
music, we lose nothing valuable either in music or literature. But it is unfortunate that so many of the greatest
poets have happened to be unmusical. Goethe, though he
once tried to conduct an amateur choral society, had no
gift for music and knew better than to trust his own judgement about it. Unfortunately he preferred a musical
adviser who would not venture to argue with him. And
the spectacle of Goethe led in musical matters by Zelter is

like a vision of Messrs. Shaw, Chesterton, and Belloc trying to keep up with science by studying Jules Verne. Stanford threw himself at Tennyson's feet in generous youthful adoration, and probably saved that poet from one or two blunders in musical matters. Browning talks cryptically and suggestively about music, but it was almost a feature of his style to call everything by the wrong name if he possibly could. In Shakespeare almost the only passage that uses musical terminology without something wrong or hopelessly obscure is the gamut of Hortensio in *The Taming of the Shrew*. Only in Milton and Bridges can the student of English literature find positive statements about music that the musician can follow up in the certain hope that the meaning is worth finding out. It would ill become a musician to compare musical culture with so vast a field as that of letters. But it may safely be said that no musician has ever ventured to remain so ignorant of the national literature, and of all that has been made international by translation, as most persons of literary culture are content to remain ignorant of music.

This was not so in England in the days of the Tudors, nor at the period of the Restoration. Nor was it so in Italy during the seventeenth and eighteenth centuries while opera was taking shape. The humblest writer of words for composers could not consider himself a hack-worker when one of the leading poets of his age and country devoted the whole of a long life and a personality of princely bearing to writing words exclusively for music. Such was the life-work of Metastasio (1698–1782). If you want a fair estimate of Metastasio's art you must turn to the historians of literature, who are somewhat puzzled to describe a poetry so exclusively designed for a kind of music that is no longer studied even by musicians. From musical historians Metastasio gets nothing but abuse. Brilliant debating points are made out of such a fact as that he 'expired in a canzona', extemporizing in neat verse on the occasion of receiving extreme unction. It is not clear why this should be more ridiculous than the fact that Bach on his death-bed dictated a figured chorale in fugue by contrary motion. The main difference in the two cases is that Metastasio wrote poetry which was set to music by composers whose works have perished with them, whereas Bach has written music that endures. There is also a spiritual difference between Metastasio and Bach which makes it seem trivial to bully poor Metastasio with a gibe. But two facts remain: first that Metastasio's poetry is still read for its own sake by students of Italian literature, and secondly that Metastasio was continually vexed at the way in which his operas were set to music. What he achieved in his dramas was a very rational musical scheme, according to which each situation was arrived at by a natural and smooth progress of dialogue and action, in order to be marked at every emotional crisis or possible point of repose by a tableau during which the emotion could be expressed in an aria set to a few lines of pregnant poetry so designed that the words would bear repetition with good rhetorical effect in a musical scheme. There is no essential difference between this and ordinary drama; indeed it reduces the conflict between music and action to the constant element of conflict between lyric poetry and action in all drama. The Metastasio formula was doomed from the outset, not because it was irrational, but because it was too easy. Hasse, who wrote operas literally by the hundred, could not remember whether he had set some of Metastasio's dramas three times or only twice. The essential tragedy of Metastasio's long career is that his operas were never once set by a great musician until Mozart himself, desperately driven under the pressure of more important works, hurriedly executed a commission for the wedding festivities of the Austrian Emperor and set *La Clemenza di Tito* in a style suitable to the occasion. The play has been said to be one of Metastasio's best. To the modern Philistine its moral seems to be 'Why cannot a hard-working Roman Emperor have three wives?' And the new Empress graciously characterized Mozart's music as *una porcheria tedesca*. But there is nothing in the structure of the play to prevent Mozart from making a fine thing of it if he could have felt a little more sympathy for the intrigues of persons with a reversionary interest in Titus's dilemmas. Otherwise there is no discoverable reason why the Metastasio plays should not have been set by great composers. The poet's only faults are those of an inveterate improvisor; and for the musician these are not faults at all. Perhaps one of the most momentous disappointments in musical history was that of the child Mozart, when at the age of twelve he was not allowed to have a libretto by Metastasio for the opera he was to produce at Milan. An alliance between Metastasio and that amazing child might have grown into a greater partnership than that of Gluck and Calzabigi. If only Metastasio instead of Varesco had written *Idomeneo*!

Raniero Calzabigi was an enthusiastic poet whose ideas on operatic reform were highly congenial to Gluck. It is quite likely that the poet induced Gluck to cross his Rubicon sooner than he might have done without prompting from a person who had original ideas as to the construction of libretti; but Calzabigi was a simple soul and betrayed a certain inflation of the head when he afterwards claimed that he taught Gluck the proper rise and fall of melody in the setting of his words. He is supposed to have been a violent opponent of Metastasio; but if this is so he must have been in disagreement with his own family, for Metastasio's favourite edition of his own works was edited by a Calzabigi. Be this as it may, Raniero Calzabigi encountered Gluck at the right moment for both of them. Gluck could no more reform opera on Metastasio's lines than he could walk up a mountain of glass. There was no need for reform. Anybody could set Metastasio to music, and everybody did. There was no aesthetic reason why Metastasio's drama should not provide a large number of characters and a complicated plot, and there were many financial and practical reasons why it should. Calzabigi attacked the problem by striking at vested interests. The subjects of serious opera were invariably classical, or at least concerned with the decline of the Roman Empire, though one of Handel's librettists once ventured as far as Richard Cœur de Lion. Calzabigi and Gluck stuck to Greek legend but reduced it to a more than Greek simplicity.

The plot of *Orfeo* is as follows: Act I presents Orpheus and the chorus mourning at the grave of Eurydice. Orpheus asks to be left alone with his grief: he communes with the echo, and resolves to kill himself. Enter Eros or Cupid, called Amor by the poet. He tells Orpheus that the gods, touched by his grief, will allow him to visit the underworld and bring back Eurydice on condition that he does not look upon her face until he reaches the light of day. Orpheus resolves upon this enterprise. The second act begins in the underworld with a chorus and dance of the furies. They are interrupted by the sound of Orpheus's lyre. He pleads with them, and at last they yield him passage. The scene changes to the Elysian fields. The happy shades are enjoying their quiet songs and dances. Orpheus enters and asks for his Eurydice. His prayer is granted, and, keeping his face averted, he leads her away. In Act III Eurydice is following Orpheus to the upper world. They are still among the underground rocks, and Eurydice is distressed because Orpheus will not look at her. Apparently he understands that he is forbidden not only to look at her but to explain why he cannot. At last, tormented by her jealousy, he gives way and turns towards her. She falls dead, and he is in despair again. Amor returns and, stating that the gods are satisfied after all, revives Eurydice, and the scene changes to his temple, where his triumph and the happiness of Orpheus and Eurydice are celebrated with ballet and chorus.

Already the first pioneers of opera in 1600 had found that in a musical setting the pathos of the Orpheus legend becomes intolerable unless a happy ending is provided.

Music concentrates its emotional effects so powerfully that either a considerable intellectual apparatus or a melodramatic callousness is necessary to make a tragic end tolerable. Thus when later Italian opera became tragic it became eminently blood-and-thunder. The story of *Il Trovatore* is gruesome; but a critic has not ineptly observed that nobody ever risked sitting down in the trunk-hose of the gipsy's foster-son. And, by the time libretti had become so tragic, music had learnt to provide common dance-rhythms for the most solemn occasions. But there is something very different from conventionality in the refusal of earlier musicians to face tragic issues in music. Their art recaptured the emotional values of childhood; and to the normal child a story that ends sadly is an outrage. That criticism is altogether too easy which condemns the recapture of the child's instincts. Nobody need trouble to justify the mechanism by which happy endings are secured, unless on these grounds, that the cruder the device the more honest is what Scots law would call the confession and avoidance. Alike in primitive, unreformed, and reformed opera, the composer was dealing with a musical apparatus that contained few elements that appeal primarily to the intellect. Beauty of musical design, beauty of harmony and tone, immediate emotional expression, these things may be directed by genius to results in which the intellect may find inexhaustible enjoyment. But they are not primarily addressed to the faculty of conscious reason. A fugue instantly draws attention to the interplay of its voices: a sonata presupposes that you will recognize its themes when they recur: a drama with an elaborate plot demands your attention to the course of events. All such apparatuses may be used to heighten the total power of emotion, but they invariably reduce its immediate shock. There is evidently nothing to reduce the shock of emotion in Gluck's *Orfeo*; and its effect is incredibly moving. Indeed, its most famous (though not really its greatest) achievement in pathos is the aria 'Che farò senza Euridice', which comes after Eurydice's annoying behaviour, and might have been expected to alienate the sympathy of any listener who had not given a holiday to the faculty of reason.

Ignore Euripides when you approach Gluck's *Alceste*. Verrall has shown that the Brownings were too literal-minded for the ironies of Euripides' satiric drama; but if Verrall is ten times as subtle as Balaustion, that interpreter is twenty times subtler than Calzabigi. The whole opera has precisely this and no more connexion with the Greek drama: that it concerns a king at the point of death, whose life can be purchased by the willing sacrifice of some other life, and is so purchased by that of his wife, who is finally brought back from death by superhuman means. Every vestige of a problem is removed from the treatment of this story. The devotion of the people to their king and their grief at his impending death are the dominant notes of the first act; and the difficulty of finding a willing sacrifice is not stressed. Admetus is horrified at the idea that any one should be sacrificed for him, and the chief tragic moment is that in which his wife confesses to him that she is the sacrifice. Thus Calzabigi secures two acts full of intense emotion without any occasion for doubt or analysis of motives. In the third act he encountered problems of dramatic 'business', and here he failed conspicuously. When the opera was remodelled for the Parisian stage the third act ruined its effect. Gluck exclaimed 'Alceste est tombée', to which Rousseau replied 'Oui, mais elle est tombée du ciel'. The rest of the opera was so impressive that the rescue of its third act was thought worth the trouble. A new part was created for Hercules, who had not appeared in Calzabigi's libretto at all. Thus, instead of Calzabigi's Apollo *ex machina*, it is now Hercules who, as in the Greek story, plunges into the underworld and rescues Alceste. Unfortunately not only the whole role of Hercules, but the supreme crisis of his conquest of the underworld was composed, while Gluck was away

in Vienna, by a certain Gossec whom musical historians mention with a respect by no means justified by
the ridiculous effect of his stiff little phrases and jejune
harmonies in the midst of Gluck's greatest music. Gluck
seems to write badly enough when he is not inspired; but
his feeblest stuff would put Gossec to shame. And the
four leaves containing Gluck's own handling of the climax
are lost! The original Italian version cannot help us here;
for throughout the opera Gluck's reconstructions are so
extensive that, in readapting the Paris version to Italian
words, not one line of Calzabigi's text can remain. And,
on the whole, the Paris version is incomparably finer, to
an extent which can be measured already at the rise of
the curtain, where the overture leads to a mighty outcry
of the populace instead of dying away almost formally as
in the original.

Yet there is much to be said for taking the Italian rather
than the French version of *Alceste* as the basis of modern
performances of the work. There is no reason why the
manifest improvements of detail in the French version
should not be grafted on the original Italian form in such
a manner as to leave the third act unencumbered by any
foreign matter whatever. The French alterations have to
some extent affected the plot; and, no doubt, if we could
recover the missing passage in Gluck's French third act
it would prove to be finer than anything in the Italian
version. But Gossec's Hercules and his music for the
combat between Hercules and the Infernal Deities simply
will not do. When one is not in the act of enjoying Gluck's
music one recollects him as an unlearned composer whose
crudeness needs some indulgence; but if we want to see
how illusory such after-impressions can be we have only
to contemplate the harmonies and rhythms which Gossec
thinks impressive enough for the Infernal Deities in the
act of yielding to Hercules. I forbear to give a musical
example, but the reader should be warned that most of the
printed vocal scores give Gossec's rubbish without the

slightest hint that it is not by Gluck. Apart from internal evidence it may be easily distinguished by the fact that it all belongs to the role of Hercules and that its choral portion is in C major.

The Italian *Alceste* contains several beautiful numbers that are not in the French version; and the French version contains, besides an enormous amount of ballet, several new arias which show the growing complexity and subtlety of Gluck's rhetoric. In the Italian *Alceste* the air 'Non vi turbate' has become almost unrecognizable in its French form 'Ah! Divinités implacables', though a close examination shows the French version to be a bar-for-bar variation of the Italian. But meanwhile the Italian version has become known as an Andantino in E flat for pianoforte by Mozart, because he copied it on pianoforte staves for some unknown purpose, possibly as theme for a set of variations. Such a work would have made an agreeably serious companion to the excellent comic variations on Gluck's *Unser dumme Pöbel meint*. The influence of Gluck on Mozart is deeper than we are ready to suppose; and in *Idomeneo* the oracle scene and the ballet music pay tribute to Gluck that amounts to something like explicit quotation. Throughout Mozart's works there are certain pathetic turns of phrase that are more probably to be derived from Gluck than from any less important maker of the musical language of the eighteenth century. Here is a 'conflation' of one of the Gluck-Mozart idioms. Mozart often uses the chromatic version (*b*) which is not in Gluck's vocabulary; but Mozart by no means neglects the severer form (*a*).

At this point it becomes interesting to inquire why *Idomeneo* is the only work in which Mozart shows the dramatic influence of Gluck in any obvious way. It is an insufficient answer that Mozart's lines of progress lay in comic opera where Gluck's contribution was insignificant: we want to know why the musical power shown in the tragic grandeur of *Idomeneo* did not improve upon this opening, developing the manifestly congenial dramatic aspect of it, and automatically extruding with growing taste the anti-dramatic elements of coloratura singing and redundant symmetry which spoilt *Idomeneo*. In his later works there are no limits to the dramatic sensibility Mozart shows when he chooses; and there are plenty of points in *Idomeneo* itself that are considerably more dramatic in Mozart's hand than the librettist Varesco had any reason to expect. But the first thing that is obvious about Mozart is that he is very fond of music. He could never have approved of Gluck's avowal in the dedicatory letter of *Alceste* that the composer's aim should be 'to restrict music to its proper function of rendering service to poetry and dramatic situations as colour and chiaroscuro serve the purpose of a well composed picture'; and Gluck's own achievement was not to restrict but to enlarge music 'to its proper function'. It never became self-evident to Mozart that any musical resource was necessarily un-dramatic. His whole development, alike in instrumental and stage music, might be traced in terms of his growing insight into the dramatic meaning of any and every musical resource. In the last resort he would probably have come to consider an undramatic libretto as unmusical, though his life was not nearly long enough for him to outgrow a readiness to irrigate Saharas with his flow of musical inspiration. Even as it was, Mozart became a dramatic reformer of opera over a much wider area than Gluck could command. But to Gluck belongs the supreme credit not only of displaying genuinely dramatic music on the stage but of creating such music at all. We only weaken the resources of language by applying the epithet dramatic to all forms of rhetoric. We may agree with Macaulay that some dialogues in *Paradise Lost* would make excellent drama, and we may remind ourselves that Demosthenes said that the three essentials of rhetoric are 'action, action, and action'; but we shall get an inadequate meaning from the word dramatic as applied to music unless we restrict it to actions less static than those of the orator, and changes of situation capable of interrupting the flow of Milton's finest dialogue.

Now we have seen that in *Orfeo* and *Alceste* Calzabigi had simplified the dramatic problem of opera almost out of existence. And there is much to be said for the view that the critical atmosphere of Paris enlarged Gluck's sense of the theatre and set him free from what might have become cramping in Calzabigi's doctrine. But this brings us to another distinction which might form the subject of a useful essay which to the best of my belief has not yet been written. Is the sense of the theatre co-extensive with the sense of drama? The history of opera in France shows that it is manifestly nothing of the kind. Every time a foreign composer has brought dramatic music into France he has encountered criticism which, whether it exasperates or pleases him, profoundly affects his style for the rest of his life. Few tendencies in musical history have been so conspicuous and so unmistakable as the vitalizing effect of French criticism upon writers of opera. And yet, who are the great classics of French opera? Lulli, an Italian; Rameau; Gluck, an Austrian; and Meyerbeer, a German Jew, the Barnum of opera; and aloof and austere, but a teacher of several famous if recalcitrant pupils, the Italian Cherubini, influenced against his masterful will by both Gluck and Beethoven. With the pupils of that much abused martinet the history of French opera becomes more obviously the history of French composers, and also passes into a very much lighter phase. But the curious thing about the classical history, whether it be French or foreign, is that with few exceptions its masterpieces have not been particularly dramatic and have, indeed, for the most part, fallen into a respectful neglect for that very reason. The 'sense of the theatre' which they show is a sense of entries, exits, and groupings.

Before Gluck came to Paris his two great 'reformed' works, *Orfeo* and *Alceste*, contained a few ballets to make appropriate resting-places in the very simple action of these works. He found that performance was out of the question in Paris unless there was at least an hour's bulk of ballet music distributed over each opera. To this we owe large masses of instrumental music in which Gluck rises to incomparably greater heights than in his few and unimportant symphonic efforts apart from the stage; and it is to this that we owe, a century later, that Wagner grafted on to the crudeness of his *Tannhäuser* a good half-hour's bulk of music in his ripest and most brilliant orchestral style. But it is quite clear that in neither case is such music a contribution to the reform of opera. It almost seems as if the arbiters of taste whose dictates were followed by the composers of French opera regarded dramatic action as a thing subversive of the art of the theatre. Perhaps that is why *Orfeo* was received in Paris with almost universal approval, while *Alceste* (having more action in it) at first failed. The few who complained of the insufficiency of action in *Orfeo* admitted in the same breath that the music carried the spectator over that defect.

Gluck did not find it necessary to reconstruct *Orfeo* to anything like the extent that the Parisian stage required for *Alceste*. The two works present widely different problems for modern performance. An entirely new opera would have cost Gluck little more labour than his revision of *Alceste*. Yet we may perform the original Italian version with the certainty that we are dealing with Gluck's own first inspiration in every detail, and without much difficulty in grafting upon it those features of the second *Alceste* which are real improvements. If, on the other hand, we base our performance on the French *Alceste*, we must find some scholarly substitute for Gossec's stuff. With *Orfeo* the case is different. Where the French version differs from the original Italian in musical content and declamation it is so incomparably finer that no sensitive judgement could abandon it. The Italian version has recently been published in vocal score and presumably adopted as the basis of performance, but none of its unfamiliar details will bear comparison with the sublime style of what may be conveniently called the authorized version. This criticism is no mere result of custom. The effect of a return to the Italian version is by no means that of a return to something more severe. In one of the greatest passages of all, the entry of Orpheus into the Elysian fields, the Italian orchestration is actually more elaborate than the French, and a glance is enough to show that Gluck has here removed superfluities. All the new French details represent quite obviously a deepening and purifying of Gluck's style. Yet, as a whole, the authentic French version, in the form given in the monumental Pelletan-Damcke edition, is intolerable almost from beginning to end, inasmuch as the whole part of Orpheus was transposed by Gluck from an alto to a high tenor voice; with the result, among minor disadvantages, that the whole scene of Orpheus's contest with the Furies has become entirely decentralized in key, and the magnificent original plan of its modulations obliterated. The famous tenor, Le Gros, in whose interest these dreadful changes were made, must have had an unpleasantly high voice, and he could sing the great Elysian recitative at its original pitch. That movement therefore remains untransposed; but the shrill tenor is quite subversive of the deep calm that Gluck originally intended for this most wonderful of accompanied recitatives.

We may take it then, that every adequate modern performance of *Orfeo* will consist of the French scoring grafted on to the Italian plan of keys and voice. Neither by this means nor by returning to the pure Italian version shall we recover exactly what Gluck intended; and this is just as well. Scholarship itself is not obliged to insist on the restoration of conditions that ought never to have existed. We may sing the cantatas of Bach nowadays without following the precedents of the *Thomanerschule* under Bach himself by giving the choir a well-deserved flogging afterwards. In graver mood we may hope that Western civilization will never again allow the voice of the *castrato* to be heard. Let us stick to our modern innovation of giving the part of *Orfeo* to a woman with a contralto voice, and let us have the benefit of Gluck's most inspired final touches on the undamaged fabric of his first and freshest essay in music-drama. It is ridiculous to suppose that the glorious voices and noble persons of Amalia Joachim and Giulia Ravogli produced a less natural and classical representation of Gluck's Orpheus than the eunuchs of the eighteenth century.

Gluck had not settled in Paris long before the French recognized in him a glorious opportunity for the development of musical party politics. Paris had not yet forgotten the great war between the Buffonistes and the Anti-buffonistes. But that was a mere matter of fine art, though it established the triumph of comic opera as represented by Pergolese's *La Serva Padrona*. The arrival of Gluck gave occasion for something much more exciting, a contest of personalities. The French operatic stage was already showing hospitality to another foreigner, Piccinni, and here was a glorious opportunity for setting up a rivalry between masters of two different schools. The wars between the Gluckistes and the Piccinnistes filled the feuilletons of the day with volumes of quite interesting literature. But Gluck's victory was decisive at the time and annihilating for the future. Nowadays, even if we take the trouble to read the contemporary literature on the subject, we have not the slightest idea what the Piccinnistes were talking about; nor shall we find that the literature becomes more intelligible in the light of Piccinni's music. None of the literature, even when it is by as good a musician as Rousseau, comes to grips with music as music at all. Rousseau was a composer, though a very poor one; but when he begins to explain the subtleties of Gluck's chorus of Furies in *Orfée* he flies in a thoroughly amateurish way to extremes of pedantry in theorizing about an enharmonic modulation which he reads into his text by mistake, and which, even if his account were correct, would have about the same aesthetic value as Virgil's masterly use of the ablative absolute. What emerges from all the literature, even before we take the trouble to consult the music, is that the whole controversy was a quarrel between the supporters of French music and the supporters of Italian music, in which the French partisans were so patriotic as to choose an Austrian champion.

In looking at Piccinni's music the first thing that is manifest is that that amiable artist has an admiration for Gluck and is working his hardest to imitate him in every particular, not always stopping short of plagiarism. I regret that I have not had an opportunity of reading Piccinni's *Iphigénie en Aulide*. Obviously the first document to consult is Piccinni's execution of the work which the Parisians arranged that both composers should set in rivalry. On the other hand, I have picked up the score of Piccinni's *Roland*, a later work, the libretto of which Gluck refused to set when he heard that it had been given to Piccinni. The subject is that of Handel's *Orlando*; but Handel's treatment is at least as dramatic. Piccinni's is well worth reading, but not worth reviving. To revive Handel's *Orlando* would be to produce some thirty pieces of music that never fail individually to move with an admirable circulation within the limits of static musical forms, and which moreover sometimes show thrilling signs of a larger dramatic life in development and juxtaposition, though the whole does not profess to cohere. Against this it is vain to urge the superior claims of a music-drama that achieves coherence for three and a half hours with a uniformly sluggish circulation and no remarkable features of composition. Coherence is not enough; the composer who wishes to fill hours with one piece instead of thirty must show power and momentum. Yet Piccinni's *Roland* quite justifies the Piccinnistes for existing. All music, great and small, would soon come to an end if it were the invariable fate of musicians as good as Piccinni to starve.

He was a considerable master of melody and had other attractive features in his style. His instrumentation is defective in its technique, and sugary in its merits. The sugary qualities no doubt helped his vogue. The defects are different from those of Gluck, but it is hard to say that they are more serious; and in any case there is no evidence that even the most learned musicians of Paris at the time were better judges of instrumentation. As has been said above, Gluck's escape from technical difficulties depends upon inspiration; and the short and sufficient description of the difference between Gluck and Piccinni is the old critical evasion that Gluck is inspired and Piccinni is not. Fortunately, criticism need not so completely abdicate as to leave the matter here. Inspiration is not a *chimaera bombinans in vacuo*, and even the most dramatic music of the most drastic reformer of opera does not attempt its task without being musical. In the last resort the greatness of Gluck reveals itself conclusively as the greatness of a composer. If this were not so, the whole business of reforming opera might as well have been left to Calzabigi and the journalists. Now it so happens that composition is an aspect of music which is never dealt with in musical literature. In this matter the technical treatises are even more to seek than the journalists; for they, one and all, take the fatal line of substituting generalizations from complete works of art for the methods by which works of art are really produced by masters.

The art of composition in music is essentially the same as the art of composition in prose and poetry, and the worst possible way to learn it is by setting up a large art-form as if it were a scenario and trying to fill it out. A composer should learn all forms of musical texture as he would learn a language, and he should then find out by experience what each kind of texture is good for. A composer as respectable as Piccinni can trust his music to proceed at a comfortable amble without breaking down. If he is more learned than Piccinni his musical textures will be richer and more interesting; but if he is a genius his music will not amble uniformly, but will show a momentum that carries everything before it, whether the intellectual and material apparatus be as primitive as Gluck's or as complex and luxurious as Wagner's. The external art-forms are the results of the various powers of movement which the composer of genius sets to work. Certain kinds of music can fill a given time with certain ranges of contrast and certain musical evolutions. For the composer of opera the times to be filled up and the ranges and evolutions to be accomplished within them depend upon the libretto, and if he is not his own librettist some of the merits of his art-forms manifestly belong to the poet. To Calzabigi, and to the collaborators who adapted Quinault and Racine to Gluck's purposes, we must give credit for a leading feature in Gluck's operatic schemes—the building-up of a long scene to a fine architectural design by means of a recurring chorus or recurring movements, such as the funeral choruses and the echo-songs which constitute the main bulk of the first act of *Orfeo*, and the choruses of the grief-stricken populace in the first act of *Alceste*. But the merit of the librettist would have availed little if the composer had not transcended it.

When the producer wishes to treat the composer with the contempt due to all who approach the stage otherwise than by the orthodox progress from call-boy to actor-manager, his first procedure is to find any two passages which repeat the same phrase or arrive at the same chord, and then to cut out everything which occurs between them, in accordance with the axiom that any cut, however non-sensical, is better than any music or any argument, however

necessary. There are works where this axiom is of some
practical use, but with Gluck it is conspicuously untrue.
I should be surprised to learn that the most Philistine of
producers ever even thought of cutting down the three
statements of Orpheus's lament to the echoes, with the
three recitatives that alternate with them. There are cases
where Gluck has used in a later work a shortened form of
an earlier piece of music. I believe that the longer form
will invariably prove to be the better. Dramatic cogency
seldom enters into the question, because, as we have seen,
Gluck's reform of opera owes most of its cogency to its
having got rid of almost all action except an emotional
tension which has more to gain than to lose by spreading
itself over a long time. For the purposes of Gluck's
reforms music did not require to be speeded up and
compressed. It did, indeed, demand release from the im-
perturbable amble of the da capo aria, and the da capo
itself was a repetition which achieved a fool-proof symmetry by a stroke of the pen and prolonged every pause
in the action by some five minutes without contributing
any architectural quality to a scene as a whole. The mere
getting rid of this convention is in itself a speeding-up;
but the total effect of Gluck's methods is not a compression,
but an expansion, of music. In modern performances we
are not obliged to agree with the eighteenth-century
Parisian in demanding a whole hour of ballet music, nor
would Gluck have provided so much ballet to suit his own
taste; but the last things that you need to cut out from
Gluck are his repetitions and expansions. It is precisely
in these that his power of climax is a musical resource
epoch-making in its own day and true for all time. Music
had to learn to expand with the kind of expansion that
does not arise from the working out of a polyphonic
argument. Gluck's power in that matter is one of the
reasons why his music is not easy to illustrate by short
quotations. This difficulty is a constant source of mis-
understanding in books on musical history, and the only

possible safeguard against it would be to compel every musical historian to produce a volume of whole compositions illustrating his points. In every art there will always be literally hundreds of artists who can say a good thing here and there, for one who can produce a whole work of art that has more momentum than that of a safe amble.

Let us see whether it is possible to indicate Gluck's power of composition by illustrations that, without ruinous expense, may show the scale on which he can work. Fortunately, there is an example in *Iphigénie en Aulide* which can be summarized in a few musical staves, which consists almost wholly of elements inconceivable to Bach and Handel, and which is on a time-scale which would not be felt to be inadequate in Wagner's mature style. Agamemnon is protesting that the gods cannot expect him to obey the command to sacrifice his daughter. He has twice sung in the plain abrupt rhythm of the words: 'Je n'obéirai point à cet ordre inhumain'. This takes five bars punctuated by pauses. Then he breaks into a cantabile: 'J'entends retentir dans mon sein le cri plaintif de la nature; elle parle à mon cœur, et sa voix est plus sûre que les oracles du destin'. This takes twenty-seven bars, with no repetition of words except 'que les oracles du destin'. Here is the ground-plan of the whole procedure. The appoggiatura of the oboe is only approximately a crotchet, being written as a grace-note which may be treated with some freedom, here preferably on the slow side.

AG. J'en-tends re-ten-tir dans mon sein   le

ORCH. *forz.*

pizz.

cri   plain - tif   de la   na - tu - re   (&c.)

f   AG. Je   n'o - bé - i - rai point   (&c.)

cres. . . . .

Nothing like this had ever been written before, and it is one of the things that cannot be surpassed by anything later. The tempo is, so far as a metronome can measure it, the same in the rhetorical passage as in the abrupt declamations: a good conductor and a good singer will take care that there is no substantial change, otherwise we should only lose the fact that the music is now moving at least four times as slowly. In terms of an earlier static music, 'le cri plaintif de la nature' would have been present throughout the whole aria in the form of a more or less florid oboe solo, if the composer happened to be using Gluck's group of instruments. A later composer might have localized 'le cri', putting it once just before the utterance of the words, or oftener, according as he chose to repeat the words. The classical procedure for musical illustration is to put the illustration first and let the words explain it afterwards. This is proof against disappointment, for if the illustration does not seem apt to the listener he will not associate it with the words at all, whereas if the words are put forward first the composer challenges criticism. At the outset Gluck obeys this rule: the audience, and Agamemnon himself, hear the cry of the oboe before it is identified with 'le cri plaintif de la nature'; but it does not remain a local illustration, though the words are not repeated; nor, on the other hand, does it explain itself away as a decorative scheme. It rises at long but equal intervals for no less than nine steps, to which it adds four more declining over the dominant and establishing it; after which Agamemnon resumes his short protest: 'Je n'obéirai point à cet ordre inhumain', and ends abruptly.

The accompaniment to 'le cri plaintif' consists of repeated quavers in the middle of the harmony, and of pizzicato basses once in two bars alternating with the cry of the oboe and giving rise to faint sustained notes of a bassoon. To the eye of a reader accustomed to enjoy polyphonic scores there is nothing to distinguish the appearance of this page from that of absolute rubbish; but with an experienced ear the score-reader will recognize that the quality of tone in the whole vast expanse is Wagnerian in depth and perfection, and the composition will overawe anybody who can feel the difference between living form and patchwork. The repeated quavers throb with a human emotion which not even our modern experience of the vibrato of the cinema organ can defile; though, as Gluck shows us all modes of instrumental vibration in their original full health, the cinema organ translates them into the now more familiar terms of every disease from which instruments and voices can suffer. The pizzicato notes of the basses, with their faint prolongation in the sighs of the bassoon, have the exact emotional value of sobs.

The whole passage is nevertheless marked by the highest qualities of Greek art and is eminently what is commonly, but misleadingly, called reserved. The term is misleading because it implies that something is withheld. This is not the case: nothing is withheld, but nothing is in excess. The simplicity is Greek, and so is the subtlety. The four last steps about the dominant of C minor are the consummation of architectural and emotional perfection. Their chief point is musical, and it would be far-fetched to find rhetoric or irony in the fact that the last clause of the words is repeated. So far as the voice part is concerned, it is a more remarkable achievement that in the whole passage the words have not been repeated before. It is no part of Gluck's aesthetic system that repetitions of words should be avoided, nor did the poets of the eighteenth century, whether they wrote specially for music or not, expect that their words could be sung without repetitions.

For my other illustration I select the substance of one of Berlioz's letters. The whole of this letter consists of a quotation not quite co-extensive with mine, and commented upon solely by four notes of exclamation. To that admirable comment I will add that this melody shows, as my phrase-numerals indicate, one symptom of Gluck's

power of movement and composition in the irregularity
and overlapping of its rhythm. The quotation is from
Iphigénie en Tauride, Act II, No. 17.

This quotation seems to lose interest as it continues, though the intention to express emotion by high notes and minor chords is manifest. But this is just where short and sketchy quotations of dramatic music become misleading. The very features which here look weak are the signs of a constant increase of power; and even the magnificent first phrase gives little warning of the cumulative effect of the whole composition. Gluck is not only never stiff; the amblers manage to get through their works without manifest signs of rheumatism; but Gluck's movement, his momentum, whether in slow or quick tempo, is always powerful. The accompaniment of this wonderful air is a little more elaborate than that of 'le cri plaintif de la nature', and quite different in effect, though it has in common the throbbing quaver movement and the deep pizzicato basses, with what one might call harmonics for a couple of horns several octaves higher. The movement is kept up for no less than 112 bars, broken by two pauses only in the last line but three; the singer is Iphigénie, joined towards the end by her fellow-priestesses

of Tauris. Note that as in the previous quotation, and in
Che farò and the echo songs in the first act of *Orfeo*,
Gluck's highest pathos is expressed in the major mode.
He uses the minor mode chiefly to express protest or
energy, and sometimes for picturesqueness or variety
with no set purpose at all. The study of Gluck's most
serious melody is a useful method of shaking modern
criticism out of its conventional values.

Both these illustrations are in a slow tempo; an illustration of Gluck's power of movement in a quicker tempo
would need more room than can be afforded. I must leave,
therefore, in a dogmatic form, the statement that Gluck
never fails to convey a sense of speed when he wishes. In
point of fact, there is more of quick than of slow tempo in
his representative works. Young composers used to be told
that slow movements were the acid test of a composer's
power, and that it was there that the young were most
liable to fail. I have never found this to be the case. In the
days when that advice was orthodox, a young composer
generally made a fool of himself over scherzos and showed
his best talent when his tempo was slow. The usual failure
of composers at the present day, and at all times, has been
in maintaining a quick movement. Modern civilization is
said to worship pace, but this does not often express itself
effectively in music. You can sleep more easily in a train
going at sixty miles an hour on a good line than in a bath-
chair. If you transcribe a slow movement, changing the
notation so that demi-semiquavers are represented by
minims and slower notes by semibreves tied to other
notes in due proportion, you will have to bar it in alla
breve bars and call it prestissimo, with semibreves at 208
of the metronome; but it will remain a slow movement in
spite of the notation and the convulsions forced thereby
upon the conductor. It is astonishing how few composers
show a grasp of this fact; and I have not yet seen the text-
book on composition which attempts to bring home to the
student that if a phrase of given length be played twice,

first in a quick tempo, and secondly in a tempo four times as slow, the slow rendering will take four times as long.

I cannot recall any passage in Gluck which does not 'go'; though there are plenty of passages where inspiration fails him. 'Les mouvements des monstres' in Armida's garden cannot in the best of productions be much more awe-inspiring than the usual pantomime dragons, and Gluck's music for them is neither better nor worse than the music Handel wrote in *Rinaldo* for the same situation as an accompaniment to those fights between Signor Nicolini and the lion at which Addison pokes fun in the *Spectator*. But whether Gluck is moving on a small scale or large, he never breaks down, nor at his dullest or most doctrinaire does his rhythm become stodgy. I have already remarked upon the ineptitude of Gossec's intervention in *Alceste*. It is like hearing a small schoolboy interrupt with his construe a recital by Gilbert Murray. 'These are indeed circumstances in which a man saying "Ah!" would speak correctly.'

Thanks largely to Berlioz, Gluck enjoys a popular fame as one of the pioneers of orchestration. It is a remarkable fact in the style of a composer who really was not a contra-puntist that Gluck's accompaniments, basses, and inner parts are never tiresome, and are almost always beautiful and thrilling in colour. Such qualities they maintain in spite of an often exasperating liability to grammatical mistakes. These, however, are often difficult to correct without removing something essential to the style. A curious case is the grammatical blunder of giving a chorus of female voices the upper fourths of a series of chords of the sixth, leaving the bass to the orchestra, as in the famous Hymn of the Priestesses in *Iphigénie en Tauride*, 'Chaste fille de Latone'. Critics will never agree whether this is a mere error, or whether Gévaert is right in think-ing it a trait of genius, showing a scholarly sense of austere primitive Greek music. Both views contain some truth. Gluck never had a scholarly sense of any kind, and his genius was as triumphant as the British Constitution or the Light Brigade in blundering from precedent to precedent. Parry, whose general admiration for Gluck would almost satisfy Berlioz, deplores most of Gluck's choruses and explains them by saying that in that department he was brought up in a bad school. The bad school was certainly not that of Gluck's Italian apprenticeship, where the choral traditions were excellent; but there is no denying that the choral traditions of the French theatre constituted a thoroughly bad influence. Yet on the whole the truth seems to be on the side of the patriotic French, to whom Gluck's choruses are the *ne plus ultra* of efficiency and point. They ought no doubt to be very bad, but they happen to be for the most part astonishingly good. And before the Furies in *Orfeo* and *Iphigénie en Tauride* criticism becomes silent reverence.

I have purposely selected details from Gluck that have not been made famous in literature. The more famous achievements of Gluck's dramatic rhetoric are neither greater than nor inferior to my illustrations. They are very much finer than the literary description of them manages to indicate, because they would all remain great music if the things they illustrated were removed without trace. They would, of course, suffer from the substitution of things they were manifestly not meant to illustrate; but it is no fair test of music to distract the listener's attention. Hence, no doubt, the failure of Gluck's early pasticcio. But when Orestes says 'le calme rentre dans mon cœur' and the violas belie him with their syncopated monotone:

the tragic irony is terrible. But the prose writer who can describe this rhetorical point might possibly have conceived it himself without being a greater musician than Rousseau.

My own experience of such interesting details in musical

history leads me to have the profoundest distrust of all such descriptions when they are attached to the works of an unknown or neglected composer. This particular passage is a conspicuous item in the architecture of one of Gluck's grandest achievements; and it depends, like all of them, on the elementary fact that, though he could talk about music in a very interesting way, he composed infinitely better than he talked. His instrumentation, primitive though it looks, contains so many strokes of genius that it supplies almost a majority of the quotations in Berlioz's treatise on that art. But here again its isolated points, impressive though they may be in themselves, have a far deeper meaning and effect as manifestations of his general power of composition. His tone-colours owe quite as much of their value to how long they last and at what moment they change as to any intrinsic quality that can impress the mind at once. Gluck summarized his own principles in the famous letter which dedicates the Italian *Alceste* to the Duke of Tuscany. He touches upon the abuses of the old opera, especially the da capo aria which often concludes the da capo where the words do not make sense, and which holds up the action in order to give the singer time to extemporize four different ways of ornamenting the same phrase, &c., &c. But the most important part of his letter is a sentence which has attracted less attention than the rest. He says that the combinations of instruments should be controlled by the passion of the situation.

This is, so far as I am aware, the only statement about instrumentation made in the eighteenth century which shows a consciousness that that art had undergone a total revolution from the aesthetic systems of Bach and Handel. It means two things: first, that the scheme of orchestration was no longer a decorative pattern, uniform and unchangeable for each movement; secondly, though in practical use no visible change was made, it implies the abolition of the continuo, the system by which the domestic

I

service of filling out the harmony in the background was entrusted to a gentleman at the harpsichord or pianoforte, while the instruments of the orchestra proper were free to make their own patterns. One of the many interesting tendencies in modern music is that of groups of musicians who, sometimes in different countries and independently of each other, aspire to return to Bach and to write musical textures in which every note has the necessity of a main or coequal part in a polyphonic design. Some of the modern aspirants to this consummation undoubtedly fail to realize that Bach himself would have been extremely discontented with the tubby thinness of those modern performances of his works that are given by unscholarly purists who make no attempt to produce his continuo, and who do not realize that the harpsichord itself produced by means of octave registers often twice, and sometimes three times, as many notes as those written. Continuo music, and harpsichord music with its faculty of mechanical doublings, made up a very aristocratic art, but had essentially the advantages, if not the disadvantages, of a civilization that relies upon slavery. The stupendous revolution that was accomplished by the art of Haydn and Mozart is not, as some of our neo-classics are inclined to think, a decadence and extravagance, but perhaps the severest and strongest economy that music has yet achieved. It means that the orchestra and the inner parts of all written music perform their own domestic service and are content to use humble formulas (suggestive, if you will, of scrubbing-brushes and pails of water) at any moment, without loss—but on the contrary with much gain—to their dignity. Gluck is far more than a pioneer of opera. He is a pioneer, and a great one, in the whole of that noble musical revolution. Haydn and Mozart seem to have achieved their task in complete independence of Gluck, but it is probable that the enormous impression made by Gluck upon dramatic music contributed more than anybody at the time was aware of to the capacity of the public to appreciate Haydn's and Mozart's purely instrumental art.

The works of Gluck which concern the present discussion are:

I. *Orfeo*, which exists ideally and practically in the grafting of the improvements of the Paris version (without the dislocations) upon the original vocal pitch and key-system of the Italian version. In this form it is perhaps the most perfect and certainly the most moving of all Gluck's works; and the scene in which Orpheus conquers the Furies is one of the supreme achievements in music-drama.

II. *Alceste*, the Italian version of which is prefaced by Gluck's famous manifesto of his principles in the dedicatory letter. The French version is in every respect finer, except for the deplorable loss of Gluck's own climax in the third act. *Alceste* is on a larger scale than *Orfeo* and, as far as mature perfections can be compared, it may be said to mark an advance in power of handling musical form in grand proportions.

The libretti of *Orfeo* and *Alceste* are by Calzabigi, as also that of another important work:

III. *Paris and Helena*, of which I have never succeeded in obtaining a full score. Gluck in pianoforte score is not an attractive spectacle to any one who has once enjoyed the touching vitality of even the most primitive features of his orchestration.

IV. *Iphigénie en Aulide*, written in official rivalry with Piccinni's work on the same subject. This work again shows 'progress', if that is the proper term for increase of range. On the other hand, the doctrinaire has to come to the rescue of the composer when he passes from Calzabigi's unmixed personified emotions to the maternal and priestly conflicts and stratagems of Clytemnestra, Calchas, and the other diplomatists of Racine's stage.

V. *Iphigénie en Tauride*, perhaps one of the most spiritual, as well as one of the most picturesque, works ever put upon the operatic stage.

Both the *Iphigénies* owe something, though not as much as has been supposed, to Racine, whose phrases are sometimes distinctly traceable in *Iphigénie en Aulide*, and whose scenario has been followed in both operas.

VI. *Armide*, derived, like Handel's *Rinaldo* and Sacchini's *Renaud*, from an episode in Tasso's *Gerusalemme Liberata*, is the last of Gluck's great works and the one of which he said that he could wish it to finish his career. The libretto, by Quinault, had been set by Lulli ninety years earlier. With a composer of Gluck's power it was a foregone conclusion that the character and style of Armida would not remain confined to that of an enchantress who produced choruses of birds warbling in a magic garden, like the 'rainbow-dyed sparrows for the opera' which Addison encountered being carried in a large cage down the Haymarket for a rehearsal of Handel's *Rinaldo*. It is not surprising that the critics accused Gluck of giving the enchantress the task of a monotonous and tiresome caterwauling; and Gluck's replies to his critics anticipated the best vitriol of Wagner's prose. Though its subject is best suited neither to Gluck nor to modern taste, *Armide* remains a work which, with pious and tactful production, is very impressive. Gluck's full power is shown in the scene where Armida summons the Spirit of Hate to extirpate from her heart her love of Rinaldo, but her courage fails her and she dismisses the wrathful spirit with her purpose unaccomplished.

After *Armide*, Gluck finished another large work, *Écho et Narcisse*. The title is enough to show that here Gluck is cramped within the limits of prettiness; and this cramping is fatal to him. Under stress of emotion he can be recklessly pretty; or rather, the beauty of his pathetic melodies has an exquisite tenderness which seems to be the inspiring source of every pretty thing that has since been achieved by lyric composers at the height of their powers. But Gluck confined to prettiness is a sad and dried-up creature, and I, who have a sinful appetite for prettiness, have never been able to take a large dose of *Écho et Narcisse*.

Gluck died before he had finished another work, *Les Danaïdes*, which was finished for him by Salieri, if I recollect rightly. Here, again, we may doubt whether the subject could have inspired him.

The five great works, including *Armide*, are manifestly majestic in their scope; and, once we become absorbed in them, all inequalities and faults of style become swept away in the essential grandeur, nobility, and adequacy of the composer's powers.

6

CARL MARIA VON WEBER
(1786–1826)

By DENNIS ARUNDELL

'THE first question put to a foreign amateur, on his arrival in Germany, was, "Do you know the Freyschütz of Marie de Weber?" "No," was invariably the reply. "Fly, then," was the response, "and get rid of your culpable ignorance, and we promise you pleasure—admiration—delight—enthusiasm!" '

Stafford, *History of Music*, 1830.

THE history of eighteenth-century art is the history of the struggle to be free from the humdrum of everyday life. Cities, which were formerly little more than feudal centres, had gradually become business centres primarily. Commerce no longer existed as a necessary part of town life, the towns began to exist because of their commerce. Finance was turning into an embryo science, and the example of the Dutch merchants led to the establishment of national banks.

For the artist reaction was inevitable. Any escape from the mud of the streets was welcome. The seventeenth century had discovered three roads to freedom. Ancient Greece and Rome brought grandeur and mythological fantasy to literature and music, pastoral simplicity brought freshness and purity to poetry and painting, and the intellectual and artistic discovery of China brought a strange unworldly beauty to architecture.

By 1635 Europe and China had established intercourse and the novelty of the strange Eastern beauties rapidly became the fashion. Blue porcelain was imitated at Delft, the copper pagoda roofs with their queer projections, myriad lamps, and coloured glaze inspired engravers and architects to embellish their prints and buildings with decorative filigree, and the weird charm of the landscape filled the theatre with gardens, 'the Architecture, the

Trees, the Plants, the Fruit, the Birds, the Beasts quite different to what we have in this part of the World'.[1] Rural beauty attracted the poets, whether tinged with the spirit of the classical eclogues at first or second hand, as with Hoffmanswaldau and the second Silesian school of poets, or welcomed as a refreshing relief, as with Herrick and his contemporary revolters from the town. Classical myths inspired the birth of opera and classical metres dominated the Racines and Drydens.

In England pastoral freedom soon became pastoral fashion. Scotland's wild unearthly music was hailed as an escape from formality and soon became a formality itself.[2] Herrick's Devon, Prue, and beer were transformed into a champagne country, Daphne, and sparkling wine, while pastoral opera with its delicate beauties charading as shepherdesses and warbling Arne's charming graces was *à la mode* till the country was rediscovered by Wordsworth. Escape from the city and everyday life turned into ardent seeking after country joys—spurious though they might be. The professional singer, at first forced by expediency to decry 'the Tumult and Smoake of the Town'[3] in spite of his personal loathing for the country, soon was unhappy if he did not have some nightingale or sheep to sentimentalize. It began to pay to ape the rustic. Ivy on ruined towers, symbolical of the triumph of Nature, was made a cult and—if not already in existence—was duly cultivated. Rural retreats, ruined grottoes, mossy pillars were jerry-built in fashionable gardens to create the illusion of careless solitude and imitated in the filigree engravings that bordered pictures and music.[4]

In France the court ballets encouraged the make-believe

[1] Purcell's *Fairy Queen*, Act V.
[2] It is curious how escape from the hard facts of reality always leads to barbarism, till the new barbaric mode becomes sentimentalized. Compare the adoption and subsequent deterioration of negro jazz in the recent revolt against the tragedies of human suffering.
[3] Shadwell's *Epsom Wells*, 1672.
[4] Cf. Bickham's *Musical Entertainer*, 1737.

of Watteau and the golden milk-pails of Marie Antoinette at the Trianon, while the Rousseaus toyed with their *Devins du Village* and thought of the simple glory of the ordinary man until the word was spelt with a capital letter and Man revolted against fairyland and guillotined its play-actors.

Italy, having been inoculated earlier with the pastoral than other countries, became artificial earlier. Tasso's imitators of the seventeenth century were followed by the Roman Academy of Arcadia, and the affectation of this mediocre school was easily outshone by Metastasio's classic grandeur and Goldoni's revolt in discovering the humanity of innkeepers and their cronies. Leporello and Pantaloon in the streets of Venice were more honest, more refreshing, more alive than the spangled heroes of the mock-classic.

Germany, riddled with petty courts which aped the Versailles manners and the Italian taste, was torn between the intellectual Leipzig school of Gottschied and the emotional Zürich school of Bodmer, and found it harder to escape. Italian music ruled the day, and imposed the form —if it could not swamp the humanity—of the Bachs, the Handels, and the Haydns. Here the revolt against the artificiality of foreign styles and tastes was naturally later in time. It was led by Klopstock with his freer metres and language, Lessing with his admiration for the bourgeois realities of Shakespeare, Wieland with his queer mixture of grace and materialism, and, above all, Herder with his love of nature and his native folk-songs.

By 1786 Goethe, inspired by Herder, had absorbed the humanity of Shakespeare, the grandeur of Gothic architecture, the romance of Ossian and old German ballads: he had written his play on Goetz von Berlichingen, the champion of freedom, his poems *Der Wanderer* and *Wanderers Sturmlied*, *Werther*, and parts of *Faust* and *Wilhelm Meister*. On September 3rd he started on his journey to see the wonders of Italy, and on December 18th Carl Maria von Weber, who was to express in music the wonder in man and the elements that Goethe felt so strongly, was born.

It is not surprising that Weber became a musician. His father, it is true, determined to make him a second Mozart, but heredity and environment more surely combined to drive him to music. His great-grandfather was a keen amateur of music and the drama; his grandfather sang and played the violin; of his four cousins, Josepha was the original Queen of the Night in *Zauberflöte*, Aloysia— Mozart's first love—was the original Constanze in the *Entführung*, Constanze—Mozart's wife—was a pleasant singer and a capable pianist; his father played the violin, the viola, and—as a virtuoso—the double-bass, and had been the musical director of the Lübeck theatre and the Kapellmeister to the Prince-Bishop of Eutin; his mother was also a singer.

At the time of Weber's birth his father was only Stadt- musikant at Eutin, but after touring with a troupe of strolling players the family settled in Salzburg for a time and the eleven-year-old Weber had some lessons from the sixty-year-old Michael Haydn.

His first opera, *Die Macht der Liebe und des Weins*— burnt with other of his early efforts—was written in 1799, and his second, *Das Waldmädchen*—composed at the age of thirteen—was performed at Freiberg in November 1800. His third, *Peter Schmoll und seine Nachbarn*, was produced at Augsburg in 1803 with little result except that Haydn commended it and Concertmeister Otter wrote at the end of the score 'Erit mature ut Mozart'.

In the following year his theatrical life began in earnest. He was appointed, through the recommendation of the Abbé Vogler, from whom he had learned how to study seriously, Kapellmeister of the Breslau Theatre. Being barely seventeen and a half he naturally made many mis- takes and his tact was not noticeable, but for more than a year he gained first-hand experience in the managing of a stage, though this allowed him little time for composition.

In 1807 Prussia was finally defeated by Napoleon, and as a result Duke Eugène of Württemberg was compelled to give up his band—of whom Weber had for the past few months been Musik-Intendant—but procured posts for his musicians as best he could. Weber, a strong anti-Buonapartist, became private secretary to Duke Ludwig and his brother King Frederic at Stuttgart.

For some time music was forgotten and Weber 'was thrown . . . into the vortex of a dissipated court'.[1] But though—or perhaps because—his emotions were strongly affected by Ludwig's frivolities and tempers, Margarethe Lang's seductive charm, the wild debauches of the young Fausts Höllenfahrt Society, and the financial difficulties of both Weber and his father, resulting in the composer's dramatic arrest at a rehearsal of his *Sylvana*, the lessons he learned were invaluable—not only morally, but dramatically. 'From this time forward I can count pretty tolerably on having settled matters with myself; and all that time has since done, or can do for me, is to rub off corners, and add clearness and comprehensibility to the principles then firmly established.'

The year 1810 was spent chiefly in Mannheim and Darmstadt, criticizing, touring, and composing—notably the comic opera *Abu Hassan*. At the beginning of the following year he unconsciously explained in the most illuminating manner the reason for his future greatness:

My path in life was cast from my birth in different lines from that of any other human being; I have no happy childish days to look back upon, no free open boyhood; though still a youth I am an old man in experience, learning everything through my own feelings and by myself, *nothing* by means of others.

Tragic though this seems at first sight to be, this solitariness forced him to feel intensely, and explains succinctly his power of characterization, his sympathetic understanding, and his fervid bursts of humanity which are so

[1] Benedict's *Weber*.

overwhelming that matters of technique and style are regarded as secondary.

After two years of touring, composing, and visiting, Weber became Kapellmeister of the Opera at Prague. This post he held for three years from 1813, reaping the fruits of his experiences of Breslau. An inflexible disciplinarian, he spared neither himself nor his company in a fervid endeavour to revive the grandeur of the Prague of Mozart's day. A first-class conductor, he also superintended the administration, the scene-painting, and the stage-managing, and even learned enough Czech to meet the native performers on an equality. His experience of humanity increased still further through his mad passion for Thérèse Brunetti and his admiring devotion to Caroline Brandt—the prototypes, as it were, of his Eglantine and Euryanthe.

The battles of Leipzig and Waterloo inspired Weber and most young Germans to a burst of patriotic nationalism, as a result of which his patriotic songs and his *Kampf und Sieg* cantata were composed, though his attachment to Caroline Brandt, a strong Buonapartist, was temporarily broken.

In the autumn of 1816 he resigned his post at Prague, having produced in a little over forty months—at least ten of which were occupied with vacations—thirty old operas and thirty new works, among which he never included an opera of his own.

In 1817 he started his battle for German opera in earnest as Kapellmeister at Dresden, which post he held till his death. Here he had to fight not only Morlacchi and the Italian performers but also their ardent supporters at court. This he did by appealing directly to the musical amateurs of the town and unswervingly persisting in his innovations with the orchestra and the stage, in spite of the hostility of the King, whom, it is true, he fed with humorous occasional pieces.

The operatic invasion of the rest of Europe by Italy, which had begun in the middle of the seventeenth century, had by the middle of the eighteenth century resulted in a tyranny. Each country tried, successfully or otherwise, to rebel after its own fashion—England with its ballad opera, France with its pastoral ballet opera, Russia with its comic operas. In Germany Keiser had made a half-hearted stand against the inevitable by introducing ordinary everyday folk and choosing a highwayman as a hero[1] as early as 1701, but merely achieved a hotch-potch of German recitative and Italian aria, while his chorus remained passive. Little advance was made in the next eighty years. Gluck in Vienna had humanized the characters of opera with his *Orfeo* in 1762 and Hiller had made a worthy effort to be German with his *singspiele*. Mozart made his chorus active in *Idomeneo* (1781) and began his subtle characterization in *Entführung* (1782), but even his later brilliant output of *Figaro* (1786), *Don Giovanni* (1787), *Così* (1790), and *Zauberflöte* (1791)—which 'owes but little to any Italian predecessor' and which is 'German to the core'[2]— are too formal to be native to Germany.[3] It is the freedom of Bach, of Haydn, of Mozart, of Beethoven, of Weber, of Wagner that is German. Their 'discords' are native, their 'structure' cultivated.

At last on June 18th, 1821, the anniversary of Waterloo, the spirit of the Rhine castles, the *volkslieder*, and mysterious legends was represented to the full in opera and the decisive blow against Spontini and the Italian school was struck by the first performance of Weber's *Der Freischütz* in Berlin.

The story was based on an old legend[4] of the demon

---

[1] *Störtebeker und Gödge Michaelis.*
[2] *The Opera*, Streatfield, edited by E. J. Dent.
[3] The music of all northern European countries is freer than that of Italy. Is this because by nature the peoples of England, the Netherlands, Germany, and Russia are hardier, rougher, and have no time for frills and manners? Purcell, Dufay, Wagner, and Rimsky-Korsakov go straight to the heart of things and have little patience with rules. Northern European composers are by nature amateurs. Compare a Hebridean tune with a Neapolitan folk-song.
[4] First published at the beginning of the eighteenth century in *Unterredungen vom Reiche der Geister.*

Samiel who barters true-flying bullets for the souls of those huntsmen who consult him. Caspar, a ranger in the service of Prince Ottokar, suggests that Max, another ranger, should make the infernal compact. Max, having failed in the first contest for the post of chief huntsman—which is to be vacated by the father of Agathe, the girl he loves—agrees to cast the magic bullets with Caspar in the Wolf's Glen at midnight, in spite of Agathe's forebodings. Agathe prepares for her wedding, but, finding that by mistake a funeral wreath has been provided instead of bridal flowers, decides to wear some holy roses given to her by the forest hermit. At the final contest Max's six shots are successful, but the seventh causes Agathe to fall senseless to the ground and is then magically deflected by the holy roses to kill the villainous Caspar. Max confesses his crime, but is saved from the Prince's wrath by the hermit and is united to his Agathe.

It is difficult for any but a German to appreciate such a work to the full. The witches of the Brocken—real enough at one time—are still strong in the imagination of the German peasant. What folk-song ever appealed fully to people of other nations? The Bridesmaids' song may seem boringly interminable to English, French, or Italians, but to the people of a country where a floral *Willkommen* still greets the return of a friend it is thoroughly genuine, for all its naivety and—critically speaking—its musical dullness. A National Anthem to foreigners or experts may seem merely a silly tune, but to the native it is traditionally and automatically inspiring.

Again it is hard to become simple enough to be thrilled by pantomime magic. Fiery wheels, winking owls, phantom hounds are nowadays nothing compared with ghost trains, cavalcades, and grand hotels. When *The Tempest* was first produced, the magic table must have made the audience gasp: now we are critical if the wrong glass is used for a champagne cocktail, and mildly hypnotized by revolving stages, Venetian-blind scenery, and four simultaneous apartments. It is important to realize this difference, for unless the audience can somehow step back into the mentality of the past it cannot start to listen to a work from the past. What is new soon becomes old-fashioned, it then turns into the naïve and later is rediscovered and presented again by scholars. Weber's forebodings, storms, and demons are now somewhat naïve and old-fashioned, but they are none the less sincere and none the less brilliant. His human emotions have not suffered to the same extent. Agathe may be too definitely 'pure' for this age, Aennchen—her cheerful little cousin—too 'winsome', and Caspar too 'evil': but for all that Agathe's pathos is still lovely, Aennchen's wit still lively, and Caspar's villainy still thrilling.

In its day there was no question of the brilliance of *Der Freischütz*. The superior critics talked slightingly of it as a mere *singspiel*, but most true opera-lovers and all audiences recognized it as a real combination of stage and music. Six months after its first performance it had been played to acclamation in almost all the opera-houses in Germany.

London went madder perhaps over the work than any other town in Europe. It was produced at Covent Garden, Drury Lane, and the Lyceum simultaneously.

Even the star of Rossini was forced to hide its diminished head at the coming of this new light. . . . Poor old Handel did now and then 'upheave his vastness', but he was wellnigh dethroned and banished, by the strepitation of *Kampf und Sieg*, or a cantata in honour of the battles of La Belle Alliance and Waterloo—. . . by *Abu Hassan*—by *Der Beherrscher der Geister* . . . and by *Natur und Liebe*—all productions of the ubiquitarian Carl Maria.[1]

Some critics presumed from the public's enthusiasm that the work was poor. It was not musical enough and was, except for the overture, too dramatic—that is, too much a theatrical drama with music and not a series of

[1] *Quarterly Musical Magazine and Review*, 1824-5.

arias, scenas, and recitatives with a story. They pointed to
Mr. Hawes's concert performance, which was ludicrous.
'How indeed should it be otherwise, with the comic songs
of Kilian and Rose,[1] sung by Mr. Terrail and Miss God-
dall, with a chorus of owls, hooted by the choristers of
St. Paul's and the Chapel Royal, and the gong struck by
Mr. Hawes himself?'

A burlesque of the opera, conceived in the same spirit
and entitled *Love in a Charnel-house*, with a trio between
two owls and a wolf, was discussed in a Covent Garden
entertainment called *Lofty Projects*, and the opinion of the
critics seemed to be that the great attraction of the work
lay in 'the romantic and mystical constitution of the story
—its magic and its scenery, its owls and its bats—all
monstrous, all abominable things. . . . The music, we are
convinced by experience, had but a slight share in fixing
its popularity, though the report of the music led the way
to the introduction of the opera itself.' Weber, they considered, 'has absorbed all the reputation that has attended
the drama itself'.

These critics—purely musical critics apparently[2]—were
so bothered, as they always are, by new sounds that they
at once presumed the music to be incoherent, disregarding
—as it did—all the rules they had learned as gospel. They
were incapable—as they always are—of criticizing the work
as a whole, and, being used to music *or* drama, found it
impossible to conceive of music *and* drama.

Yet in the correspondence resulting from the account of
the concert already quoted 'An Admirer of Consistency'
admirably took up the cudgels on Weber's behalf:

Can any thing more forcibly illustrate the unjustness . . . of
performing music expressly written for the stage, at a concert,
totally detached from its story—severing, as it were, the soul
of the music from the body, and thus rendering it liable to such

[1] Aennchen? Hawes had introduced extraneous ballads.
[2] When will it be realized by editors that to criticize an opera a
knowledge of both music and stage is necessary?

a critique as the above? . . . It proves the composer to have
entered so thoroughly, heart and mind, into the spirit of the
subject, as to have completely identified the two; so much so,
that either without the other is comparatively nothing. The
music . . . appears to have flowed spontaneously as the story
unfolded. M. von Weber . . . is purely a *dramatic composer*,
and as *such* ranks . . . second to few, if any, that have preceded
him. . . . The difference between Weber and the generality of
modern composers is, that he writes to his story *only*, and *that*
so intently, that the music cannot with safety, or at least with
propriety or justice, in a critical point of view, be separated from
it; while others, on the contrary, turn all their attention to
general effect, their first and indeed almost only aim being to
hit upon a pretty melody that shall please the public, and be
sung here or there, or every where, and with equal effect. . . .
The contrary of this system, as I have already observed, forms,
in my opinion, Weber's greatest eulogy, and leads me to repeat,
that it is unfair, that it is unjust to perform such operas at a
concert in the first place, and more particularly so to form and
write a critical opinion and judgment on the merits of the
music *so performed* in the second.[1]

Weber himself listened too carefully to the adverse
critics and at once set out to prove his worth by writing a
full opera. If he failed, the blame rests partly with his
librettist, Helmina von Chezy, and partly, as Spitta
sensibly pointed out,[2] with the composer himself. As
Weber admitted, 'Do you suppose that any proper composer will allow a libretto to be put into his hand like an
apple?' The chief flaw in this new opera, *Euryanthe*, is
that it relies too much on events outside the action of the
opera. This would not matter if the story were universally
known (though this would not excuse it),[3] but when
the story is not widely known and is anyway somewhat

[1] A letter that might often be adapted nowadays—for instance, concerning Alban Berg's *Wozzeck* performed at a Philharmonic concert
on March 14, 1934.
[2] Grove's *Dictionary*.
[3] Recently accounts of 'What happened afterwards' to the Sleeping
Beauty and other fairy-tale characters have been broadcast, and these
naturally needed no explanation.

complicated, the reliance on previous events is unfortunate
at the least.

Adolar and Lysiart in medieval France are rivals for
Euryanthe, who possesses two mysteries—a ring and a
secret. Eglantine, a protegée of Euryanthe, is in love with
Adolar but is ready to marry Lysiart in return for stealing
the ring and telling him the secret. Lysiart produces these
at court as proof that he has won Euryanthe's love. She is
condemned to be killed by Adolar, who, however, has not
the heart to kill her, but leaves her to perish. Meeting the
bridal procession of Eglantine and Lysiart he is told by
the bride that she ruined Euryanthe in the hope of winning
him herself. Lysiart stabs Eglantine, Euryanthe revives,
and the lovers are united.

In spite of all that has been said against it, *Euryanthe* is
a fine work—it is a really grand opera. If it does not appeal
as directly as *Der Freischütz*, this may be because Weber
was essentially a composer of the storm and stress of
human emotions, and their allegorical counterparts in
nature and the supernatural. The massive, the great, were
not for him. He needed no big canvas for his work: his
music is full of intimate touches, delicate and subtle points
of detail. Every word, every mood and shade of mood, are
reflected in his music. He is happier when the French
Court is an incident—as in the later *Oberon*—than when
it pervades the whole atmosphere.

The production of *Euryanthe* was received with mixed
feelings. The public were enthusiastic, it is true, but
musicians considered it 'hard to understand and harder
to sing such music', Schubert—who had equally dis-
liked *Der Freischütz*—summing it up with 'This is no
music. There is no finale, no concerted piece according to
the rules of art. It is all striving after effect.[1] And he finds
fault with Rossini! It is utterly dry and dismal.' The
anti-Weberites were only too ready to name the work

---

[1] How often this is said nowadays about new music—and, presumably, will always be said even by intelligent musicians!

K

Ennuyante, as the composer himself had once inadvertently remarked, not knowing that Euryanthe's child was to be Lohengrin with even harder music to sing.

Adverse criticism so worried Weber that all his energy deserted him. 'I have not an idea, and do not believe I ever composed anything. Those operas were not mine after all.' But in the autumn of 1824 he was encouraged to start composing again after fifteen months' silence by an invitation from Charles Kemble to write a new opera for Covent Garden.

Whether Kemble's reason was artistic or financial—and the correspondence over terms seems to imply the latter— the fact remains that Weber was invited to compose an opera on the subject of *Faust*, from Goethe, or *Oberon*, from Wieland, and that the composer enthusiastically undertook to set Planché's libretto on *Oberon*.

The story of this opera is such as must have appealed immediately to Weber, with his love of human emotions, medieval chivalry, and supernatural fantasies. Oberon, having as usual quarrelled with Titania, has vowed never to be reconciled with her until he has found two constant lovers, but repenting his vow sends Puck to search for such a pair. He learns that Sir Huon of Bordeaux, having slain Charlemagne's son for attempting his murder, has been condemned to go to Baghdad, slay the man who sits at the Caliph's right hand, and claim the Caliph's daughter. By Oberon's magic Huon falls in love with a vision of Rezia, who is unwillingly betrothed to Babekan, and is transported to the Tigris with a magic horn which will summon Oberon if need be. Huon kills Babekan and Oberon wafts the lovers to the port of Ascalon, where they set sail for Greece, only to be wrecked by a magic storm to test their constancy. Pirates capture Rezia and mermaids carry Huon to the piratical Tunis. Here Roshana, wife of the Emir, falls in love with Huon, who is therefore condemned to be burnt at the stake with Rezia, who claims him as her husband. Oberon and his reconciled queen inter-

vene and transport the lovers to Charlemagne's court in
triumph.

The overture to *Oberon* is an epitome both of the opera
and of the whole of Weber's music. The magic horn, the
fairies, Charlemagne's court, Rezia's aria to the ocean,
Puck's invocation—all are here. The music is not only
'romantic', it is 'atmospheric', and above all it is—like all
his music—essentially drama.[1]

The first Act is fine enough—with its magical fairy
opening where the delicate voices seem to be part of the
moonlit orchestra, with the passionate regret of Oberon's
fatal vow, with the strange simplicity of the vision of
Rezia with her lute, with the ingeniously heroic farewell
to Huon,[2] and the finely picturesque finale—Rezia waiting
confidently for her saviour while the harem slaves march
away into the darkness to their rest.

But how can the second Act be even hinted at in words?
First comes the grandly barbaric entry to the Caliph's
court, then the eerie wood-wind chords of magic, then a
moment's contrast with Fatima's delicious little flirt-song
'A lonely Arab maid', and at last the quartet 'Over the dark
blue waters', which is one of the most beautiful pieces in
the whole work. The scene changes to the seashore, and
Weber is in his element. Puck's invocation of the spirits
and their reply is in its musical drama little short of marvellous. Here is pure poetic fantasy, yet not all weird and
exciting: the most eerie moment is surely the two-note

[1] A late Victorian once confessed to me that as a girl she foolishly
fancied a romance and sentimental conversation when playing Weber's
Invitation to the Valse. She need not have apologized: the need for
some such fancy was inevitable. As Spitta wrote in Grove's *Dictionary*,
'To form a right estimate of Weber's music it is necessary to look upon
him as a dramatic composer. Not that his other compositions are of
no importance—quite the contrary; but in one and all may be discerned
more or less plainly that dramatic genius which was the essence of his
nature, and which determined their form, and gave them that stamp
whereby they differ so strikingly from the productions of other artists.'
[2] Weber was right in disliking the florid 'Yes, even love' written to
show off Braham's voice. The original 'From boyhood trained in
battlefield', which it replaced, is far superior.

harmony on the words 'Obey the spell'. It is easy to make a full skirling orchestra thrill with a diminished seventh, but it takes a genius to cast enchantment with a mere unexpected diminished fifth.

The magic storm then bursts in all its fury; a moment's relief with Huon's movingly simple prayer, and Rezia's justly famed scena 'Ocean, thou mighty monster' begins.

The scena represents the gradual calm of the troubled waters, the breaking of the sun through the gloom, and the arrival of a boat to the succour of the distressed Rezia. All these natural circumstances, with the sensations they create in her bosom, form the subject of the scena, and the composer has strictly adhered to the intention of adapting it to the sole purpose of dramatic effect. The recitative . . . is powerfully conceived. The allegro then presents to the ear (as the scenery to the eye) the distant rolling of the yet angry billows, and the gradual re-appearance of light. . . . At the end of the allegro there is a recitative to describe the bursting [1] forth of the sun, and the very fine *andante maestoso* which succeeds seems to catch at the instant a portion of the warmth and light of the glaring orb, and to increase in dignity as the object it depicts increases in splendour. . . . An animated movement, at the appearance of the boat, contrasts with the andante, but the last part of this song is decidedly too instrumental. . . . The immense effect sought in this scene requires a far more powerful agent than the voice,[2] but every possible assistance from the orchestra is given, and it is in descriptive music that Weber's forte lies.[3]

Again Weber, the true dramatist, is not afraid to end the act quietly with the beautiful delicacy of the voices of the mermaids floating on the calm sea in their 'emerald cars'.

The last act is practically a lively scherzo with occasional contrasts. Fatima's 'Oh Araby' is a jolly ballad, and her duet with the comic Sherasmin, 'On the banks of sweet Garonne', is as wittily human as the humours of *Die Meistersinger*. A break for the heroic trio 'And must I then dissemble', Rezia's expressive cavatina 'Mourn thou, poor heart', and Huon's lively rondo 'I revel in joy and hope again', and we return to jollity, first with the long Eastern choral ballet that fails to seduce the hero, and then with the magic horn that sets all the slaves jigging and jogging irresistibly while Oberon wafts the virtuous lovers to safety. For the end—Oberon's noble farewell and the grand finale at Charlemagne's court.

Weber may not have been a great composer, but he was without doubt a great opera composer. Unlike the majority of those who have written works for the theatre he understood stagecraft from the inside, and his operas are therefore unities. The academic critics of his day and since were to a great extent right when they disparaged his music on musical grounds. In Weber's music there is

[1] 'busting' in the original!
[2] What would this critic have said of *Die Walküre*?
[3] *Musical Review.*

little musical development, and when he repeats, he repeats for the most part baldly without the little extra touches a Mozart would give. His music will not stand alone, a cunning collection of notes, like Bach's, or even Beethoven's to a great extent: it is so sensitive, responsive, and apprehensive that it depends largely on the dramatic tone-colour of the instruments of the orchestra, their combinations and contrastings: it is cramped if it is confined to a single instrument or two. Weber never produced a prize bloom nor perfected a single species, but the luxuriance of his colours is supreme, and ranges from delicacy to exoticism.

Above all Weber's music is wedded to the stage. His music does not reflect the action and the emotions of the drama, nor does it transcend the drama: it is part and parcel with it. It is dangerous to draw any line, but what other opera composers have consistently understood the theatre so well as Monteverdi, Purcell, Weber, and Puccini? Their music as such may be criticized academically, but they live drama in their music and their music is filled with human sympathy. Without Weber music since his day would have been a different thing. 'Judged by the standard of Beethoven his melody, harmony, and rhythm are often commonplace and trivial in the extreme; but we cannot read the work of Schubert, Schumann, Mendelssohn, Chopin, Liszt, or Wagner without finding frequent traces of his genius'.[1]

[1] E. J. Dent, 'Italian Chamber Cantatas' in the *Musical Antiquary*, vol. ii.

7

HECTOR BERLIOZ
(1803–1869)
By TOM S. WOTTON

ERLIOZ differs from every other composer who has contributed to the development of his art, in that he may be said to have commenced his musical life in mid-career. It was at once his glory and, in some respects, his undoing. And it has much to do with the fact that the adverse criticism lavished on all reformers has in his case been so persistent. It is one of the curiosities of musical history that sixty years after his death, Berlioz still holds a debatable position amongst composers, and that there are still conscientious musicians who deny him genius, or, admitting grudgingly that he had some small share of it, insist that his eccentricity and faulty technique obscure it too much to allow of his being counted amongst the greatest masters. His detractors may declare that the curiosity is that he survives at all. But the fact that he does survive, and has a number of warm admirers, many of whom are competent to speak with authority on things musical, seems rather to point to the possibility that his opponents have viewed his works from a wrong angle, and that their lack of appreciation is due to something inherent in themselves.

Although instances may be adduced of youthful works of great originality, in the usual course the earliest productions of a composer are more or less reflections of those of his predecessors. Step by step he hammers out his own individuality, together with a technique peculiar to himself for expressing it. Gradually he discards or modifies the methods of his predecessors, until he may be considered as the principal of them, and thus he reaches his *Eroica*, his *Tristan*. And this slow unfolding of himself, the evolution

of his means of expression, have an important bearing on
his final general acceptance.

The average man is inclined to be suspicious of originality if it be thrust too suddenly upon him. His mind cannot
grasp it, and he has nothing to aid him in determining
whether it be good or bad. Originality *per se* has nothing
particular to commend it. Any one who will take the
trouble to study current ideas carefully can easily concoct
something diametrically opposed to them. The only
originality of any worth is that which conveys to the world
some verity it had not previously realized. And the world
realizes truth slowly! Hence the desirability of the development of the composer as outlined above.

The composer also owes something to his imitators—his
successors in point of fact—who, paradoxically, prepare
the way for him in devious directions. Long before the
later works of Wagner were applauded at the Grand
Opéra, the French public was familiarized with the Bayreuth master's ideas and methods through certain compositions of their own musicians. Before Brahms's symphonies
were enjoyed by concert-goers in England, some of our
own composers had given them glimpses of his mode of
thought. Even minor makers of music accustom the
public to chords and progressions that are faint echoes of
the master.

Berlioz received assistance neither from predecessors
nor imitators, and therefore an unknown or rarely heard
work of his strikes many of his listeners much as it did its
first audience eighty or a hundred years ago. They are confronted by that same originality that perplexed their forebears, and like them are without a standard to test its
worth. The only difference between then and now is, that
at the commencement of Berlioz's career some were
inclined to regard him as a charlatan. But few would
dream of bringing that charge against him nowadays. Of
his sincerity there can be no doubt. His divergence from
accepted views was not deliberate. His originality was

both born in him and fostered by his upbringing, in which it might be said there was no music except that which he himself created.

Attempts have been made to consider Berlioz as a sort of musical sign-post which pointed to roads he had not the ability to explore himself. Thus, he has been dubbed the unconscious inventor of the symphonic poem, of which Liszt had the wit to perceive the possibilities. This, however, is a misleading label. Liszt no doubt learnt from the *Fantastic* Symphony the effectiveness of modifying a theme to fit it to varying moods and situations, but he worked out the idea on different lines. Nor were his views on 'programme music' the same as those of Berlioz, who, in spite of his reputation, and the erroneous notion that he was unable to compose without some definite story in his mind, really only approached it in one number—the Death Scene in the *Romeo and Juliet* Symphony, the omission of which, in a sarcastic note in the score, he recommends for ninety-nine performances out of a hundred. We shall return to the subject, and I would merely remark here that the dragging-in of the *idée fixe* at the end of the March to Execution, and other touches of realism, can hardly be classed as programme music of the same order as Liszt's *Die Ideale* or Strauss's *Don Quixote*.

Some have endeavoured to regard Berlioz as being in some degree a precursor of Wagner, and Jean Marnold,[1] one of the fiercest of the French master's adversaries, would trace a connexion between the *Tristan* prelude and the long-drawn-out melodies of the older composer. But Wagner's knowledge of the works of Berlioz was derived simply from hearing some of them during his stay in Paris (September 1839 to April 1842), and afterwards in Dresden, when he assisted Berlioz with his rehearsals. He heard all the four symphonies, and though he tells us in *My Life* how portions of them pleased him, he confesses that 'though ravished by his compositions, I was at the

[1] *Mercure de France*, Jan. 15 and Feb. 1, 1905.

same time repelled and even wearied of them'. Scarcely the attitude of a devout disciple! Wagner owns that 'at first the grandeur and masterly execution of the orchestral part almost overwhelmed' him, and he must have learnt much from hearing it. He, however, applied his knowledge to his own methods of orchestration, which were completely different from those of the French composer, without, I would add, necessarily showing any advance on them. Each master adopted the vehicle best suited to his purpose.

Probably Berlioz's influence was felt mostly in Russia, where Wagner's ideas were only tardily accepted. But here again we can find no direct imitators. Weingartner's dictum, however, that 'without Berlioz we should not be where we are' is true. And Masson is correct, when, in his admirable book on the master, he says:

If France has not always encouraged his efforts, she has profited largely from his influence. He revivified our music. He liberated melody, dislocated obsolete models, cast prophetic lights on harmony, coupled tone-colours with an audacity that foreshadows contemporary impressionism. . . . There is not a single living French musician who does not owe some little to Berlioz.

His influence may not have been so great in countries swayed by Teutonic ideas, but still it has been felt. He opened windows in the temple of music—smashed them, if you will—and thus cleared the atmosphere from that stagnation which was threatened after the death of Beethoven.

While still a student, Berlioz produced *Les Francs Juges* Overture, and this, laid out on the grandest scale and ablaze with new tone-colours, was alone sufficient to place him at a bound among the leading composers of France. Then, immediately after his emancipation from the classrooms of the Conservatoire, he presented to the Parisian public perhaps the most revolutionary work of the nineteenth century—the *Fantastic* Symphony, one of his best-known compositions, and that which perhaps is most closely associated with his name. It is to be regretted that, amongst musical masterpieces, it should exhibit, in the midst of so many pages that proclaim the genius, some signs of immaturity and inexperience. It could not have been otherwise! Genius may achieve much, but it cannot express itself fully without experience, even though it be armed with a perfect technique, which at that time Berlioz most assuredly did not possess. Although the work was retouched for several years after the initial performance, it would have been better, as regards Berlioz's future status, if the five movements of the symphony had lain fallow for the sixteen years that separate the *Eight Scenes from Faust* from *The Damnation of Faust*. In collating the earlier with the later versions of the *Scenes*, we can perceive not only an improved technique but the experience derived from a larger view of life. It is not advisable to start in mid-career! But just as we often love our friends more for their weaknesses than their virtues, many admirers of the Symphony would not have a note of it altered, preferring, with Louis Ehlert, 'the errors of giants to the verities of dwarves'.

The imperfection of Berlioz's technique is often brought against him by his opponents. But we have no reason for supposing that he was idle during his four years at the Conservatoire. It required no great intelligence to learn the rules that governed harmony and counterpoint as taught in Paris in the 1820's, and the young musician would have worked industriously at his exercises, if only to oblige his teachers—Lesueur, to whom he owed an immense debt of gratitude and for whom he had a real affection, and Reicha, whom he at any rate respected. He knew the rules, but his musical instinct told him that many of them were antiquated or absurd. Their observance irked him in the expression of his ideas, and so he broke them, often clumsily, since he had not then worked out a technique of his own. His detractors deny that he ever possessed one, and impute to ignorance his divergences from accepted usage. This view can only arise from an unsympathetic study of his works. His harmonic sense may not have been so highly developed as that of some of the other masters, but countless passages in his works can be adduced to prove that he was very far from being devoid of it. It is unfortunate that Cherubini did not grant him that professorship of harmony for which he applied. We should have learnt definitely what his system was, and, in laying down rules for others, he would have been compelled to set his own house in order.

As Ernest Newman has pointed out in his *Musical Studies*, in some respects Berlioz's earlier compositions evince more agreement with academic rules than his later ones. Even Jean Marnold (*op. cit.*) admits that Berlioz wrote better at the age of twenty-seven (*Fantastic* Symphony) than Wagner did at twenty-eight (*The Flying Dutchman*). (In considering this we must remember that Wagner commenced a systematic study of harmony some few years earlier in life.) If we take Mr. Newman's statement as authoritative, the suggestion that Berlioz's harmonic methods arose entirely from ignorance makes him an almost incredible personage. Here we have a man who commences his musical career cognizant of certain rules which he may at times have broken: as a critic, he is constantly attending performances, listening to music based on those rules, and writing notices of the various works, in which he often drew particular attention to the harmony in a technical way which no modern critic would dare to do in a daily paper, as he then did: and while he has perforce to study the works of others, he is engaged in writing music of his own and in testing the effect of it at rehearsal.

Yet, in spite of all this, he gradually forgets the rules he had been taught and had himself previously largely practised. This is surely an impossible view, and in its place it is more logical to conclude that he evolved a system of his own, as has been the custom of every other composer. Whether it were a good one, or one adapted for general use, is another question. Before condemning it, we should recall Schumann's words apropos of the 'faults' in the *Fantastic* Symphony: 'Should one attempt to correct the harmony, or even make some modifications —for a practised harmonist it would be child's-play—one would see what tameness would result'. Possibly Berlioz preferred breaking an accepted rule to running the risk of being tame.

This is not the place to enter into a discussion of Berlioz's system of harmony, beyond touching on three characteristics—his fondness for chords in root position, his objection to appoggiaturas, and his hatred of enharmonic modulation such as is found in the works of Wagner. He himself employed enharmonic modulations, but, as Saint-Saëns has pointed out, they were based on a different principle. Those which stud the pages of *Tristan* he abominated. They offended his ears quite as much as those of his adversaries are pained by any progression that he ever penned. And, it might be added, in the 1860's a great many highly respectable musicians shared his objections. His ideas on the employment of the appoggiatura were equally pronounced. In his celebrated attack in 1835 on *Zampa* (a favourite opera of the Parisians), he protested against 'the abuse of the appoggiatura, which denaturalizes every chord, gives to the harmony a vague colour without decisive character, weakens the harshness of certain dissonances or augments it to the verge of discordance, transforms sweetness into insipidity, makes grace lackadaisical, and appears to me the most insufferable of the affectations of the Parisian school'. In 1860—twenty-five years later— in his notice of the two concerts that Wagner gave in Paris, he says of the *Tristan* prelude: 'It is a slow piece, commencing pianissimo, gradually increasing to a fortissimo, and returning to the initial nuance, without any theme save a sort of chromatic groan, but crowded with dissonant chords of which the long appoggiaturas replacing the real note of the harmony augment the cruelty.' Tarring Hérold and Wagner with the same brush may cause a smile, but the two extracts show how tenaciously Berlioz clung to his opinions as regards harmony. Indeed, this fixity of purpose is one of his characteristics, as it has been with other reformers. The fault in his case was that, owing to his precocious originality, he was inclined to adopt these rigid opinions too early in his career.

It is difficult to explain his partiality for chords in root position—Gounod called him the apostle of false basses. We may impute it to his early love for Gluck and Spontini, neither of whom cultivated a flowing bass-line. Or we may trace some subtle connexion between the practice and his methods of orchestration. It is perhaps simplest to look upon it as a mannerism, the evil of which his detractors have exaggerated: they have done the same with other 'faults' in his technique. Were that technique impeccable and in accord with every academic rule, it is quite possible that many of them would still have no great liking for Berlioz as a composer—we fortunately have not all the same tastes—and they find in his occasional stiff basses something to justify their antipathy. Few of us have the courage to declare our hate for this or that without attempting to explain it.

If Berlioz's system of harmony differed from that of his contemporaries, the same might be said of many of his melodies. Though we can find in his works tunes of regular construction, often the second halves of his melodies do not correspond with the first. And at times they run to many more bars than is customary, and so merge into 'continuous melody'. Hence Marnold's remark, cited above, that Berlioz foreshadowed the prelude to *Tristan*. Berlioz's *chant récitatif*, however (of which much of Faust's part in *The Damnation of Faust* is a good example), based on song, differs from Wagner's *Sprachmelodie*, which is based more or less on the inflexions of ordinary speech. Expressive melody, or (better) melodiousness, is one of the essential qualities of the French master's music, and to some extent accounts for certain features of his harmony. The melodic line often so fully expressed his thought that anything more than a rudimentary accompaniment would tend to disturb rather than enhance it.

It is possibly on account of the irregularity and length of many of Berlioz's melodies that some have denied him the possession of the melodic gift. An admirer finds it difficult to argue the point. He may appreciate some of the objections to Berlioz's harmony, though he may wonder why slight defects in it should apparently blind a listener to the many wonderful qualities of the music. But to have a thing flatly contradicted which to him is as obvious as the unclouded sun in the high heavens, leaves him at a loss for words. When Berlioz, in his *Memoirs*, summed up the predominant qualities of his music, as dispassionately, maybe, as it is possible for a composer to criticize his own works, he stressed his melodiousness, and while admitting that it is open to any one to question the value or beauty of his melodies, insisted that to deny their existence is either dishonest or foolish. I do not think that it is necessarily one or the other, though no doubt during his lifetime many musicians abused his music by way of retaliation. They had suffered the pricks of his critical pen, and here was an opportunity for hitting back. But it is not the same to-day. His detractors most certainly cannot all be considered foolish, and there is no reason for doubting their honesty, unless indeed it be dishonest to criticize a musician adversely without having made more than a superficial study of him.

As I have suggested above, I am inclined to attribute the attitude of most of Berlioz's adversaries to his astounding originality, which was sprung upon the musical world unheralded either by others or by himself. The very intensity of it is sufficient to disturb a certain type of mind. How often, after hearing an eloquent speech or sermon has one turned to one's companion, anticipating enthusiasm, only to be met by words of disparagement? Some slight error of statement, some trifling mispronunciation or unhappy trick of gesture had struck him more forcibly than anything else. The message was nothing to him, because the delivery of it did not conform to certain precise ideas of his own. Since that particular type of mind will always persist, I doubt whether Berlioz's position in the musical hierarchy will ever be definitely fixed. If ever it were, it will be by the ordinary concert-goer, to whom the critics will defer, as they have deferred before. The untrained music-lover, whatever his type of mind, is less likely to be troubled by questions of technique, especially as those details are often condoned, or even praised, by many musicians quite as competent as those who criticize adversely.

The ordinary concert-goer, however, is at a disadvantage in that he cannot pursue his study of Berlioz's orchestral music at the keyboard. With the echoes of the orchestra still ringing in his ears he may find some satisfaction in the arrangements of Liszt, Holbrooke, or Stradal. But they are very difficult, and simpler versions are often downright misleading. The concert-goer is dependent on performances,[1] and at them, I would venture to suggest, he does not always hear the real Berlioz. There is a tendency of conductors to treat him too sensationally. And for this perhaps Berlioz himself is partly to blame. He *felt* music to an extraordinary degree. His description, in *A travers chants*, of his sensations when hearing music suggests some kind of cataleptic fit. And this while listening to the music that he loved! With music that he hated his feelings approached physical nausea. Naturally his emotions were

---

[1] It is to be regretted that the gramophone companies have not shown more enterprise as regards Berlioz's works. Beyond three records of the *Fantastic* Symphony, and several of the *Roman Carnival* and *Cellini* overtures, little else has been reproduced. Apart from the other overtures and symphonies, and the bigger vocal works, such scores as *The Flight into Egypt* and *Summer Nights* should be popular.

more intense on hearing his own works, and often, when conducting them, he seems to have been on the verge of a collapse. In an endeavour to convey these abnormal sensations to others ordinary speech was inadequate, and so he had to resort to far-fetched similes or a string of superlatives. As I have said, the summing up of his qualities in the *Memoirs* is calm and collected, but elsewhere he uses language in regard to the effect of his music which has misled both admirers and detractors. He did, indeed, at times depict horrors, and in so doing may be said to have introduced a new element into music. The portrayal of the horrible had been attempted before, but, for lack of his wonderful skill in orchestration, not convincingly. Thanks, however, to his own descriptions, and to the fact that half a dozen bars of horror or terror are more likely to impress an audience than a hundred treating of softer emotions, his tendency to dwell on the former has been grossly exaggerated. Your true admirer of Berlioz has no objection to his treating of the gruesome on occasion, but he objects to the finding of it where it does not exist, and to the conductors who seek to accentuate the non-existent.

The March to Execution, for instance, which was originally a Marche des Gardes in the unfinished opera *Les Francs Juges*, has been deemed horrible from a mistaken idea that it illustrated some painful situation. As a matter of fact, we do not know what it was at first intended to depict. There seems to be no place for a march in such of the libretto as we possess. We merely find in Act III a direction—'recall of the March of the Guards . . .' to show that it had been played previously. More than probably it was intended to be a processional march of no more moment than is to be found in many of the grand operas of his day, and merely represented the assembling of the *francs juges*. Berlioz, carried away by his musical ideas, may have found that he had composed a piece of more sinister effect than was in keeping with the situation, and so transferred it to his symphony, although at that time the fate of the opera was not definitely fixed.

Wagner believed that, divorced from Berlioz's own conducting, none of the French master's works would survive, with the possible exception of the *Symphonie funèbre*. And though the opinion has been proved to be erroneous, there can be no doubt that much of the original success of his works in Germany was due to his wonderful powers as a conductor. That his works lend themselves to so many different 'readings', and have not been killed by the unsympathetic, is a testimony to their greatness. The ideas of sympathetic conductors are always of interest, but nevertheless, as Wagner knew what he was talking about, if we would have the true Berlioz, his methods of interpretation ought to be imitated as much as possible. He detested the rubato, for instance, and when both he and Wagner were conducting in London, opinions as to their respective merits turned largely on the question of the use (or abuse) of it. He also held to the marked metronome time throughout the movement, except where he indicated in the score some variation. When, in the 1870's, there was a revival of his works in Paris, both Reyer and Saint-Saëns objected to some of the tempi of the undoubtedly enthusiastic conductors, not from any desire to throw cold water on their efforts, but simply and solely because the works sounded better as they remembered the composer conducting them. There is no necessity, for example, to take *The Roman Carnival* at breakneck speed, obliterating in the general scramble many of the finer details. And Liszt, knowing Berlioz's wishes, in his arrangement of the March to Execution warned the player against quickening the pace at the end of it. Berlioz the conductor followed implicitly the directions of Berlioz the composer, and a celebrated conductor of the present day has shown us how effective such a method may prove.

Interpreters are too often inclined—perhaps unconsciously—to mould their conception of a man's music on their impression of the man himself. For instance, until quite recently Handel's music has been performed in a manner considered befitting to his portly form and full-bottomed wig. And this possibly has happened with Berlioz. He has been pictured as a highly nervous being, whose brain was at times excited to the verge of madness, and therefore as best served by sensational or even hysterical interpretations. In reality, Berlioz the man was very different from Berlioz the musician, who was remarkably sane, working out his inspirations with infinite patience and retouching them more than is customary with composers. When, maddened by an attack of quinsy and an insulting letter from Mme Moke, telling him that his engagement to her daughter was broken, Berlioz the man set out from Florence determined to commit both murder and suicide, the musician was collected enough to remember his symphony, and left directions to Habeneck as to the coda of the waltz, should the work ever be performed 'in the absence of the author'.

It is difficult to gather what were Berlioz's precise ideas on the subject of 'programme music'. Like every other composer his inspiration was at times aroused by some external object, some tale or scene. But, once aroused, purely musical considerations usually held sway, so often that attempts to connect this or that passage with a particular personage or incident are doomed to failure. He might be said to have been the musical equivalent of a mathematician, who, having translated something tangible into an algebraical formula, proceeds to develop the latter regardless of its original signification. His custom of using melodies that had belonged either to early works or to those with which he was dissatisfied is sufficient to prove that he attached no rigid meaning to a theme. A melody in the *Rob Roy* overture which we may take as having some connexion with Diana Vernon becomes later a musical portrait of Mary, Queen of Scots, in a piece at first intended for the viola d'amore of Urhan and afterwards for the ordinary viola of Paganini (the actual facts about these two contemplated works are obscure), and finally is associated with Childe Harold in the *Harold in Italy* Symphony. Many other examples of this re-using of old material might be given—on the four cantatas he composed in his efforts to gain the Prix de Rome he drew largely—and there is no reason why he should not regard his still-born works in the light of note-books. Other composers have done the same. But the method is not that of an uncompromising writer of programme music.

The Death Scene from the *Romeo and Juliet* Symphony cited above can certainly be considered as programme music. It illustrates Garrick's version of Shakespeare's scene—a strange instance of *lèse-majesté* on the part of Berlioz!—and we have Juliet's awakening, the reunion of the lovers (a metamorphosis of the principal theme of the Love Scene), and their deaths, all realistically depicted. But even here the musician betrays himself. The beautiful Invocation, though not exactly inappropriate to the situation, impresses one rather as having been the germ of the number. The ridiculous programme attached to the little violin piece, *Rêverie et Caprice*, had not anything to do with Berlioz. When it was revived in Paris, some dozen years after the composer's death, Julien Tiersot, then quite a young man, with mistaken zeal and at the instigation of Pasdeloup, concocted the rigmarole, and the publishers placed it on the title-page of their reprint of the work. Tiersot explains the incident in his *Berlioziana*, and may be forgiven. But it is strange how often an earnest disciple, anxious to aid the interests of his master, will do things contrary to his wishes. Sensational performances, from which Berlioz is not the only sufferer, no doubt are often due to the same misplaced anxiety.

Space forbids our dealing with Berlioz's form and orchestration, although the latter is the one thing connected with his music that is approved by most of his adversaries. I say 'most' advisedly, since recently an anonymous foreign conductor has objected to the master's music on the grounds that it contains so many orchestral 'stunts'—the conductor's own expression, which he did not attempt to define. Taking the word in its usual acceptation as tricks introduced for their own sake, the conductor's idea may possibly be that of many, though they may not share his objections. They are inclined to connect Berlioz with the drums, the brass orchestras and trombone 'pedals' of the *Requiem*, the effects in *The Ride to the Abyss* and the 'Sabbat' of the *Fantastic* Symphony, rather than with his many pages that contain nothing more startling than an unerring *flair* in his choice of instruments and a perfect balance. And those many pages form nine-tenths of his work.

Musical people generally seem to lose their sense of proportion in the face of Berlioz's music, and the reason for this must be sought in his baffling originality. If one would understand him—and he would repay any earnest attempt a hundredfold—one must disabuse one's mind of much that has been written about his music, a great deal of which is mere repetition of what was brought against him in his lifetime, and which, though possibly more or less justified by the current ideas of that day, now seems old-fashioned in the light of the experimentalism of modern music. Parenthetically I would observe that one thing that bewilders a listener to the French master's works is the difficulty of dating him. Even if the hearer *knows* that the March to Execution was composed less than a score of years after Haydn's death, his ears give him the lie. On the other hand, it is obviously unfair to Berlioz to treat him as in some respects a comparatively modern composer. His musical career had ended before Wagner's later works were performed.

Berlioz is an isolated figure, and we must judge him as such, without reference to any other composer. If this be done conscientiously, perhaps even some of the scoffers might be brought to echo Mr. Bernard van Dieren's opinion expressed at a Berlioz Conference that the master was 'with the sole exception of Mozart the composer of the most stupendous native gifts of the last few centuries'.

In conclusion, I would emphasize what I have said above, that Berlioz's future status will be decided by the ordinary concert-goer. When Colonne gave in Paris (practically in succession) more than a hundred performances of *The Damnation of Faust*, few amongst his enthusiastic audiences troubled themselves about Berlioz's views on the appoggiatura or enharmonic modulation, nor were they distressed by chords in root position. They simply submitted themselves to the glamour of the music, and, without preconceived ideas, submitted to its spell. Unfortunately, in England our concert-givers seldom imitate the admirable methods of the late M. Colonne. Here, although a work may meet with rapturous applause, its next performance too often does not take place until six months later, and then probably at the other end of the kingdom. Still, English audiences can follow the example of those of Paris by exercising their own judgement when hearing the music of Berlioz, and by not allowing themselves to be biased by the opinions of critics on technical points which no ordinary audience could appreciate.

That every concert-goer will include Berlioz amongst his favourite composers cannot be expected. But there is so much variety in the master's works that, given opportunities for hearing them and listening with unprejudiced ears, every lover of music ought to find sufficient to admire to warrant him applying the epithet 'great' to the man who wrote them.

8

FELIX MENDELSSOHN-BARTHOLDY
(1809–1847)
By HUBERT J. FOSS

THERE is nothing to which the old saying 'so near and yet so far' can be applied with greater aptitude than the passage of history, for it is an undoubted truth that a period of fifty years marks a greater break between the sympathies of the times it divides than the same number with a hundred added. As men die and fade from our present view, they pass through the purgatory of recent times, and the respectable Elysium of antiquity, eventually to reach an enviable heaven of uncritical admiration. Generations bring laughter, before, becoming centuries, they bring comfort. We are amused at the bulbous sleeves, the bodices, the bustles, and the weepers of the 'fifties, not surely any of them intrinsically more funny than spats, or the ruffles, brocades, and buckles of an earlier period, nor yet than broadcloth, tabard, chiton, or woad. So we are less diverted by the knife-axled chariot than by the earliest motor-car, and less by the wax writing-tablet than by the early 'telegraphic message' of Trollope's novels. It is not only that there is no medium of comparison between a remote and a present moment, such as there is with times nearer our own; there is also that divine provision, reaction.

The group-consciousness of a time reacts no less against its previous age than an individual child against its fogey parents. It is a purely parental, and not in the least an intellectual, desire that children should either inherit or accept as eternal verities the experience of their forebears. No one who cares for life can desire it with his mind. We may, we do, wish that this reaction should mean a striving to attain a higher point than our fathers.

Possibly the gravest difference between Greek ideals and
ours is that their youth attempted such a thing as an ideal,
and ours assumes it, unattempted, as an inherent prerogative. Yet however admirable this aim, we can recognize
in this world only a progress that leads not from better to
worse but from one thing to another; things neither consistently better nor consistently worse, but only different,
and with what a blessed difference!

In music this repeated reaction is to be found equally
with any other part of life, and we need look no farther
than Brahms to see it. His transformation in our modern
minds is not unlike (if less sudden than) that of Cinderella
at midnight, and we may hope a similar halo of general
acceptance will be conferred in the future upon one or two
of our living English composers whom, to-day, we are
inclined to treat as enterprising apprentices. It is possible,
however, that our reaction against our fathers is rather
more intense than that of certain earlier generations against
theirs, for music, always a rapidly moving art, has jumped
particularly swiftly in what to us are modern times. It is
not only that the ideals have changed, which indeed they
have, but that the means have changed too. There is a
strong physical as well as spiritual difference come about
in the last fifty years—a change which often has hurt our
ears more than our hearts, and which, while convincing
some of its utter superiority over its forebears, has
convinced others more reasonably of a hope for the
future, and others, as exaggerated as the first, of its utter
madness.

So we find to-day three parties—the small number of
the open-minded, the larger party which is shocked at
consonance, and the largest of all which is horrified at
a broadened system of dissonance, or, in other words,
a wider definition of consonance. In the main there are
the two well-marked types—those on whom the reaction
has laid a violent hand of welcome, and those whom it has
neglected even to nod to in the street. The one school is

still wedded to tonic and dominant; the other to anything but.

Mendelssohn provides in some senses a Tom Tiddler's ground between the two parties. As representing in a characteristic way an important phase of our immediate forebears' life, he is as saintly in the view of one party as he is diabolic in that of the other. There is nothing to choose between the values of the criticisms of these two parties; both are equally uncritical. There is, however, an advantage on the side of the diabolic school, that at least it is subject to a natural and healthy reaction which has a chance of producing something for the future. Examples of the degree of anathema are as common as blackberries, and a good instance of the other school's attitude is the musician who, when he saw a reference to Mendelssohn as 'of the second rank', accused the writer of using a meaningless tag. It did not occur to him that the words chosen exactly conveyed an exact meaning.

The object of criticism is not to await the verdict of time, which is, virtually, to wait for the verdict of those who do not wait for time. That is an easy method, sometimes followed but not to be commended.

With reservation, if with no actual doubt, one declares Mendelssohn to be typical of his age. What man, indeed, could typify all of any age, and of such an age? And the figure of Liszt rises before our eyes at the mention of the idea. For it is one of the strangest things in musical history that the attention of nearly all English musicians should be open so wide to Mendelssohn and shut so tightly to Liszt. There is the parallel of English poetry, where Tennyson and Swinburne are both types of Victorianism, yet as removed as any two poets could be. So, even if it is allowed that in romanticism Mendelssohn falls behind and that in originality he is a small figure, he may be called not only a product but also a type of his age.

And the first testimony to this is his productiveness. It is a comparison commonly made between the nineteenth century and ourselves that it was of a bigger build, and the epithet 'spacious' if hackneyed is true. This is no criterion that the century was truer, better, or of a more permanent achievement; while that is in debate, there is little doubt that it was bigger. An age when Hofmann was a minor and Gissing and Collins among the second-best, when Mrs. Browning could write her voluminous love-letters as well as *Aurora Leigh* and the Brontë children novels instead of theirs, when Trollope could flow with his interminable fiction in the intervals of a busy post-office life—such an era is planned upon a big scale. So it is with Mendelssohn from the beginning.

'He is a mature artist', Moscheles said, 'and he is yet only fifteen', and at this age he was indeed not only a mature but also an experienced composer. Of none other save Mozart is there such a profusion of youthful music recorded. The year 1820, Mendelssohn's twelfth, saw the beginning of serious composition, and the inauguration of the series of forty-four manuscript volumes which records most of his writings, in autograph and with carefully noted date and place of completion. To this same year 'are attributable', says Grove, 'between fifty and sixty movements, including amongst them a Trio for pianoforte and strings (three movements); a Sonata in F for pianoforte and violin (three movements); . . . two full Sonatas for pianoforte solo; the beginning of a third in G minor, finished the next year, and published (posthumously) in 1868 (as Op. 105); six pieces for pianoforte solo; three pieces for the same instrument, four hands; four pieces for organ; three songs; two part-songs for men's voices; a cantata . . .; and a *Lustspiel*, or little comedy, for voices and pianoforte in three scenes'.

The year 1821 produces 'five Symphonies for string quartet, each in three movements', and 'nine Fugues, also for string quartet', as a beginning. So the composition proceeded, until the Symphony published in 1824 is inscribed 'simphonia XIII in C', to be known to the world as Op. 11, Mendelssohn's 'first' Symphony. Before he was of age, he had produced several important and some even lasting works—the *Rondo Capriccioso*, the Quintet and Octet for strings, the *Midsummer Night's Dream* Overture, and the Pianoforte Sonata (Op. 6), for example. It is said that in his later life a composition pupil brought to Mendelssohn a setting of some words. Mendelssohn's advice was that the pupil should set the same words twelve more times and choose which setting he liked best. The story, even if not true, is entirely in keeping with its subject's own fluency.

The same characteristic is retained all through his life; where to-day we would produce songs, he produced symphonic works. Mere magnitude of form had no fears for him: he had by instinct a mastery of length and size and a capacity for designing a mould or form and then pouring music into it without hesitation. There is the *Ruy Blas* Overture, which, together with a chorus for sopranos, was conceived, written, copied, rehearsed, and performed all within one week—and indeed tends in places to sound like it. There is his power of improvisation, which played so large a part in producing his phenomenal popularity in England. His memory was no less prodigious. In April 1829 Mendelssohn came to England for the first time to produce his *Midsummer Night's Dream* Overture, and Thomas Attwood left the manuscript full score in a hackney coach and lost it. When Mendelssohn heard this, he said, unperturbed, that he would make another from memory, and on a comparison of the second score with the orchestral parts no errors were found. It is also recorded that he sat at the pianoforte and played to Spontini, before the latter had ever heard it, the entire Ninth Symphony of Beethoven, a work which Mendelssohn continued to remember by heart until his death.

Critically, this may have little to do with the value of his music, but it is at least an indication of the age and of how Mendelssohn was part of it. One relation, however, it does bear to his musical production, and that concerns technique; in fluency and accuracy Mendelssohn's technique never failed him, but to speak of him technically as a master, as he is sometimes described, is to exaggerate as well as misunderstand. Theoretically we may divide a composer's invention from his technique; and it is no less possible to judge his technique by its conformity to accepted principles. But in practice there must be times when a composer's invention is whipped up by his technical capacity, and times when his invention is actually a matter of technique; and this statement, if extended so as to mean that technique needs invention and not only acquired skill, applies with equal truth to both the above theoretical suppositions. There is a conspicuous lack of originality about Mendelssohn's technique. One can of course point to small virtues—to the slight twist he gave to the book-recorded concerto-form in his Violin Concerto; to his crystallizing the 'Songs without Words' form in a way that has made him responsible for too much; particularly to his ability to reintroduce his first subject in first-movement form. Otherwise we can only find efficiency—a remarkable efficiency, displayed in the very earliest of his compositions, but not surprising in so clever a Jew. Here again, in his possession of ease, ability, efficiency, and certainty of touch—all, mind you, on a broad scale—but not originality, Mendelssohn is a characteristic child of the nineteenth century. Again, I recommend doubters to make a close examination of Liszt's truly creative technique, as a contemporary basis of comparison.

Mendelssohn was the centre of one of those whirlpools of popularity which at intervals broke the current of the nineteenth century. When machinery made the people greater in number they came into a quite new existence. But the fact that there was then a public with whom a figure could be popular, essential to the time as it is, does not stand alone. Nor was the sole cause of this particular popularity only what must have been the startling personal magnetism of this little man, nor yet even the surprising instinct of both himself and his father for discreet publicity. There was also the fact that popularity, becoming once more a physical possibility, produced a type of art which it could grasp. So in literature there are the growth of the novel and the entry into literature of the ordinary man as a subject as well as an object. But while admitting that there is a tendency in the art that deals with the problems of the ordinary as opposed to the exceptional to attain a greater universality, we must avoid confusing the universal idea with the kind of idea that most men might conceive.

It is in the production of this second class of idea that Mendelssohn is related to the economic revolution of the early century. His ideas are commonly popular ideas, but they are rarely universal ideas. That is to say, they are ideas that are familiar and near to the ordinary man, but they are not ideas which are fundamental to the human nature which is in the ordinary man. Mendelssohn's music had the faculty of sounding new but not unfamiliar; it must always have been flatteringly like a pleasant reminiscence. There are certain tricks of Liszt's which are to-day spoken of as hackneyed, and to-day are hack-neyed—not by any fault of his—but then were not. That is something different. The characteristic of Mendelssohn's music to which I refer is the inherent popularity of his methods and motifs, which have just sufficient novelty to interest and just too little to excite.

It is in this lack of surprise and excitement that Mendels-sohn is finally found to be an exposition of his age. With machinery came wealth, and with wealth came, but for certain things, luxury. What prevented it was, first, the strong materialism of the age, secondly its inherent hope-fulness ('O yet we trust that somehow good Will be the final goal of ill'), and thirdly that high moral tone which was the first lesson which parents gave their children—

except for a few black sheep. So we had comfort, which is to luxury as cocoa to whisky, and to poverty as cocoa to water. 'Comfort—a person who saves one trouble; cause of satisfaction; conscious well-being', says the *Concise Oxford Dictionary*, pregnant with suggestion. Comfort is that compromise which at once gives the body ease and the mind the assurance of no evil responsibilities. Comfort, like love, is blind; comfort is heaven brought to earth, but with truth left behind.

In music none has been more comfortable than Mendelssohn, save his lesser satellites. The easy financial circumstances of his life reacted in the strongest degree upon his mind, and became a visible characteristic from end to end and in every aspect of his music. There stands this pretty figure of a man who could sketch, play all games, dance, ride, and swim, improvise and play and memorize anything, all with consummate grace and skill. Just so, too, he could compose, and nearly always, as he remained content with his circumstances, so he remained content to express them in his music. Mendelssohn was nothing if he was not a gentleman.[1] A more polite musician has never been. The roughness of Bottom and the Bergamask dancers is portrayed indeed, but with the gentle air of drawing-room charades. Occasionally through the mists of pleasant gentility there could be seen a natural human being; of these times I can speak later in high praise. But frequently the central ideas are infected; the fundamental law of contrast becomes merely an *agitato*, causing a pleasant flutter until placidity is restored by the returning suavity of the familiar first subject (familiar, indeed, when born). So, too, in construction, there is along with a genuine architectural ability, an unwillingness to press things home, and often the moment comes when, though grace sanctions the recapitulation, common sense con-

---

[1] See Samuel Butler's comments, and the last of the letters collected in his essay 'The Aunt, the Nieces, and the Dog' in *The Humour of Homer*.

demns it; form is too often a technical and not a spiritual thing in Mendelssohn.

The desire for comfort can be traced farther. There is that endless outpouring of sweet melodies, a stream that never brings itself to cease, however poorly it trickles. Sometimes it is like the water that, falling over the concrete rocks at the exhibition, flows down the vent and so up the pipe to the head of the fall, to do its decorative task again. How we long for some harmonic idea, some pure rhythm, some simplicity of musical conception! Then, too, the rippling and beating accompaniments, the production of sustained tone with a percussion instrument. Morsel follows morsel in 6/8 time till the pulse dies on the ear from its very repetition. Apart from the endless procession of tonic, dominant, and subdominant, producing an effect like that of a marching column of soldiers which stretches out of sight, there is the absence in the composer of a simple rhythmic belief in the figures he has created. They are background, and the musical idea of them never seems to seize his brain nor the rhythmic element in them to beat his imagination into a passion. For all his faculty of utilizing to the full his material, Mendelssohn seems never to have thought musically of his ideas once he had decided on them as 'subjects'. Finally, there is the continual reliance placed upon the sixth and third—most easily appreciated of all intervals, and therefore most easily tired of. Compare with Chopin's tenth, or Schubert's low third, or Brahms's heavy triads, or Liszt's full chords, these recurring thirds, figures in sixths, and common chords broken into the same intervals, that endlessly contented Mendelssohn. One longs again for the bare fifth, the unaccompanied melody, the clear point of physical assonance given by an isolated chord.

There are obvious points of touch between Mendelssohn and another true Victorian, Tennyson, and a closer examination than can be hinted at here would lead not only to an interesting study, but also to the revelation of several good points which our modern reactions and our fathers' adulation have equally hidden. There is indication that Tennyson to-day is being treated by both parties as a poet rather than as a saint or a sinner, and the same is beginning to occur with Mendelssohn. The criticism of Mr. H. C. Colles, that Mendelssohn 'just missed appealing strongly to men of all times because in the greater number of his works he was content to have expressed himself in the most perfect way possible', has an obvious application to Tennyson. Further, we see a lack of intellect in both men that compares oddly with their artistic positions. Browning seems to have begun writing at an intellectual point far ahead of that at which Tennyson had said his say; and so with Berlioz and Mendelssohn. In this connexion comes again our point of popularity. Tennyson is clearly comparable to Mendelssohn in the matter of common and universal ideas. But we can enlarge this point. Both had unseeing eyes, not in observation, but in the deductions that follow it; for both combined with their gentlemanlike nobility and high-minded superiority natures that accept rather than inquire, that receive rather than discover. Neither was touched by that healthy spirit of scepticism which came upon men as tongues of fire as the century wore on. Both were inclined to believe what they were told, and not to use their faculties of sensation to discover the truth or knowledge of the letter. Other points of contact are their respective stocks of humour, and their avowed philosophy of the perfect mean.

We can even press the point down to moods. The poem, *Ask me no more; the moon may draw the sea*, closely corresponds, artistically, to the *Lied ohne Worte*:

and the *Notturno* is indeed near in feeling to:

> And oft in ramblings on the wold
> When April nights began to blow,
> And April's crescent glimmered cold,
> I saw the village lights below.

Compare the beautiful, useless verse in some of the *Idylls* with the perfect suavity of the *Reformation* Symphony. Again, how Tennysonian is *Melusine*, and how like Mendelssohn the all-too-admirable *St. Agnes' Eve*!

The careful examination for critical purposes of all Mendelssohn's output is too long a process to justify the slender material value it would yield. That is not to say that there are no musical discoveries to be made in his extensive production, but it is an assertion that neither Mendelssohn's musical characteristics, nor the places where he transcended his normal self and capabilities, are considerable in number or scope. A closer examination, therefore, of a few of his works will give a big enough basis for judgement to allow any one not engaged on an exhaustive survey to select and generalize. I propose to discuss here only the *Hebrides* Overture, the Prelude and Fugue in E minor, and the Violin Concerto, with a passing glance at the vocal works, and to derive from them enough musical practice to exemplify the theory displayed above.

It is an impressive fact that Mendelssohn's *Elijah* has survived over eighty-six years and still holds the field in England. Does it elsewhere? I have no evidence that it does. Without ignoring the smallest portion of its massive popularity, I think that, from the critical point of view, the success of *Elijah* is more illuminating of the state of musical taste in England then and now than it is of Mendelssohn's position in history as a composer. Some of this work is dramatic in a fine manner: some is lyrical and some solidly effective. The whole represents Mendelssohn at his worst and at his best indiscriminately. Its popularity has many elements that are not musical.

M

There are the other vocal works—*St. Paul*, *The Hymn of Praise*, the psalms, the motets, the stage works, the male voice works, and the unfinished *Christus*.

Mendelssohn's writing for the voice, in one or many numbers, was always fluid. He had the sense of flow, as well as of the congenial curve which gives the human voice what it wants to sing. But the dramatic opportunities given by the words or the situation or the emotions of the moment led him away from his musical to his social mood. When fronted with words his critical sense of music went away. The 113th Psalm has a poor fugue; the *Hymn of Praise*, as well as the *Sorrows of Death*, is full of clichés; even the *Elijah* contains *O rest in the Lord*.

The songs for solo voice have their place: they opened a door for others, and they contain one or two gems—'On wings of song' and 'By Celia's Arbour' notably.

On the whole, however, the vocal output of Mendelssohn shows him at what was his most pleasing and his weakest. I do not decry these works for what they are, but I consider that the three compositions discussed below bring one nearest to that musical mind which, however overcome by worldly attractions, still could inspire his lesser moments towards a popularity unachieved by many finer minds.

Of Mendelssohn's overtures, those that have breath left in them breathe it only in the concert-room and not in the theatre. They are then virtually symphonic poems or one-movement symphonies. It is significant that the four big and successful overtures were written when Mendelssohn had produced only one orchestral three-movement work that has survived at all, the Pianoforte Concerto in G minor —not one of his important works. His three symphonies and the Violin Concerto came later, and it would be possible to consider the overtures as examples of the successful handling of a smaller form in preparation for bigger symphonic work. In the region of symphonic music, however, Mendelssohn never surpassed the

Hebrides Overture, and it is clear that aesthetically he needed both a shorter space than the full symphony to fill with the development of his ideas, and also the stimulus of outside suggestion—either that of a subject, as in these overtures, or that of words and dramatic situations, as in *Elijah* and *St. Paul*.

The *Hebrides* Overture is the best exponent in all Mendelssohn's music of the influence of external objects upon his imagination. The term programme-music has come to be expanded with an unpleasant vagueness of meaning to music which is better called characteristic, and even to dramatic music—to all music, that is, which has a definite and stated connexion with any objects outside its own province. Such a use of the term programme-music might include in its embrace the three symphonies of Mendelssohn's maturity, and an enormous quantity of the music written since Mendelssohn's time, from Schumann's *Carnaval* down to Delius's *First Cuckoo*. But as Parry says, in Grove's *Dictionary*, in his article on the Symphony:

. . . though Mendelssohn often adopted the appearance of programme, and gained some advantages by it, he never—in order to express his external ideas with more poetical consistency—relaxed any of the familiar principles of structure which are regarded as orthodox. He was, in fact, a thorough-going classicist. He accepted formulas with perfect equanimity, and aimed at resting the value of his works upon the vivacity of his ideas and the great mastery he had obtained in technical expression and clearness and certainty of orchestration.

This sentence, written about the Symphonies, applies forcibly to the overtures—and particularly to the *Hebrides* Overture. In the *Hebrides*, Mendelssohn wrote music whose conception had been influenced by things seen, and though that influence had been strong, and had produced an occasional effect in the written music which approaches the imitative, yet the music is music, and nothing more, from the first to the last bar, and in no sense a fulfilment of a programme. This conception is only slightly different in degree and not at all in kind from the normal conception of Beethoven and other composers. The attitude of Wagner throws some light on both the question of programme-music and the musical value of the *Hebrides* Overture. 'I dislike', he said on one occasion, 'everything in music that requires a verbal explanation beyond the actual sound.' Another time he said: 'Mendelssohn is a landscape painter of the first order, and the *Hebrides* Overture is his masterpiece.' The passages in the work which may bring images or reminiscences to the minds of the hearers, such as that which Wagner picks out as descriptive of the sea winds over the seas, have musical beauty, and their communicative power, however full of association, is not based upon imitation or even association, but is purely musical. A good example is the tremolando passage that lies between the first and second subjects.

The *Hebrides* Overture as a whole, then, is fine music with a definite character lent it not by its title, but first by its conception and secondly by its scoring. Built upon a simple rhythmic phrase, it is a complete development of this idea, and it stands as a highly imaginative and full statement of that phrase's possibilities. The work shows more of Mendelssohn's good qualities and less of his bad than any other in his catalogue. But while it can be said that in the *Hebrides* Overture Mendelssohn had beautiful things to say and said them beautifully, with the result that the overture is of the first interest, it is equally true that in emotional range and content it does not rise to comparison with such works as those of Bach, Beethoven, or Mozart which we would not be without. The place of the *Hebrides* Overture in music is that to which Wagner has assigned it. It is a masterpiece of landscape painting, and so, only of its own kind, a masterpiece of music.

Of the technical points which arise in connexion with this work, the first is the fact that Mendelssohn, employing the traditional first-movement form, has managed with great constructive skill to make of the one movement a complete, whole, and sufficient work. We observe, further, that analysis of the work has to rely more upon the actual sound than upon accepted formal principles which too often guide the analyst. For, at the outset, the principal subject is a mosaic of phrases: yet, withal, one virtue of the overture is its economy of material—a virtue Mendelssohn frequently displayed. The first slight motive has something about it both descriptive and characteristic, a pregnant simplicity which at once catches the attention; it is a significant musical utterance. But the inspiration cannot last. The second subject when it appears is only a pleasant tune. It provides material for emotional ebb and flow, is even in some ways descriptive, but its content is summed up by that weak and typical cadential phrase for which common sense, one would have thought, would have asked for some alleviating colour in the scoring. It is interesting that the first phrase should throughout arouse Mendelssohn to a finer treatment than all the rest of the material. The conventional major close with the assertive triads on the brass is the only stumbling-block I find in the whole work; and even so, Mendelssohn puts this flamboyant and vulgar passage, so doubtfully introduced, to intelligent use in the development.

The phrase:

is one that seems to me to sum up in its inherent energy the force of the whole overture. The natural force of this—again a simple—motive is far greater than that usually displayed by Mendelssohn. Immediately after its introduction we have two curiously conflicting passages— the re-entry of the second subject, than which nothing conceivable could better display its natural unfitness, and then the tranquillo section, perfect introduction of familiar notes in unfamiliar guise, perfectly laid out, and continuing for exactly the perfect length. Another exquisite touch is the long scale which brings us to the *reprise*. The continuation of the flute-run here, and the immediate trill on the strings, are beautiful points of colour. Again, heralding the tonic statement of the second subject, there is that long oboe note—bold in a work so full of oboe colour—to which Wagner drew attention. Finally, there is the coda, a section with a greater importance and length than most codas, for it is used to put finality to the work in its single movement. It is, musically, a *tour de force*, largely consisting of very able passage-work reminiscent of the matter already heard, and constantly employing the semiquaver phrases on the strings that have done so much already to link the work together; but it would be hard to find a passage in classical music where matter apparently so unrelated was used to form an effective ending to a work. The long trumpet notes, the loud staccatos, and the flute-run, make a close of great beauty.

It is the oratorios and pianoforte works of Mendelssohn that form the basis of that fundamental love which the English still bear towards him.

The pianoforte works may without arbitrariness be divided into three very characteristic moods: the suave, the agitated, and the capricious. The third category is important, for Mendelssohn could always write a 'scherzo', whether for piano or for other combined instruments. His classical sense of form helped him to a prodigious achievement in, for example, the Scherzo of the *Midsummer Night's Dream* music—a far more lasting and original work than the more famous overture, whose merits are discounted by its obvious indebtedness to Weber. That is absolute music—and yet there is a blood relationship between it and the *Hebrides* Overture, for somehow there is an 'airy-fairiness' in this mood which is not of purely musical origin, however much the texture of the music is purely woven of sound. Principal among the piano works of this class stands of course the *Rondo Capriccioso*, as nearly perfect (in its quick section) for its medium as anything ever written. Other pieces of charm there are too, but is one crapulous to find in many of them a sense that their function was really to engage and amuse well-bred young ladies of a strict and decorous régime?

Mendelssohn, himself a concert pianist, wrote for the pianoforte with no less, perhaps even with greater, skill than for other instruments. But while suited to the instrument, in technique his pianoforte works were neither original nor particularly interesting. There is in his pianoforte music not only a limitation of mood but also a limitation of technical interest: there is no novelty of effect, nor many passages which require really expert playing. There are indeed few things in all his numerous pianoforte compositions fit to compare with even the early Octet, and particularly with the bigger orchestral works.

But in contrast with the mood of quick and pretty nothings appears the Prelude and Fugue in E minor. Mendelssohn seems to stand outside himself here. For it is a work in which, in addition to the fact that it has a meaning far deeper than his habitual mood, he is able to display his skill in counterpoint. This his worst enemies cannot deny him, although they may assert with justice that it was frequently vitiated and even dismissed by his desire for harmonic sufficiency: that, in other words, his desire for horizontal interest was too often tempered by his desire for the sleek vertical effects for which his works are notable. An early interest and education in Bach's music is not alone responsible for this contrapuntal efficiency; it was a seed that fell upon the good ground of his precocious technical facility.

The turbulent Prelude is conceived in one short sweep from start to finish. Closely allied in subject-matter to the Fugue, it seems to give the spirit of the latter in a full blast of breath, a shout, while its successor is a reasoned and controlled statement of the same idea, no less forceful though less forcible, and achieving a greater strength by its more careful and deliberate progress.

The Fugue itself is comparable to the first movement of
the later Violin Concerto in its abandonment of that conventional reserve which makes Mendelssohn's ordinary
utterance graceful rather than profound. The earlier work
is nearer the hysterical than the later, but it is also nearer
to the elemental, if indeed still rather far from it. Built
upon a subject of considerable inherent beauty, the Fugue
is cast in the form of a great increase of power, speed, and
personal feeling, until the climax has to be provided by
means utterly outside the realm of the fugue, a Chorale in
the major, which is again followed by a major statement
of the main fugal subject, slightly developed up to a too
characteristic ending.

As a fugue it does not strictly follow the rule. Nor is
there only one deviation, for first there are several points of
pianistic and not fugal effect; secondly, there is a place
near the middle where fugal methods give place finally to
those which—however strictly they conform to the idea
of double counterpoint—are simply not a part of fugue,
the crescendo getting the upper hand of the formal idea.
On purely academic grounds it is best to consider the
E minor Fugue as a work of fugal opening, employing later
a contrapuntal but also almost symphonic method to attain
its object. As a criticism this distinction may be considered
a refinement upon academicism, but it sets aside the
necessity of quarrelling with fine music for its conflict with
academic formulas.

This Fugue has been said to show the influence of Bach.
There is no doubt that Mendelssohn was indirectly influenced by Bach, be it ever so little. His Bach love was
fundamental, and it must not be forgotten that the B minor
Mass owes its resuscitation very largely to him; nor is that
the only work of Bach and Beethoven for whose popularity
to-day Mendelssohn was responsible in the first instance.
Nevertheless the precise influence of Bach on the work
is negligible if not non-existent, for the romantic spirit is
inseparable from the work, one of whose virtues is the

application of the purely musical idea of fugal repetition to achieving a more or less personal effect. The two elements are skilfully wrought together, but not as Bach would have wrought them. Fine as it is, this Fugue does not show the intellectual power—the control of matter by mind—that the master had. Its simplicity, its variety of treatment and unity of conception, its structure, its skilled use of counter-point and the pianoforte, its light and shade, its unswerving march towards the end in view, its suspense—all these isolated points, which are but a few out of a big whole, go to make it one of the half-dozen works that stand out from Mendelssohn's available outpourings as fit to compare with the greatest music, and indeed are only short of it by a little way. It is regrettable that Mendelssohn had need to use the device of the Chorale and major statement, but even so it must be admitted he used it with success. We may without laying a finger on the Fugue wish that Mendelssohn could have forgotten his sweeter moods long enough to have written a coda more in keeping with the rest of the music. As an end to his rugged thoughts the coda is almost an anti-climax, though just redeemed from that by the interposition of the Chorale. Opening with two major statements of the subject it becomes merely a harmonic trifle of the 'Songs without Words' type, and the last five bars are distinctly banal.

The juvenile concertos of Mendelssohn (two for two pianofortes and others for other instrumental combinations) have not survived, and of the three concertos of his maturity, that for violin, in E minor, is musically by far the most satisfying. It is more: it is an important contribu-tion to the literature of its form, and the first movement at least, which shows Mendelssohn's good qualities at their best, is a masterly production in the musical sense. The Violin Concerto is important because, although Mendels-sohn here displays no less of his usual clarity, neatness, and precision of musical expression, he shows too a forget-fulness of his ordinary politeness of speech, at least in the first movement, and this makes of it one of his least restrained and most significant conceptions. The first movement is Mendelssohn at his emotional highest. There is an emotional as well as a musical use of the form which is extraordinarily telling, even more than the character of the musical material itself; the form becomes a direct means of expression, and is not only used as a means of balance and clear statement. In addition, the solo part is proof that purely 'virtuoso' effectiveness is by no means only to be found where the musical value is low. Nothing could display the violin's capabilities better than this work, but the solo part has a high musical significance of its own, an inseparable part in the development of the musical material, and a wholly effective interrelation with the orchestra. Spohr's skill is used with more intensity than he possessed. As a whole the work is highly characteristic of Mendelssohn's musical mind. It is a work, as the date shows, of his maturity, and a comparison of the score with earlier works will reveal on a very short study exactly in what this maturity consisted.

The first movement's superiority over the other two has already been postulated. The only addition to make here is a comment on its pace: meaning thereby not only speed, which it indeed has, but also its logical persistence, its unfailing inevitability, its 'drive'. The second movement leads us to reflect on the difference between Mendelssohn and the Mendelssohnian. Having a sweetness that immediately attracts, it is a movement of which the appreciation does not last. But it should be criticized only in its effective juxtaposition and contrast with the swift first movement, and not, though it is frequently so played by amateurs, as a solo piece standing in its own ground. Regarded in the former light it has, of course, a greater value as music. The third movement, exemplifying the 'airy-fairy' side of Mendelssohn's mind, may be described as dependent for its climax on the repetition rather than the development of themes. It has not the clinching quality that is now (but was not so much then) demanded of a last movement, and at the end of it we have a feeling of doubt whether its material is presented in the right form, whether that material is not too light to fill out a whole developed ternary movement, with solo instrument and orchestra. The subjects are certainly handled with dexterity, but not with finality.

There are not many points of detail that call for comment. The first movement shows again economy of material —in the use, for instance, that is made of the unpromising material contained in the triplet figure of the soloist after the first subject has been stated. The second subject exactly exemplifies Wagner's remark when he said, 'His second tunes, his slow movements generally, where the human element comes in, are weaker'.[1] But even here, Mendelssohn was harmonist enough to exploit some of the richness of the discords made by pedal notes—and there is too a clever interlacing of the wood-wind parts. Orchestrally it is a fine moment. Immediately after there is a relaxation, and the soloist's counterpoint, though clear, shows a failure of imagination.

The curious weakness of the opening of the development section is again highly characteristic. To introduce here the first subject in the major is so obvious a backsliding, so mechanical a device, and so ineffective a treatment, that even a student would instinctively shy at it. Then the pendulum swings the other way, when the soloist has a diminished statement of the 'bridge-passage' theme. This simple, delicate, dropping phrase for the violin is extraordinarily effective. There is a repressed emotional intensity here, which breaks out in a crescendo orchestral passage with a drum-roll as we approach the cadenza. The cadenza itself, apart from its perfect position, has curiously little to commend it.

[1] The scherzo element comes to the top again here. Was the pattern mind the real Mendelssohn mind, and was he vitiated only by circumstances or partly by character as well?

The moments at the end of the repeated bridge-passage
are of high emotional interest, and well exemplify both
Mendelssohn's constructive ability and the strength of
his ideas when writing this work. The attention is held in
suspense until the music resolves into the calm second
subject, which is given by its position a significance far
beyond that of its mere notes. And this import is strengthened by the soloist's stating at the end the first phrase
of the theme, in a low register and in the minor against
held strings and staccato brass and drums, all pianissimo.
This is not merely a convenience, a modulating phrase:
it is an integral part of the recapitulation. The repetition of the Codetta (in E minor) now appears like a
sudden flame bursting out of ashes that seemed to be
dead, particularly since from its start to the end of the
movement there is an unbroken sweep of music in a great
stretto.

At the end we have the feeling that the musical material
has been given its definitive treatment, that upon it has been
built a structure that is a logical result of that material.
It is a lastingly fine movement, which makes us regret
deeply the falling away of the two that follow. Apart from
the flimsiness of their material and its undecisive use, how
can we regard from such a musician egregious errors of
style like the modulation from tonic to dominant that occurs
in the last movement? In a hymn-tune it would be poor,
but in an attempt to establish a key of the structural
importance which the dominant bears in this form, such
a procedure is an unpleasant commentary upon the musical
methods of its author. Then again the use of the first-
subject rhythm as a counter-phrase to the second subject
is, in practice, a turning back upon his purpose which
seems like sheer bad invention. This florid last movement is perhaps better to hear than to think about. It has
an air of extravagance and lightness that are taking in
performance, but it cannot be said to provide a fit ending
to a Concerto with so fine an opening.

To express the intention of examining the solid achievement of Mendelssohn is to draw the enfilade fire of both
flanking parties—the reacted upon and those who are
not even reacted upon. But such fire can always be turned
away: from the first side by appealing to its merely
critical sense, which has enabled it to transcend the
Mendelssohnian; from the other by two even more
pertinent questions—What is a master? and why, by what
right, is he accepted as a master with no fear of investiga-
tion? What, especially, do we admire in these three
works? First, their strong feeling for life as well as music:
they all have 'drive'. Secondly, their revelation of the man
Mendelssohn: in all he has abandoned the conventional
for the real, and if, perhaps, the real is not very important,
it is at least real. But, thirdly, we admire their sheer
music; the economy of material never palls because there
is development, wholeness, a use of actual and not conventional form, in an emotional and not an academic way. In
all three there is inspiration of musical energy that produces the sweeping movement of them. They have a bare
relation to life. The staid feelings of the drawing-room
have been thrust away for feelings that at once sum up and
transcend humanity. Further than that, there is a universal
idea in them, and not only a common idea; and it is because
this universal idea does not appear integrally through the
other parts that make up the music, does not always show
its pure nakedness through the veil of decency that is the
music's texture, that these three works are not superlative,
but only master works of a composer of the second rank.
The nearness of them to the first rank is their remarkable
feature, although to so many it still appears remarkable
that they are not hailed with the highest acclamation.

The responsibility of our age to Mendelssohn and his
music is to bare our minds of the Mendelssohn idea, the
Mendelssohn instinct, the idiom in which he wrote, the relation he bore to the music of his predecessors, and the
influence he wielded over his followers. It is a matter of

taking such a thing as 'the Mendelssohn ending' as a part of music, not as a part of a welcome or despised environment. Do we like, as music, that cadence, or not? Or do we merely like it as Mendelssohn? Only so can we discover Mendelssohn's relation to this age, which is the beginning of his relation to ages to come, and only so can we discover whether he was a real or only an accepted composer, a man of skill or a man of strong if tempered passions, a man who made pretty or a man who made individual music.

And it was not Mendelssohn's least virtue as a composer that he was not startling: if he showed individuality without being exaggerated, which he did in his best moments, then he is the greater composer for that.

9

FRÉDÉRIC FRANÇOIS CHOPIN
(1810–1849)
By H. P. MORGAN-BROWNE

NEW-lit fires of knowledge are for ever consuming ancient art, yet from its ashes, Phoenix-like, art arises in its own appointed hour, with a different, a more ample splendour!

Often art resists these encroaching fires, just for how long must depend upon how much the works of art are self-enclosed orbs, shutting out from our consciousness those relations which prevail amongst things in the world. For in some measure every work of art is a window-less world, complete in itself, and in such measure as it fulfils these conditions it is a convincing work of art.

There is a real difference between works of art in what we call their scale or size, and though it argues a more powerful mind and a more comprehensively developed art to work on a large scale than on a small one, nevertheless the larger the scale of a work the more dangerously it courts contact with the world outside; the more it seems to be about life the less it seems to be purely about itself. Consequently, the large-scale or great works of art are the first to be consumed by the advance of knowledge.

For the bigger composers gave the world to understand that the merit of their music resided in its power of expressing their general attitude to life, and since our attitude towards life is apt to change with every fresh advance of knowledge, the world is likely to pass on any newly acquired contempt for an abandoned attitude to the music which was supposed to represent it. Many critics to-day, for instance, finding that Wagner's views were 'bourgeois', condemn his music as 'bourgeois'. That such condemnation shows hasty and confused thinking in no way protects the music against its arraigners.

Chopin's art, however, is the nearly perfect 'window-less' world; and so, though (or perhaps because) it is restricted in scale, and perfect within itself, it escapes and probably will continue to escape the dangerous fires of new ideas. The new ideas or values which Chopin's compatriot Nietzsche discovered for himself soon caused him to revolt against the art of Wagner, but until, perhaps at some remote day, the advance of knowledge or ideas bids us to admire in music only that which is inelegant, that which has neither poetry of motion, novelty of harmony, or charm of melody—until that day the music of Chopin is safe from the taints of progressive views. Throughout his career of varied enthusiasms and subsequent disgusts, Debussy retained his admiration for the music of Chopin.

Perhaps the most outstanding quality of Chopin's music is its elegance. Elegance may be simple, or again it may be infinitely luxurious, as we find it in the music of Chopin. Profusion of elegance is perhaps characteristic of Polish taste: we meet with it in the prose of Nietzsche, and in a lesser degree in the violin music of Henri Wieniawski. This elegance Chopin seems to achieve by heaping up a multiplicity of fine touches rather than by swift, sudden strokes of analysis or inspiration, by sinuous contortions of melody which are easy for the ear to follow but difficult for the mind to devise. In no other music, perhaps, are the melodies so closely knit, and yet so long drawn out, as in the compositions of Chopin.

It would indeed be hazardous to sketch out the individualities of character and taste which differentiate the Poles from other peoples, but it seems true that they are peculiarly lambent-witted and prone to moods of violent elation and profound depression. A quick and incalculable pride made of their nobles subtle, fearsome creatures. Polish pride is a different thing from the amorphous megalomania of Nordic brain-storms, and is equally removed from the orderly, dutiful, but unremitting self-confidence of the English: nor has it aught of the logical, polite, 'please admire me' pride of the French. It is never found divorced from the picturesque, the lyrical, in life; it is intermittent, and plays round the humble mind as summer lightning against an inky horizon. The elegance of the Polish intellect is opulent, sinuous, and secretive, and exhibits none of the parsimonious craftsmanship of the French.

Some such ideas must have passed through the mind of Robert Schumann when in 1839 he was led to exclaim 'Chopin is the boldest and proudest poetic spirit of the times!' Indeed he was; but he was no untutored child of inspiration. He had undergone intensive orthodox training in composition and was moreover a piano virtuoso who moved Franz Liszt to special admiration. As to the judgement of posterity in grading men of genius, although rare instances do occur where one man's fame has been assessed above his merits and another's fame below his merits, posterity does not go markedly astray in its rough general estimates of men of genius. It will often happen, however, that though a correct degree of importance has been assigned to a great man, yet a very wrong impression prevails as to the special grounds on which the man's fame should rest. Thus Chopin has been overestimated (if you prefer it, underestimated) as a light and airy sit-at-the-piano, fairy-improviser young man, and underestimated as a hard-working craftsman-composer of very considerable, if narrow, musical scholarship, and a paragon of elegant accuracy. Chopin was no more an airy-fairy romantic of superficial scholarship than W. S. Gilbert was an illiterate slap-dash genius 'dragging his sentences by the hair and the heels down the worm-eaten staircase of terrified Syntax'. Chopin and Gilbert gambolled within narrow limits; the more narrowly they limited themselves the freer seemed their movements.

Similarly Schubert has been admired for writing music with the same freedom and unconcern with which a baby dribbles down its bib. Professor Donald Tovey in his essay on Schubert dispels the popular illusion that this amiable genius gave his pen the reins, trusting to luck. In place of a Schubert who was wont to seize the nearest scrap of brown paper on which absent-mindedly to dash off a couple of immortal songs, that best of scholars puts before us a Schubert who already at the age of thirteen had played the sedulous ape to learned composers.

When we consider a list of Chopin's compositions—e.g. 42 mazurkas, 27 études, 24 preludes, 18 nocturnes, 17 Polish songs, 8 waltzes, 7 polonaises, 4 scherzi, 3 impromptus (and 35 posthumous pieces), and 1 great fantasia— we realize more clearly the close lines within which his genius proved itself inexhaustible. Custom had imposed a certain type of rhythm and melody on such dances as the mazurka, the polonaise, bolero, tarantelle, &c., yet never did they weigh down his invention—his skill taught us to forget the limitations under which he so willingly laboured. Virtually he compelled himself to say again and again the same thing, and this he did without the least sign of exhausted fancy.

But in seeking to estimate his greatness as a composer we must not allow the seeming ease with which he triumphs over these difficulties to blind us to the greatness of the strain they imposed. Try to compose a dozen mazurkas and see what happens to your inventiveness. On the other hand we must not overestimate the difficulty of working within closely circumscribed limits. In literary composition, for instance, where a subject, say 'Courage', is proposed for an examination essay, we are often confounded by the extent of the ground we have to cover, and nothing enters our minds save a few trite and barren generalities; whereas a point blank question, such as 'Does the fireman need more courage than the soldier?', may enable us at once to get a grip on the matter in hand—our gaze has, as it were, become more sharply focused and the various points of view over this narrower field of vision stand out in much finer definition. It seems probable that this limitation was natural to Chopin, or at least, if not entirely a device for doing better work, it doubtless banished from his mind the paralysing feeling that 'one idea' as the Irishman expressed it 'is as good as another, and a jolly sight better'.

Chopin was a man whose sensory-nerve system was of the highest degree of delicacy and precision: he longed for brilliant and luxurious musical utterance, and after tense exertions he achieved a large measure of satisfaction for his desires, and for ours too. Though Chopin was a virtuoso he had not the virtuoso's failing, the tendency to rush to express his inspirations. He had early acquired the habit of working at composition instead of the habit of immediate expression, and sometimes he would spend six months polishing a single page. The virtuoso's urge is to express at once what comes to his mind and to do that in the most striking manner possible. He does not long retain and elaborate within his brain his germs of ideas; his 'vintage' is of the same year as his 'crushing', and must indeed be good if it is for one moment to compare with ancient wines. Dr. Emanuel Lasker, philosopher, mathematician, and for twenty-six years chess champion of the world, interestingly remarks in his extraordinary book *Struggle* that probably throughout his career he has found that the first moves which suggest themselves to a masterplayer are little if at all superior to those which might occur to any beginner, and that it is only through a long series of rejections that he comes at last upon the move which his experience and intelligence can accept—clearly a case of first thoughts being the worst. So it is perhaps with all intellectual operations: the mind must be allowed time and opportunity to churn the crude elements of its first promptings. This, however, Liszt rarely allowed himself, and nothing more clearly shows the prodigious natural ability of the man than the excellence of his immature inventions. Though Liszt had perhaps a larger share of wide-ranging inspiration than any other musician, he was, it seemed, incapable of maturing his first conceptions. Chopin and Wagner, each in his own very different way, inhibited or retained his first thoughts for further cerebration.

Elegant as Lionel Palairet, Chopin, after a few trial balls, opened his brilliant innings with a polonaise.

The polonaise, according to Sowinski (*Les Musiciens polonais*) derives from the ancient Christmas carols still sung in Poland, but the general opinion now seems to be that the polonaise is of courtly origin, and that it came to Poland when Henry III of Anjou was elected to the Polish throne in 1578. On that occasion at Cracow, the wives of the nobles marched in procession past the throne to the sound of stately music. This 'stately music' was probably a survival of the pavanes of the French Court of the fifteenth century, and there is evidence that this dance had not always so marked a national character as it assumed in later times. However that may be, it is generally supposed that whenever a foreign prince was thereafter elected this ceremony was repeated, and that out of the music which accompanied these processions the polonaise was gradually developed. The rhythm of the polonaise is characteristically spondaic.

J. S. Bach wrote two polonaises, Handel incorporates one in the Concerto Grosso No. 3 in E minor, Mozart has a rondeau polonaise in his Sonata in D minor, Schubert wrote polonaises for four hands, Weber (Op. 21), a Polacca brillante (Op. 72); Wagner composed one for four hands (Op. 2), Beethoven (Op. 89) also wrote one, and the two Polish composers Kupinski and Ogniski wrote several. It was, however, Chopin who made the polonaise peculiarly Polish and at the same time singularly his own. With the sole exception of the *Fantaisie Polonaise* (A major, Op. 61), his polonaises either have a strong and martial rhythm or they are dreamy and melancholy—compare Op. 40, No. 1 in A major and Op. 44 in F♯ minor with the E♭ minor Polonaise (Op. 26) and that in C minor (Op. 40, No. 2).

The origin of the mazurka is far less doubtful, and few would deny its Polish origin. The name is said to derive from the ancient Palatinate of Masovia. This dance admitted of very varied and somewhat peculiar steps and was in the nature of an improvisation, usually in $\frac{3}{4}$ or $\frac{3}{8}$ time. Chopin polished the music of this dance out of recognition and removed from it all elements of heaviness and vulgarity. It was as though some contemporary engineer, having examined Stephenson's Puffing Billy, had straightway designed a locomotive the equal in speed and grace of those which now draw our royal trains.

Though Chopin invented neither the polonaise nor the mazurka he did carry them to a point of naturalness and perfection which effectually discouraged further efforts along those lines.

Nor did Chopin invent the nocturne; for if any one may be said to have done this it was our own musician Field, who really seems to have been the first to discover that wide-spread chords accompanying slow liquid melodies are singularly effective in expressing the limpid silence of summer nights. Throughout, the music of Field bears prophetic resemblance to Chopin's music, yet the older man felt little sympathy for Chopin or his music; 'un talent de chambre de malade' was his inadequate verdict. But composers, with the very brilliant exceptions of Liszt and Schumann, are poor and prejudiced critics, even to the extent of being prejudiced against their own style of music when they meet with it in others. It can be taken for granted that Chopin was familiar with Field's nocturnes and it is likely that Liszt, who wrote an appreciation of them, had at some time played them to Chopin and even discussed them with him, as also his polonaises and mazurkas, and there can be little doubt that Field's music helped to confirm Chopin in his own musical tastes. That must be the mildest assertion of Chopin's indebtedness to the 'pale, melancholy, awkward, lanky, Irish boy'. When one considers the difference in their upbringing and general circumstances it is impossible not to feel that the resemblance in their music must have sprung from deep-seated similarity of talents and temperament. Chopin all his life, and we have George Sand's testimony for it, loved no one save the members of his own family. Field, on the other hand, relates how, owing to the harshness of his father and grandfather, he was tempted to run away from home. Chopin, as a boy, was a welcome visitor in the halls of Polish nobles; Field was apprenticed to Clementi, and drudged as a piano-salesman for the firm of Clementi & Co. In Poland at that time the artist was doubtless often glad he was 'not as other men are'; in England he was sorry.

Field and Chopin were not only piano-virtuosi but also players of a markedly similar character, as all descriptions of their style go to prove.

Chopin was a Pole; he resembled more his mother than his father. His mother was a calm, fair-haired girl, sweet, very pretty, full of charm with dark blue eyes, straight nose, and prominent chin, thrifty, practical, and modest. She loved poetry and had some skill in its composition. She was a clever linguist and had an inborn love of music. Her voice was beautiful in speech and song, and she played the clavichord charmingly.

Concerning the nationality of the father there has been much futile debate; he may or may not have been a Frenchman, he certainly loved Poland and seemed Polish in all his sympathies. When first we hear of him he was book-keeper to a firm of snuff-factors; subsequently he was professor of the French language in the newly-founded Lyceum at Warsaw. He appears to have been a man of good general education, and versatile or adaptable. Both father and mother were good and thoughtful parents, although indeed the young Chopin was allowed to overwork through being encouraged to keep abreast of his class in his general studies whilst not neglecting his music. He was born at Zelazowa-Wola ('Iron Will') on February 22nd, 1810, six Polish (that is to say thirty English) miles outside Warsaw, in a low-ceiled room of the long left annexe of the house of the Countess Sharbeck, to whose three children, the father, Nicholas Chopin, was household tutor. The rooms occupied by the Chopin family had the beamed ceilings and white-washed walls customary in Polish country-houses in those days. The second or drawing-room had two long windows looking out across the river Utrata which flowed almost under the windows of the house; beyond, wide expanses of cornland spread around the house to the far horizon intoxicating the eye with a sense of light and unbounded freedom. Fruit trees too abounded in the neighbourhood and the manor gardens in the summer were resplendent with flowers. In these surroundings young Chopin lived till his seventeenth year.

His father was loved and respected by the people and nobles alike; his mother, a cousin of Countess Sharbeck, was charming and talented; his three sisters, Louise, Isabella, and Emilia, were lively, pretty, and intelligent. Perfect understanding and affection held sway in that household. The parents were very happy when little 'Fryderyk' was born. But soon his mother was bitterly grieved to find that the boy was quite unmusical. He wept inconsolably whenever she sang to him—Louise, his elder sister, had gurgled with joy whenever her mother crooned over her. 'Never mind', said the father, 'we will none the less make a good man of him.' The father played quite well on the violin and the flute—the mother sang exquisitely; they certainly were entitled to expect a musical son! They did not, however, have long to wait to discover that they had been overestimating their own talents and underestimating their son's.

At the age of two he began to take a deep interest in his mother's high-backed clavichord and to fumble with the notes, and between the ages of four and five he was making up his own little tunes. At eight years of age he played in public a piano concerto by Gyrowetz. Of that concert the boy joyously told his mother 'Everybody was looking at my new collar'. Chopin's first musical education was received from Adalbert Ziwny, a Czech musician, a violinist who is said to have been a passionate admirer of J. S. Bach, but as soon as he was twelve years old Ziwny declared it was time to send his young pupil on to Josef Elsner, the learned musical director of the Conservatoire at Warsaw. In 1827 Chopin discontinued his general studies at the Lyceum and devoted himself to music. When, in 1829, he left his native town to make his début in Vienna as a piano-virtuoso he was in all respects a perfectly formed and, as it happened, a finally developed artist.

It would indeed be ridiculous to try to divide Chopin's compositions into periods as has been found advisable in the particular case of Beethoven, and subsequently in a lesser degree with many others. Chopin's art shows no perceptible gradual progress nor even any change at all. Already in his set of variations on *La ci darem mano* (Op. 2) which so excited Schumann's admiration, the style and individuality of Chopin's music are clearly made manifest. Not until we come to his final compositions does his manner in the least alter. In his last pieces he would, however, at times appear to have taken a leap forward into our present age: he subtilized his progressions out of all keeping with the taste of his day. He was, it is true, at all times a daring harmonist, but the results of the discordant elements in his work—the harsh modulations—went by unnoticed, so Moscheles tells us, when Chopin played his own music owing to the lightness of his touch when passing over the offending passages. This unremittingly rhythmic, flowing phrasing and his singing tone reduced the sharpness to a pleasant stringency which served to keep the richness and uniformity of his melodies from cloying through excess of sweetness. 'When I play these modulations myself I dislike them', said Moscheles, 'but when Chopin plays them he makes magic with them.'

In 1831 Chopin left Vienna with the idea of visiting London. He passed through Paris, where he found himself in such a congenial atmosphere that he remained there for the rest of his life. In Paris it was only natural that he should become the favourite musical hero of society, as he had been in Poland.

It was here and through Liszt that he met Mme Dudevant (George Sand), and at first it was antipathy not liking that they felt for one another. But the stumpy ogress whose normal diet was men of genius was soon to have her appetite whetted by the tantalizing aroma of Chopin's fame. His evasive personality, polite amiable reserve, and distinguished appearance also played their part in challenging her possessive instinct. How soon this determined spoiler of genius grew tired of her new toy no one can ever know—probably very soon, but she hid her ever-growing boredom for a long while.

Chopin, for his part, declared that the destruction of his relations with Mme Dudevant in 1847 broke up his life. As for George Sand a genius was for her two things; first, good copy for her novels; secondly, a man, and she was soon done with her geniuses in both capacities. The general view, however, is more charitable, and likes to pretend that her motherly care fostered his musical genius. It is here suggested that her coarse camaraderie often threw the evasive Chopin back on his music and his piano for consolation, and admitted that in this unpremeditated and indirect way George Sand may have aided his genius. The last ten years of Chopin's life were nothing but a continual struggle against the illness which at last carried him off. The year before his death he visited England, where he was received with every mark of admiration and esteem. On October 17th, 1849, he died in the arms of his sister, who had hastened from Warsaw to be at his side. He was buried in the cemetery of Père Lachaise. Chopin always spoke French with a Polish accent and is said to have thought the

French language hard and unmusical by comparison with his own.

A recent and rather surprising find of death masks of Chopin reveal his head and features to be what physiognomists and phrenologists would probably agree were those of a craftsman-dreamer. The fine fashioning of the features bespeaks ancient, sensitive material, possibly a Jewish strain from the father. The portraits by Ary Scheffer, Kolberg, and his friend Delacroix show him delicate, translucent almost, ivory tinted with touches here and there of mother-of-pearl reflections, of medium height, elegant springing carriage, long hair in ringlets pale or ash-coloured with no touch of gold—deep clear eyes, limpid and lustrous of fine spirituality, a long slightly Roman nose, fine and thin at the nostrils, the whole appearance distinguished in unusual measure and almost ferociously aristocratic. Indeed Liszt said of him 'Quand il était dans la société des princes, il semblait être le plus prince'. Liszt, however, was disgusted that Chopin and his artist friend Delacroix could speak of nothing together but their tailor and their bootmaker. With others Chopin was often animated and entertaining and so good a mimic that the well-known English actor Parry, as well as several French actors of repute and other discriminating judges, had repeatedly assured him that as an actor he had a career before him. In giving music lessons, which unlike most musicians of genius he liked doing, he was kind, patient, and tactful, constantly, however, urging his pupils to put their whole soul into their playing. Often he would play to them himself.

He tolerated mistakes, but mechanical playing brought him to despair. Animation, lyrical liveliness, indeed, were the very essence of his genius in rhythm and melody. His appearance, his character, his playing, his compositions were all in harmonious keeping with one another as perhaps they never before had been in any man.

Though his tone was not powerful, as large concert-

rooms proved, yet in favourable circumstances it created
an illusion of great power in the forte passages by contrast
with his perfect pianissimo touch; and the brilliant, ardent
quality of his notes in rapid passages led some one to speak
of them as 'molten pearls dropping on red velvet'. He
produced a soft flowing upper-voice to the accompaniment of deep fundamental bass tones, and his use of the
pedals gave to the piano the sobbing tones of an aeolian
harp, whilst his rhythm had an incomparable rocking
quality which strangely quickened the spirit of his
listeners.

Berlioz, Moscheles, and Mendelssohn declared Chopin
the most original and interesting pianist of the day.
Elegant melodies came almost unbidden to his fingers, but
he would work sometimes for several months over the
harmonies of a single page before he would even consider
sending them to the printer. Yet when the proofs came
he could scarcely bring himself to look at them, and
perhaps no composer ever left so many printers' errors in
his proofs. Hence partly the great interest attaching to
M. Edouard Ganche's authoritative recent work in which
he undertook to restore, so far as is humanly possible,
Chopin's music as he gave it or presumably intended to
give it.

Chopin had a fortunate childhood and a youth singularly
well-calculated to keep him from dissipating his genius
along lines alien to his highly specialized temperament.
He had too a singular gift for evasion, polite evasion at that,
so that people who, like George Sand, were in a position to
force upon him their uncongenial natures, left very little
mark on his character. He thus remained, in the over-
worked phrase, true to himself, kept his artistic integrity
and his apparently exhaustless faculty for achieving variety
within uniformity. Consider his fifty mazurkas all so
different, and as Mr. Eric Blom has wisely said, 'from all
we know of him, had he lived, he could have written five
hundred without repeating himself'. At an early age

Chopin put his hand to the piano and never thereafter looked back—or forward. The orchestra may or may not have tempted him but it was never able to lure him from the piano. The orchestration of his piano concerto is thin, and indeed seemed specially designed in no way to obscure the solo parts. As Chopin used the piano constantly while composing he had the advantage, one would think, of knowing exactly what his works would sound like when played as he wished them played. It scarcely seems possible that orchestral composers can know exactly how their music will sound. This, however, is a matter in which perhaps but few musicians will concur. Mily Alexeivitch Balakiref orchestrated some of Chopin's pieces; they are, however, very little known in this new guise.

For other men's music and other men's playing Chopin does not seem to have felt much enthusiasm. Like Liszt he was astounded and delighted by Paganini and he composed a piece, *Souvenir de Paganini* (A major), in the violinist's honour, which Paderewski told Huneker he had seen, adding that it had only historic interest. Handel's *Ode to St. Cecilia's Day* is said to have deeply impressed him. Schubert he found 'rough', Schumann he does not trouble to mention, and for Berlioz he reserved his only rude and violent criticism—'his music was such that it justified any one who wished to break with him'. Compelled of course to recognize the genius of Liszt he yet found him extravagant, excessive!

Chopin has been described as having looked over the shoulders of the German musicians towards the Italians. But the mightiest of the Germans, J. S. Bach himself, took a few sly peeps in the same direction.

Chopin loved dancing and himself tells how he strained his ankle in a frantic rush to join in a mazurka; one does not readily imagine Bach, Beethoven, or Schubert pressing eagerly forward to join in dancing the mazurka. Chopin compressed the widespread waters of musical feeling into the narrow channel of certain Polish dance rhythms, and

in consequence of that compression those waters flowed
with ebullient animation and irresistible force. His music
has some of the firmness and all the glitter of highly
polished gems in the martial polonaises, and in his sadder
music his melancholy is lustrous.

In musical 'ornamentation' he is more lively and to the
point than any of his predecessors. To choose but one
instance, how apt is his use of the quick stamping triplet
in the mazurka! He not only invented new ideas in
music but it would often seem that he has also given them
their final form, and to invent so that your invention may
not be improved upon by successors is rarely the lot of
innovators in any branch of human activity. One may,
perhaps, recall the case of Aristotle, from whose brain the
science of Deductive Logic is said, by Archbishop Whate-
ley, to have leapt full-fledged.

One may not pretend that Chopin's moral nature was
exalted, or that his intellectual faculties, though penetrating, were either profound or wide-ranging. Ingenious
he was and witty, and his moral nature was at least good.
He had very considerable powers of concentration which
helped him in imparting finality and closeness of texture
to all his work. He was a poet but not an absent-minded
poet—a dreamer, at times, but a strangely definite dreamer.
His works up to Op. 74 may be compressed into a few
thin volumes, yet they represent an enormous amount of
labour—their musical value is rare and peculiar. His
works may be arranged as follows in the order of their
artistic importance: the études and preludes; the mazurkas
and polonaises; the ballades and scherzi; the nocturnes
and valses. In a sense Chopin was the purest of pure
musicians, for he is very little concerned with illustrating
intellectual ideas or moral grandeur; he is concerned with
no theory but the theory of music. He is indeed deeply
touched by the beauty of nature, and the beauty of women;
but only by way of a start—all is soon forgotten when he
begins composing, all but the need for gratifying the ear in

accordance with the laws of consonance and the demands of rhythm.

In the days of Schumann and Liszt Chopin was valued as a magical musician of deeply poetic nature; later on many people came to regard him rather contemptuously as a composer of 'salon music' in contradistinction, mark you, to 'chamber music'. To-day theorists probably esteem him chiefly for his consummate musical craftsmanship. Very significant too is the fact that Debussy never tired of proclaiming the influence of Chopin on modern composition.

Although Chopin himself was fond of saying 'My manner of playing greatly pleases the ladies' we must not use this jocular remark in evidence against him. If we are to make any just estimate of this man we must remember only that he was a very refined poet by temperament, a supremely gifted musician of limited sympathies, and perhaps above all, an incomparable musical stylist.

10

FRANZ LISZT
(1811–1886)
By CECIL GRAY

THE prestige of a universally accepted dogma is often so great that it is exceedingly difficult, even for the most alert and discriminating critic, to throw off its hypnotic influence and arrive at an independent point of view. It is, indeed, somewhat depressing, though none the less highly salutary, to consider what a large proportion of one's habitual standards of judgement consists merely of prejudices and preconceived notions, so hallowed by tradition and sanctified by incessant repetition as to have attained to the status and dignity of incontrovertible truths. In many cases we maintain and give utterance to them unthinkingly, merely because it has never even occurred to us to question them.

Suppose, for example, that one were to ask any average intelligent music-lover for his opinion concerning the music of Palestrina. One can be perfectly certain that he would straightway begin to discourse eloquently and reverently upon its wonderful simplicity and perfection of style, its depth of devotional sentiment, and so forth; but if one were then to ask him what works of Palestrina he knew or had even only casually heard, it is exceedingly improbable, to say the least, that he would be able to mention the name of any one, except perhaps that of the *Missa Papae Marcelli*, and still more improbable that he would even recognize this if he were to hear it, or that he would be able to distinguish it from the work of any of Palestrina's innumerable predecessors, contemporaries, or successors who wrote *a cappella* Church music. Even the few critics and scholars—and how few they are!—who are sufficiently acquainted with his music to be entitled to an opinion concerning it are inevitably influenced to an incalculable extent in their judgement by the formidable prestige conferred upon it by centuries of unremitting and enthusiastic praise.

A similar example of precisely the opposite order is afforded by the music of Liszt, the mere mention of whose name is enough to evoke in response a string of epithets such as fustian, tinsel, pinchbeck, rhodomontade, tawdry, shoddy, garish, bedizened, and so on; but you will generally find that those people who are most lavish in their employment of this vocabulary know just as little of Liszt's music as the conventional admirers of Palestrina do of his. Even those who do know his work sufficiently well to be in a position to judge it for themselves almost invariably approach it with an adverse prejudice against it which is none the less, perhaps all the more, strong because it is to a great extent quite unconscious, the outcome of several decades of steady vituperation of Liszt on the part of musicians of every conceivable creed and tendency. The inevitable result is that they find in it precisely what they expect to find, what they have been taught to find, what they subconsciously wish to find.

Incidentally, this prejudice against Liszt is particularly strongly in evidence in this country. Professor Dent, for example, has said somewhere, quite rightly, that English musicians in general have an aversion from the music of Liszt amounting almost to horror, and adduces in support of his depreciatory estimate of Elgar the fact that he, almost alone among his compatriots, shows traces of his pernicious influence; and certainly nothing is calculated to damage a composer more completely and irretrievably in the eyes of the English musical public than a suspicion that he is infected by the Lisztian contagion. We shall have occasion later to inquire more closely into the reasons for this peculiarly national hostility to Liszt, the violence and intensity of which is always a source of bewilderment to foreign musicians, even to those who do not themselves care greatly for his art and share the general prejudice against it.

Now, it need hardly be said that such hard-and-fast, cut-and-dried, ready-made, preconceived notions as these we have been examining have always a certain basis of justification. It is no doubt perfectly true that, on the whole, the music of Palestrina deserves the encomiums which are lavished upon it by people who have in all probability never heard a note of it, and would care nothing for it if they did; similarly it is undeniable that some at least of the music of Liszt, and certainly most of it that is best known and most frequently performed, thoroughly merits the denigratory epithets set forth above. Liszt's admirers, however, set little store by the greater part of the works by which he is commonly known; in fact they might even agree with the conventional view of him in so far as it is based upon such works as the Pianoforte Concerto No. 1 in E flat, the symphonic poem *Les Préludes*, the étude *La Campanella*, the *Hungarian Rhapsodies*, and *Liebesträume*, which are about all of Liszt that is familiar to the average concert-goer, and all of which are amongst his least successful productions. It is, or should be, a truism to say that a composer should be judged by his best work, but Liszt, up to the present time, has been condemned on account of his worst. It is true that the musical public frequently displays a disconcerting propensity for taking to its heart the least significant productions of a great master; in our time, for example, Elgar first achieved recognition through *Salut d'amour* and *Pomp and Circumstance*, and Sibelius similarly through *Valse triste* and *Finlandia*.

In the course of time, however, their more important works have come to be appreciated at their proper value, but although Liszt has now been dead for nearly fifty years this consummation has not yet taken place with regard to his music; in concert programmes he is still represented by works of the same order as those of

o

Elgar and Sibelius mentioned above. *Les Préludes* is of all his large orchestral works the weakest, *La Campanella* is the least admirable of his studies in pianistic virtuosity, the *Hungarian Rhapsodies*, if hardly deserving the abuse to which they are habitually subjected, are quite unimportant, and the E flat Concerto is admittedly a somewhat vulgar and flashy composition which, moreover, is played far too often. Indeed, the only great and important work of Liszt which is comparatively well known to the ordinary concert-going public is the piano sonata, and the fact that this truly superb work should still elicit from many critical pens, whenever it is performed, the same stale old *clichés* that I quoted at the outset of this essay, provides the best illustration possible of my contention to the effect that the writers of such nonsense are listening to the music—if, indeed, they are listening to it at all, which is perhaps an unduly charitable assumption—with a subconscious prejudice against the composer. To call such music as this 'tinsel' or 'pinchbeck'—the two favourite words in the anti-Lisztian vocabulary—is a critical aberration of the first magnitude. The piano sonata is pure gold throughout, probably the most outstanding achievement in piano music of the entire nineteenth century.

In this connexion one is inevitably reminded of the famous experiments with dogs recently conducted by Professor Pavlov (whom God preserve!) of Moscow. The eminent Russian scientist, it will be remembered, after having for some time fed his dogs to the accompaniment of bells, made the momentous discovery that after a time copious salivation could be induced in the unfortunate animals by the ringing of a bell alone. This is what is termed a 'conditioned reflex'—a phenomenon to be encountered as frequently in the domain of musical criticism as in that of canine alimentation. The music of Liszt is a case in point: the inferior works which are all that we ordinarily hear of him have so accustomed us to expect the worst from him that his name alone, irrespective of any

particular work in question, has come to symbolize all that
is basest in musical art.

Whenever, then—and it is very often—one finds any one
giving vent to the customary *clichés* concerning the music
of Liszt, one can be fairly sure that he is either totally
ignorant of Liszt's work as a whole, or else so hidebound
with prejudice that his reaction is not to the music itself
but only to an associated idea, as with our Pavlovian dogs.
As I have already said, they may be applicable to a certain
restricted number of his works, which happen unfortunately to be his best-known ones, but that is all. So far,
indeed, are they from being true of his work as a whole
that the exact opposite is very much nearer the truth,
namely, that a chronological survey of his entire output
reveals a steady and consistent diminution in brilliant
externality, ending in a bareness and austerity of utterance
almost without parallel in music. Moreover, even in many
of those works which may seem to merit the opprobrious
epithets habitually cast at them, the faults lie entirely on
the surface and do not affect the sound core of the music.

In this respect there is a very close relation between the
artist and the man. In the earlier part of his career in
particular, with all his splendour, brilliance, and generosity, one feels a certain element of ostentation and display in his character which are not entirely sympathetic,
suggesting the artistic equivalent of a *nouveau riche*—he
is altogether too conscious of his genius. Underneath this
slightly vulgar exterior, however, there lay always the
fineness and nobility of character which, in his maturity
and old age, have perforce been recognized even by those
who were, and are, most hostile to his art. In this connexion there is an interesting and instructive anecdote
told by his friend Legouvé, to the effect that on one occasion when Liszt was posing for his portrait to the French
painter Ary Scheffer, the latter said to him rudely, 'Don't
put on the airs of a man of genius with me; you know well
enough that I am not impressed by it'. 'You are perfectly

right, my dear friend,' replied Liszt quietly, 'but you must try to forgive me; you cannot realize how it spoils one to have been an infant prodigy.' The reply shows all the greatness and fineness of sensibility which underlay the superficial pose involuntarily, unconsciously assumed, out of sheer force of habit and upbringing. Precisely the same phenomenon is to be observed in his art; the element of vulgarity and display in it which has always aroused such violent critical censure is just as superficial and skin-deep as it is with the man, and if his critics had reproached him with it to his face he would no doubt have replied to them as he replied to Ary Scheffer, saying that it was the inevitable outcome of having begun his artistic career as a pianoforte virtuoso.

For this reason the music of Liszt constitutes one of the most searching tests of critical acumen that the art presents. The hasty and superficial critic fails to penetrate through the frequently meretricious outer shell to the solid worth beneath, and only the most experienced and discerning assayer is able to determine correctly the proportion of pure metal to base in the complex alloys which many of his works are. Some of them, again, are admittedly mere pinchbeck, as I have already said; others again, however, are pure gold throughout.

The chief reason, in fact, why critical opinion generally goes so completely astray over Liszt, particularly in this country, is to be found in a definite *parti pris* against brilliance and virtuosity as such. In the same way that we are reluctant to believe that a painted, powdered, and bedizened damsel can be as 'good' as her plain, homely, and unadorned sister, so we find it difficult to admit that the brilliant and magnificent piano sonata of Liszt, for example, could be as good as a drab and dingy one of Schumann or Brahms. It is at bottom a Puritanical prejudice; at least one certainly finds it most highly developed in those countries where Protestantism is strongest and most firmly established, in Northern and Teutonic countries chiefly. The Southern, Latin attitude is very different; the Roman Catholic Church, of which Liszt was a loyal son, teaches that magnificence and splendour are positive and desirable qualities. See, for example, the *Summa Theologica* of Saint Thomas Aquinas, Part II, qq. cxxxiv, 'Of Magnificence'.

Even if one were to admit, however, for the sake of argument, that the brilliance and glitter of much of Liszt's music are intrinsically condemnable, the stricture only applies to a part of his work. For in the same way that Liszt began his career as a triumphant and opulent virtuoso and then gradually and progressively withdrew himself from the world until he finally took holy orders and died in poverty, so his work, viewed as a whole, exhibits precisely the same steady, unbroken process of recession from all that is superficial, decorative, external, until in the writings of his last years he arrives, as I have already said, at a bareness and austerity of utterance which have no parallel in music. Needless to say, these later works are entirely unknown to those who prate so glibly of Liszt's flashiness and so forth. Not that I would necessarily suggest that they are his most important compositions, any more than that his assumption of holy orders was the consummation of his earthly life. On the contrary, it is probable that the devout churchman in Liszt damaged and grew at the expense of the artist, and that the asceticism of the later works denotes a similar weakening and impoverishment of the genius exhibited in some of his earlier works. The fact remains that to ignore this process of development and its ultimate phase is to misunderstand Liszt entirely; to speak of him as an artist exclusively preoccupied with effects of superficial brilliance and showiness is as if one were to represent St. Augustine as the Don Juan of antiquity and St. Francis as the Casanova of the Middle Ages, simply because they lived loose and worldly lives in their youth. Again, it may well be true that the Tolstoy of *Anna Karenina* and *War and Peace* is a greater artist than the pietistic Tolstoy of the naïve and simple peasant tales with which he occupied his closing years, but to ignore the process of spiritual development which led to this is to miss the whole meaning and significance of his career. Similarly, to concentrate almost exclusively on the early Liszt, or even the Liszt of complete maturity, and to ignore the latest works: to dwell at length on his dazzling triumphs as a virtuoso in his youth and to forget the twilight of his closing years and his tragic end, neglected and penniless, at Bayreuth of all places—this is to misunderstand him altogether. That the composer who, of all composers that have ever lived, has gone farthest in the direction of austerity and asceticism, and finally pushed the modern doctrine of the elimination of non-essentials to such an extreme pitch that he often ended by eliminating essentials as well—that he should invariably be held up to derision and contempt by musical historians and critics and represented as the supreme charlatan and trick showman of music—this is surely the most consummate stroke of ironic perversity in the history of music; for in such works as the symphonic poem *Von der Wiege bis zum Grabe*, the third and last volume of the *Années de Pèlerinage*, the later piano pieces such as *Nuages Gris*, *Prélude funèbre*, *Sinistre*, *La lugubre Gondole*, and others, the last songs such as *J'ai perdu ma force*, *Sei still*, *Gebet*, *Einst*, *Verlassen*, *Wir dachten*—in all these works with which he concluded his creative career one finds a quite disconcerting bareness of idiom and a complete sacrifice of every means of effect to the purposes of expression. The conceptions, moreover, to which expression is given in these later works are almost invariably of a gloomy and tragic order, and again in this respect also one finds merely the ultimate point of a constantly growing tendency throughout his entire creative activity. The real, fundamental Liszt, indeed, is not the brilliant and facile rhetorician that he is invariably made out to be, delighting principally in grandiose sonorities and triumphant apotheoses; the essence of his art, on the contrary, consists in a sadness, a melancholy, a disillusion, a despair, of a depth and intensity unequalled, perhaps, in all music. No composer has ever ventured farther into that City of Dreadful Night of which the poet Thomson sings; none has expressed with greater poignancy

> The sense that every struggle brings defeat
> Because Fate holds no prize to crown success;
> That all the oracles are dumb or cheat
> Because they have no secret to express;
> That none can pierce the vast black veil uncertain
> Because there is no light beyond the curtain;
> That all is vanity and nothingness.

This is the essential Liszt. It is here that his true greatness lies, here that he is original, unique, unsurpassed. Too often, however, as a dutiful son of the Church, he felt himself constrained to give the lie to his innermost convictions, of which perhaps he was not himself fully and consciously aware; hence his pompous, triumphant finales which are almost invariably the weakest sections of his works. Hostile criticism, in fact, is fully justified here in a sense; it rightly perceives in such things a certain hollowness, lack of conviction, and seeming insincerity, but errs in diagnosing the cause of them. Too often, indeed, Liszt went a long way towards spoiling his best works through his assumption of a facile and shallow optimism which is in opposition to his real self and stands in flagrant contradiction to what has gone before. The ending of the *Faust* Symphony is a case in point. The work should logically have concluded with the Mephistopheles movement, and I believe I am right in saying that such was the original conception, but scruples of conscience and ethical considerations generally led him to tack on to the end of it a choral epilogue, a kind of 'happy ending' depicting redemption through womanly love, which not only impairs the profundity and originality of the conception as a whole, but also constitutes a blot upon the otherwise perfect form and musical logic of the work. This fault, however, does not prevent the *Faust* Symphony from being probably, on the whole, his greatest work and one of the highest achievements of the nineteenth century; for the rest, however, his most completely satisfying compositions on a large scale are those in which the sadness and despair which are the core of his thought and feeling are not thus contradicted, such as the symphonic poems *Ce qu'on entend sur la montagne*, *Héroïde funèbre*, *Hamlet*, and the great piano sonata, the closing page of which I never hear without thinking involuntarily of that terrible little sentence of Pascal, 'Le silence éternel de ces espaces infinis m'effraie', of which it always seems to me to be the perfect musical embodiment and equivalent. Even the finest of his sacred music is not that wherein he celebrates the glories of the Church militant and triumphant, as in so many grandiose pages of the *Graner Festmesse*, *Die Legende von der heiligen Elisabeth*, and *Christus*, fine works though they are in many ways, but in such things as his deeply moving setting of the thirteenth Psalm, 'How long wilt thou forget me, O Lord? for ever? how long wilt thou hide thy face from me?' Here again, however, the beauty of the work is somewhat impaired by the exultant conclusion, which does not seem to ring entirely true.

Another widely prevalent misconception regarding the music of Liszt is that, in the words of Dannreuther in his volume on 'The Romantic Period' in *The Oxford History of Music*, 'he devoted his extraordinary mastery of instrumental technique to the purposes of illustrative expression'. All the symphonic poems, with the exception of *Orpheus*, are, Dannreuther says,

impromptu illustrations, corresponding to some poem, or picture, or group of concepts expressed in words. They are mere sketches arranged in accordance with some poetical plan, extraneous, and more or less alien, to music. ... From the point of view of musical design, a lax and loose conception of art prevails more or less through all the *Poèmes symphoniques*.

. . . In lieu of musical logic and consistency of design, he is content with rhapsodical improvisation. The power of persistence seems wanting. . . . The musical growth is spoilt, the development of the themes is stopped or perverted by some reference to extraneous ideas. Everywhere the programme stands in the way and the materials refuse to coalesce.

The two chief accusations made against Liszt here, namely, a lack of formal cohesion and a reliance on programmatic ideas alien to music, are both absolutely and entirely untrue. Out of the twelve symphonic poems, which are the objects of these strictures, *Hungaria* and *Festklänge* have no programme at all, *Hamlet* has no other than is contained in the title and makes no attempt to illustrate the drama, *Hunnenschlacht* is merely a battle-piece, also with no further indication than the title, *Tasso*, *Mazeppa*, and *Prometheus* are merely variants on the simplest of all possible musical formulas—*Lamento e Trionfo*—the alleged programmes of *Les Préludes* and the *Héroïde funèbre* are the vaguest kind of romantic *schwärmerei* and contain no concrete images susceptible of illustration, and *Orpheus* is specifically exempted by Dannreuther himself from the strictures above quoted. Only two out of the twelve can be truly said to be programme music in the strict sense of the words, namely the first and last, *Ce qu'on entend sur la montagne* and *Die Ideale*, to which may also be added the *Dante* Symphony, which is only a gigantic symphonic poem in two movements. The first of these is based upon a poem of Victor Hugo which it no doubt follows closely enough in general outline, but the poem itself is nothing more or less than a preliminary sketch for a musical composition, as the few lines which follow clearly show:

> Ce fut d'abord un bruit large, immense, confus,
> Plus vague que le vent dans les arbres touffus,
> Plein d'accords éclatants, de suaves murmures
> Doux comme un chant du soir . . .
> Bientôt je distinguai, confuses et voilées,
> Deux voix dans cette voix l'une à l'autre mêlées,

L'une venait des mers; chant de gloire! hymne heureux!
C'était la voix des flots qui se parlaient entre eux;
L'autre, qui s'élevait de la terre où nous sommes,
Était triste; c'était le murmure des hommes.

This is hardly a programme that can be called 'extraneous and more or less alien to music', it will be admitted. Rather is it true that Victor Hugo was guilty of writing a poem which is based upon a musical programme that is extraneous and more or less alien to poetry.

In *Die Ideale* the composer follows an entirely different scheme from the poem of Schiller on which it is ostensibly based. The order of the verses inscribed in the score is not that of the poet, but an arbitrary arrangement made by the composer; even then he does not by any means follow the poem line by line, or even verse by verse. Still, it is true that the literary element in *Die Ideale* remains considerable, and without a knowledge of it the work is apt to seem somewhat unintelligible. The same is true of the *Dante* Symphony, but neither of these two works, though they are certainly among Liszt's most ambitious efforts, is among his best. Of them it may be admitted that the musical development is conditioned, and sometimes hindered, to a great extent by extraneous literary ideas, and that the form is, in consequence, loose and unsatisfactory. But to say of the rest of his large orchestral works, as Dannreuther and many others do, that they are completely formless and consist chiefly of 'rhapsodical improvisation' is entirely untrue, and can, indeed, be proved untrue. This has in fact been done in a recent book written by a German musicologist, Joachim Bergfeld, *Die formale Struktur der symphonischen Dichtungen Franz Liszts*, in which the writer conclusively shows, by means of a most Teutonically painstaking and searching analysis, complete with elaborate diagrams, that the symphonic poems of Liszt are exceedingly carefully, methodically, even pedantically, constructed. How any one can ever have thought otherwise is beyond comprehension. If Liszt is not one of the great masters of form—and he certainly is not—the reason is not that he relies on 'rhapsodical improvisation' but precisely the opposite, namely, that his form is often, perhaps generally, too mechanical, precise, logical, and symmetrical, lacking in the living, spontaneous, organic quality which is characteristic of the highest achievements in musical form. In some of his best works on a large scale, however, he does attain to formal perfection, notably in the piano sonata, *Hamlet*, and—apart from the slight flaw already indicated—the great *Faust* Symphony, to name only three.

This widely spread delusion concerning the formal looseness and invertebracy of Liszt's major works is, of course, merely another example of Pavlovian caninity. Most of the lesser pianoforte works of his which are generally known have a certain improvisatory quality, and this characteristic has in consequence been unthinkingly applied to his work in other fields, even when it is almost painfully laboured and precise, as Bergfeld shows it to have been very frequently.

The immense quantity of fine music that Liszt wrote for the piano is almost entirely neglected by concert pianists, and is in consequence virtually unknown to the general public, apart from a few well-worn and hackneyed show-pieces which are frequently included in the final groups of recital programmes solely in order to display the technical accomplishments of the performer. Many of his best pieces, however, notably in the collections *Années de Pèlerinage* and *Harmonies poétiques et religieuses*, are not exceptionally difficult but, on the contrary, for the most part well within the scope of the ordinarily proficient player, and among the finest in the pianistic repertoire. On the other hand, the difficult *Études d'exécution transcendante* are by no means mere virtuoso pieces, but works of intrinsic merit as well, and even many of the greatly abused operatic fantasias are in their way perfect masterpieces. Saint-Saëns has well said that such things are not necessarily any more negligible artistically than overtures, which are generally little more than fantasias on the themes of the opera which is to follow. One might say that, while the overture prepares the listener's mind for the drama which is to come, the Lisztian fantasia is in the nature of an epilogue, a commentary or meditation upon the drama after it is over. The transfiguring imaginative power which Liszt brings to such things is seldom recognized by criticism. An honourable and noteworthy exception is to be found in the writings of a shrewd and penetrating critic of the 'nineties, named George Bernard Shaw. Speaking of the great fantasia on the *Don Juan* of Mozart he says:

When you hear the terrible progressions of the statue's invitation suddenly echoing through the harmonies accompanying Juan's seductive 'Andiam, andiam, mio bene', you cannot help accepting it as a stroke of genius—that is, if you know your *'Don Giovanni'* au fond.

Even more remarkable in its critical acumen is his appreciation of the fantasia on Meyerbeer's *Robert le Diable*,

one of those prodigious opera fantasias of Liszt's which few pianists can play and fewer understand. . . . That on 'Robert' is a pungent criticism of Meyerbeer as well as a *tour de force* of adaptation to the pianoforte. To anyone who knows the opera, and knows the composer thoroughly, no written analysis of 'Robert' could be half so interesting as this fantasia in which Liszt, whilst vividly reproducing Meyerbeer's cleverly economised and elaborated scraps of fantasy, grace, and power, picks up the separate themes apparently at random, and fits them to one another with a satirical ingenuity which brings out in the most striking way how very limited and mechanical the Meyerbeerian forms were.

Two other neglected aspects of Liszt's phenomenally versatile genius are the few, but superb, works which he wrote for the organ—probably the finest written for the instrument since Bach—namely, the fantasia and fugue on the theme B.A.C.H., the *Evocation in the Sistine Chapel* based upon Mozart's *Ave Verum*, the variations on *Weinen*, *klagen*, the fantasia and fugue on the choral *Ad nos, ad salutarem undam*; and the fifty or so songs with piano accompaniment, some of which, such as *Kennst du das Land?*, *Es muss ein Wunderbares sein*, *Kling leise*, *Ein Fichtenbaum*, *König im Thule*, *Vatergruft*, *Ich möchte hingehn*, *Ich scheide*, *Enfant, si j'étais roi*, and many others too numerous to mention here, are among the best songs written since Schubert. Above all, however, does Liszt excel in his settings of Heine, whose combination of sentimentality and irony, of lyricism and cynicism, was particularly congenial and akin to his own temperament.

This strain of irony and cynicism which so often underlies the suave and sentimental exterior of his music is the active aspect of the weariness and disillusionment which we have already noted in much of his best work, and particularly in his later years—the combination of medieval *accidia* and modern *weltschmerz* which we find in his *Hamlet* for example, and in the last songs and piano pieces. There it is passive, despairing, almost resigned; in its more positive manifestations it takes the form of a withering and pitiless mockery of which the most perfect expression is to be found in the third movement of the *Faust* Symphony, the *Mephisto* Waltzes, the *Totentanz*, and other similar essays in the musical *macabre*. It runs like a leitmotiv, however, throughout his entire work; as Busoni says in an essay on Liszt in his book *Von der Einheit der Musik*, 'Für Liszts Ausdrucksvermögen bezeichnend ist die Wiedergabe zweier Gefühlsmomente: des diabolischen und des katholisch-gläubigen.' This, incidentally, helps further to explain the Anglo-Saxon dislike of Liszt to which reference has already been made. The national taste is not sympathetic to Catholicism, and intolerant of Diabolism; not unnaturally, therefore, the combination of the two in one personality is felt to be altogether too much. To oscillate perpetually between the saintly and the satanic, as Liszt does, is ungentlemanly and un-English, to say the least. Similarly, the dazzling brilliance of one part of his

work and the intense austerity of the other are alike
uncongenial to a race which seeks in all things the *via
media*, the happy mean, the compromise between two
extremes. This is not necessarily an unworthy ideal, I
hasten to add; it has certainly made the British Empire
what it is, but it undoubtedly constitutes a formidable
barrier to the due appreciation of the art of Liszt for whom,
in the words of that regrettably un-English man, William
Blake, 'the road of excess leads to the palace of wisdom'.

Whatever one's opinion may be concerning the intrinsic
merit, or the reverse, of Liszt's music, there can be no two
opinions concerning the immense influence his work has
had, for good or evil, and possibly for both, on the history
of the art—greater in all probability than that of any other
composer who has ever lived. No musician has more
generously lavished such superlative interpretative gifts,
as pianist, as transcriber, as conductor (during the Weimar
period), on his great predecessors and contemporaries;
similarly none has more richly endowed his contemporaries
and successors with the fruits of his creative activities.
Liszt, indeed, quite simply, is the father of modern music.
There is no composer of any importance during the latter
part of the nineteenth, or the beginning of the twentieth,
century who has not been influenced by him in some way
or another. The first and most important of all was, of
course, Wagner. The Wagnerians have always attempted
to minimize and gloze over this debt, but Wagner himself,
greatly to his credit, never tried to do so but, on the contrary, openly proclaimed it. See for example the well-
known letter written to Liszt in which he says: 'Ich
bezeichne dich als Schöpfer meiner jetzigen Stellung.
Wenn ich komponiere und instrumentiere denke ich immer
nur an dich . . . deine drei letzten Partituren sollen mich
wieder zum Musiker weihen für den Beginn meines
zweiten Aktes [Siegfried], den dies Studium einleiten soll.'
Even before he had come so far it is generally recognized
to-day that the immense step forward that Wagner made

between *Lohengrin* and *Rheingold* is in large part due to the influence of Liszt.

There is no need even to mention the enormous extent of the debt that is owed to him by the most eminent modern German composers; it speaks for itself. The Richard Strauss of the symphonic poems, for example, could not have existed without Liszt, and the same applies to innumerable others. Even Brahms himself, it is interesting and instructive to note, was influenced by Liszt in his early works such as the first and second piano sonatas, where he adopts the Lisztian device of thematic transformation, and in the clearly poetic elements of the third. In France Saint-Saëns was, of course, one of the most fervent admirers and disciples of Liszt, and one of his most sedulous imitators, César Franck, is no less demonstrably and effectually indebted to him, not merely in his symphonic poems but in all his work, and the so-called impressionists were anticipated by him in many of their most characteristic effects and procedures, sometimes by as much as half a century—see, for example, such things as 'Au bord d'une source' and the 'Jeux d'eaux à la Villa d'Este' in the *Années de Pèlerinage*, and the 'Prédication aux Oiseaux' of the *Légendes*, also the augmented fifths and whole-tone scales encountered in works written as early as the 'thirties. Again, the American critic Huneker has described Liszt, not without justice, in his book on him, as 'the first cosmopolitan in music', and as such he has a numerous, if somewhat undistinguished, progeny in every country in Europe—the Moskowskis, Glazounovs, Rachmaninovs, Dohnanyis, and so forth are all direct descendants of Liszt; equally justly, however, he can be regarded as the first of the nationalists, not merely by virtue of his *Hungarian Rhapsodies* and other similar works, which were practically the first of their kind, but also on account of the encouragement and inspiration he gave to the formation of national schools in many countries. Balakirev, the founder of the Russian nationalist school, and Borodin, to say nothing of Rimsky-Korsakov, were deeply influenced by Liszt; so also were the Bohemian nationalists Smetana and Dvořák, Albeniz, and through him the modern Spanish nationalists, and even the Norwegian Grieg. Other eminent composers possessing no distinctively nationalistic traits or anything else in common who have likewise been deeply influenced by him are Busoni, who is in many respects the very reincarnation of Liszt, Scriabin, whose witch's cauldron contains many ingredients stolen from him, and, as we have already seen, Elgar. Traces of his thought can even be perceived where no direct influence exists. For example, the passage of interlocking common chords of C natural and F sharp in Stravinsky's *Petrouchka*, described in the score as 'Malédictions de Petrouchka', is basically identical with an episode in the posthumous and only recently published concerto for piano and strings of Liszt, entitled *Malédiction*—a strange and arresting coincidence, this, by the way. Even Arnold Schönberg and the atonalists derive in many respects from Liszt. The perverse and ironic romanticism of *Pierrot Lunaire*, for example, is only a development of that in the amazing third movement of the *Faust* Symphony, and in his last works Liszt clearly foreshadows the principles of atonality. Incidentally, in this connexion it is amusing to note a passage in Dannreuther's volume on the Romantic Period already referred to, in which we are told that even as early as the 'thirties Liszt earnestly worked at the conception of a possible *ordre omnitonique* which might be destined at some distant date to supersede our present tonality. 'It is a fact stranger still', continues Dannreuther with sublime innocence, 'that Liszt, all his life long, should have retained such a notion, and that he desired to make, and was ever ready to encourage, experiments in tonality which led to effects of interesting ugliness.' Strangest of all, however, is the fact that Liszt's *ordre omnitonique* has to-day become an accomplished reality. Assuredly, that much maligned lady, the Princess Wittgenstein, was not far wrong when she wrote that 'On ne le comprend pas encore — beaucoup moins que Wagner. Liszt a jeté sa lance beaucoup plus loin dans l'avenir. Plusieurs générations passeront avant qu'il soit entièrement compris.' There are many clear indications, however, that the day is at last approaching when Liszt will be recognized as not merely the most potent germinative force in modern music, but also, in his own right, as the inspired creator of some of the greatest and most original masterpieces of the nineteenth century.

GIUSEPPE VERDI
(1813–1901)
By F. BONAVIA

VERDI'S last opera when first performed won a very qualified success. Indeed, when it was known that he was writing *Falstaff* the general impression was one of surprise not so much because of the composer's age—he was nearly eighty years old—but because of the comic subject chosen by the author of *Trovatore*. *Otello* had been eminently successful; but popular opinion still held to the belief that the secret of the good fortune that attended Verdi's operas lay in an almost inexhaustible vein of rich, flowing melody. *Falstaff* was received with every outward sign of favour. Congratulations poured in from every part of the world, the press published enthusiastic eulogies, but the public showed a curious disinclination to go to the theatre. With that marvellous sense of reality found only in the perfect idealist, Verdi soon discovered how things stood and answered his admirers by pointing to the box-office returns—'the true barometer of success'. Time did justice to *Falstaff* and confounded those who had suggested that its composition had been undertaken merely to solace an old man's leisure. The freshness of this great comedy, its tenderness and good humour, not only cleared away prejudices but opened the way for closer and more sympathetic study of an art as simple and as difficult as that of Mozart.

There is, of course, nothing more bewildering than simplicity for the very good reason that no one can gauge its depth. It may be shallow, it may be profound—only time and temperamental affinities can help us to discriminate. Complexity, on the other hand, inevitably attracts both the thoughtful and the thoughtless, since the former can exercise their ingenuity, and the latter, profiting by the other's researches, lay claim to a knowledge they do not possess.

The slow but certain rehabilitation of *Falstaff* led to a revision of former opinion and vindicated critics who, like Sir Charles Stanford, had made no secret of their profound admiration. But earlier operas also profited by the favourable atmosphere thus created. Performances became less casual than they had been. Singers could not easily be weaned from the affectations and abuses which had gone so long unchecked, but a more earnest and thoughtful attitude came to be expected and the possibility of revising earlier works was seriously considered.

In time the movement culminated in the revival of *Macbeth* in Germany—a significant move since it could not be mistaken for a passion for those sometimes coarse but full-blooded melodies of the early Verdian period— and pointed to a new appreciation of qualities not generally supposed to be characteristic of Verdi's work. A gift for vigorous, popular melody was never denied him any more than it had been denied to Bellini or Donizetti, whom he was held to have beaten at their own game. The charge most frequently proferred against him was of having allowed lyrical expression a greater and more important share than musical drama can stand—if it is to be a drama and not a succession of songs. It was admitted that his melodies had greater vitality than those of his predecessors; but it was urged, and with truth, that melody alone could not support the weight of dramatic action.

Macbeth, produced three years before *Lohengrin* and forty before *Otello*, shows clearly and unmistakably how quick Verdi's mind was in appreciating the needs of the music drama and how well he knew that, if trills and flourishes do not make a melody, sweet or impetuous tunes do not make an opera. It was characteristic of him that he revealed it not in a manifesto but casually, in a letter protesting against the choice of a singer who seemed to him unlikely to understand what he required of Lady Macbeth. 'Mme Tadolini,' he wrote, 'whom you have chosen, sings to perfection and I prefer the interpreter of "Lady Macbeth" not to sing at all.' Rather significant, this demand for a singer to refrain from singing in an age when singers did not scruple to ask composers to add another aria or two and refused a part like that of Senta if they thought it unworthy of their talents.

One wonders how many who heard *Macbeth* when it was first produced, or even later when it was revived in Paris in 1865, realized all it meant to Verdi. There is authority for asserting that the dilettanti of the time cherished above all else the baritone aria—probably the least individual and interesting piece in the whole opera. Verdi, however, knew well where its strength lay. He pinned his faith on the duet between Macbeth and Lady Macbeth and the sleep-walking scene; if these failed in their effect, the whole opera, he said, must collapse. And, it is important to note, in the aria which 'was not to be sung'—the sleep-walking scene—the orchestra becomes the protagonist. The whole musical interest is there.

We need go no farther to see where Verdi differed from his Italian contemporaries. With them it was the eloquence of melody that counted; with him its dramatic fitness. Before Verdi a melody could be transposed from one situation to another without seeming irrelevant. With him and after him music acquired richer but also more definite expression. There could be never again a question of adapting, and still less of 'borrowing'. A melody such as that in which Gennaro reveals himself to Lucrezia Borgia in Donizetti's opera could fit equally well and equally vaguely any other occasion. Lady Macbeth's aria cannot be translated elsewhere without making nonsense of it.

Not all in *Macbeth* is of a piece with the sleep-walking scene. Passages and whole pages, if scored with greater ability, yet recall the earlier manner. But once the principle of dramatic fitness had begun to dominate Verdi's mind, it never again allowed him to stray from it. The operas which immediately followed in rapid succession, *I Masnadieri* (1847) and *Il Corsaro* (1848), are less important in this respect. But dramatic aptness is well in evidence in *Luisa Miller*, in *La Battaglia di Legnano*, and gives all their force to the finest pages of *Rigoletto*. Once the critical world accepted without scandal the substitution of one mistress for another; the true marriage of words and music allowed no such latitude.

To avoid wrong impressions, let us say that we do not agree with that contemporary of Gluck, quoted by Hanslick, who maintained that the famous aria of Orpheus, 'J'ai perdu mon Eurydice' would be better mated to verses which ran 'J'ai trouvé mon Eurydice'. M. Boyé cannot have had a very keen perception of musical sentiment if he missed the sense of loss and sorrow which inspires this song—not less poignant for its undemonstrative opening. Any piece of music can be so divided that some part of it, some small fragment, can be twisted to serve another purpose. Some characteristics of Verdi's style, for instance, some turn of phrase, can be seen in his first opera, *Oberto Conte di San Bonifacio*, and equally in *Otello*. Points of resemblance between the new and the old there may be, just as sometimes we discover the same thought in two different writers. These things are due to chance, they are inevitable; no one thinks less of Shakespeare because scholars have traced some of his ideas to other writers. What was urgently needed, and what Verdi did for Italian as Wagner for German music, was to put an end to real abuses. The practice of lifting a piece, an aria or a chorus, from an opera and inserting it into another opera or an oratorio, which Handel himself occasionally practised, endured till early in the nineteenth century partly because no one objected to it and partly because composers found it very convenient when time ran short. The public who accepted it never looked upon opera as anything more than a peg for singers, something like a cantata to which scenery had been added with opportunities for eye-pleasing action and movement.

Such a view of opera is hardly removed from the masque and the pantomime. It still exists in the minds of many concerned with opera. Where the directions of the composer are not carried out, when the score is curtailed arbitrarily, where conductors distort the tempo, when the singers are allowed to disport their vanity by making a show of lung power, where the scenery takes precedence of strictly musical considerations, when opera thus resembles a picture cut at the edges, daubed here and there, half hidden by shadows—where these conditions prevail the appeal is no longer that of music drama. It is not impossible, however, that an age which believes that one may dispense with romantic life and colour will return to the colder but still diverting forms of the masque and the pantomime; but to this Verdi would never have subscribed.

A good deal of ridicule has been cast on the works of Donizetti, as on the early operas of Verdi, by critics who in other days would have championed the unities and seen in opera only an extension *ad absurdum* of the licence of the drama. As a matter of fact all theatrical ventures are based on conventionality. The test of a drama or of an opera is not in the number or in the gravity of its offences against the laws of time, place, and action, but in the skill of the poet or composer and in his ability to convey a plausible picture of events and people in spite of them. Some conventions, some make-believe, cannot be avoided in the theatre any more than a painter can avoid presenting objects on a flat surface. The so-called 'weakness' of an ensemble—a duet, a trio, a concerted piece—is no weakness but strength when by such means the composer can express what goes on in the mind of two or more persons at the same time. It is true that this does not happen in real life where, in a dialogue, while one speaks another must, or at least should, be silent. But we do not cease to think when we cease to speak. Any art which can express both the words of one and the thoughts of another is surely entitled to do so, as dramatists have tried to do, by means of 'asides', often far more artificial than duets or quartets.

But Donizetti and others who, like him, revelled in the new liberty and range which the romantic impulse had given to music were apt to overrate the value of a melodic style. It could not alone provide sufficient contrast; it could not depict some degrees in the gamut of passion; it could not discriminate with sufficient clearness between different characters. That is what of all the Italians Verdi was the first to learn.

He was not very well equipped by fortune for such a task. Born and bred mostly in a small community where, we may be sure, no one ever thought of questioning the existing order either in music or in the drama, nothing could be farther from his mind than to challenge it. But he had, apart from his musical genius, two immensely valuable qualities—artistic honesty and an unusual amount of common sense. His honesty prevented him from pandering to what was thought to be public taste. His common sense showed him where reform was needed and how far it could be carried out. Paradoxical as it may seem, this composer who so early won popular applause had never to compromise with his conscience to meet it and passed the greater part of his life away from the masses who acclaimed him. When an opera was ready he appeared in public, trained his singers, perhaps conducted and certainly supervised the first performance, and then disappeared. Such a naturally modest and retiring disposition does not suggest the eagerness of the born reformer. If he came to carry out reforms it was because common sense showed that they were indispensable. Nothing is more significant than the answer he gave to a singer who asked for another aria: 'I cannot; for I have already done my

best. It may be little; but I can do nothing better.'
Verdi's whole character is summed up in those brief
sentences. He was strengthened in the conviction that
sincerity is the best policy by an almost superstitious
reverence for 'inspiration', for those moments of exaltation
in which new ideas flashed into his mind. This criterion
is not wholly sound; mediocre ideas may also be conceived
in moments of unnatural excitement. The minor composer,
even the unknown composer, may think of a new idea,
believe it excellent, and continue so to do, unless he happens to be one of those exceptional men who accept the
world's verdict. But in Verdi's case this belief was confirmed by success, and helped to steel the determination
never to listen to the advice of outsiders. Once convinced
that he had done his best the public could, as far as he was
concerned, take it or leave it. Undoubtedly the system
suited his genius to perfection. His own revisions were
seldom happy, and operas which were completed in the
shortest time have survived many a revolutionary period
in the history of music—the revelation of Wagner's genius,
the recognition of Brahms, the new impressionism of
Debussy, the invasion of the picturesque art of Russia—
and have lived into an era when the really advanced discuss,
like Milton's fallen angels,

> Fix'd fate, free-will, foreknowledge absolute,
> And found no end, in wand'ring mazes lost.

We speak of Verdian reform, but it would be more
accurate to speak of development. It is true that in comparing the formal divisions into which the acts of the early
operas fall with the later operas, where the only law is that
of dramatic development, one is struck by the difference
of shape, outlook, and craftsmanship. But his reform was
as gradual a growth as his technique—even more, since
at no time did he take up a position from which he later
found it desirable to withdraw. The development was as
gradual and as continuous as that of the child into the man.

It was, above all, a deepening of the understanding, a widening of sympathies, a quicker and more generous, more intelligent, response to the appeal of whatever passion sways the dramatis personae of the plays.

The unequal quality of the early operas was due partly, no doubt, to a conventional conception of musical theory, but also to Verdi's inability to conceal the fact that some situations did not quicken his genius so well as others. There is no sin in this, since when Verdi began writing recitativo was still in use, long stretches of which were never meant to be treated otherwise than in a conventional fashion. In *Nabucco* as in *Conte Oberto* his finer powers are awakened by situations meant to appeal to a warm and generous rather than a very sensitive nature. Only occasionally does he prove to us that his nature was highly sensitive as well as generous, that his musical instinct could be equal to subtlety of expression. Neither *La Battaglia di Legnano* nor *Luisa Miller* shows anything like the range and the sure touch of the later operas. Yet if we consider them together—they were both produced in the same year—we cannot but marvel that two such different subjects should appeal to him in exactly the same degree, that the hand which wrote the scene in Sant' Ambrogio of the former opera (outshining the once famous conspiracy in *Les Huguenots*) should also have written the delicate, sensitive arias of *Luisa Miller*.

These operas suffer to-day from the somewhat unadventurous nature of the harmonies, which frequently repeat a more or less conventional pattern and set limits to the melodic invention. To appraise them it is necessary to approach them by different ways and bear in mind the limitations of analysis and criticism so clearly defined by Sainte-Beuve:

However well the net is woven, something always remains outside and escapes; it is what we call genius, personal talent. The learned critic lays his siege to attack this like an engineer. He trenches it about and hems it into a corner, under colour of surrounding it with all the outward conditions that may prove necessary. And these conditions really do serve personal originality; they incite it, they tempt it forth, they place it in a position to act and react, more or less; but they do not make it. This particle which Horace entitles divine (*divinae particulam aurae*), and which in the primitive, natural sense of the term really is such, has never yet surrendered to science, and abides unexplained. That is no reason for science to throw down her weapons and renounce her daring enterprise. The siege of Troy lasted ten years; and there are problems which perhaps may last as long as human life itself.

Verdi's genius is all in that particle which abides unexplained. He is not the great grammarian whose discoveries may be analysed and discussed: nor is he the symphonic composer whose essays in form can be made the subject of profound study. His harmony is always controlled by that more personal factor, taste. His conception of symphonic form is evident only in the string quartet, which, admirable work as it is in many ways, pales in importance by the side of the operas. Nor is our task made easier by the curious standard applied by those who deny the name of music to anything which does not conform to a preconceived pattern and make extravagant claims for the easy melodies of the early period because they are more extended in form. These fail to see what Verdi himself saw as clearly as Monteverde—the essential difference between the dramatic and the lyrical style. As long as the subject of opera was a mere excuse for music, when the heroes were traditional figures of mythology, Achilles or Alexander, the treatment did not matter very much. The action was entirely conventional, and all the musician was expected to do was to choose from the text those situations he thought best adapted to his talents and temperament. When, however, the theme is Othello or Lear the lengthening effects of music at once become apparent; thoughts which should move quickly are arrested by lyrical treatment and a mean must be struck between the aria and the recitativo; the gulf must be bridged somehow if a constantly recurring anti-climax is to be avoided. The only alternative to Verdi's is the Wagnerian plan, with its deliberate cutting down of the action to its bare essentials so as to make full allowance for the expansion of music. In choosing a different way Verdi was wise since in all his operas the action is swift and better suited to his temperament.

Admittedly the expediency of a system is no proof of its worth. The more dramatic style of *Otello* would be inferior to the more lyrical style of *Aïda* if its only justification lay in aptitude to express more fittingly certain emotions. But if there is a beauty of lyrical there is also a beauty of dramatic expression, even though the apostles of lyricism or 'pure music' may not agree to it. They differ as the song of Schubert differs from that of Hugo Wolf; but they both have beauty and their character is essentially 'musical'. The one moves us with the wonder of a single perfect idea, the other with a succession of thoughts more brief but not less poignant. The old operatic style with its subdivisions of the scene into set pieces, arias, duets, and the like, favoured the first form; the second is exemplified by the love duet in *Otello* where the music changes with every new image that flashes in the mind of the characters.

Are the love duets of *Ernani* or *Rigoletto* or even *Aïda* finer musically than that of *Otello*? No one can seriously suggest it. In part, the superiority of *Otello* can be traced to finer workmanship—greater wealth of technical resources, surer and more masterly touch in exploiting them. But its chief merit rests mainly in a lyrical impulse which, controlled, gains immeasurably in vigour and originality, in depth and swiftness. It is not in the least necessary to deny virtue and beauty to the melodies which enrich the scores of *Ernani* or *Trovatore* in order to establish the claims of the later operas. But the essence of the Verdian reform is just this schooling of the lyrical instinct; and its

evolution led to the fullest development of a genius who
began his career amongst the arrangements for brass band
found in the library of his patron, Barezzi!

No wonder Verdi was at first reluctant to leave the safe
path of the plainest of harmonic gambits. And perhaps
to-day we are apt to give too much importance to 'freedom'
of harmony; at any rate some modern composers, for all
their airs of independence and dexterous camouflage, have
already gone back a considerable way towards simpler
formulas. However this may be, it should be remembered
in attempting to gauge the extent of Verdian reforms that
amongst Verdi's immediate predecessors and contemporaries there was no one to stimulate his genius, no one
akin to him in temperament. Rossini, who should have
taken the place in Verdi's mind and heart which Beethoven
had in Wagner's, was of a temperament so different as to
preclude the possibility of intimate understanding. Thus
he had to work out his own salvation and go step by step,
from the buoyant but undistinguished *Nabucco* to *Macbeth*,
where first he searched and found a dramatic effect
removed from lyricism; to *Rigoletto*, conceived, as he said,
'without arias, without final tableaux, just as an endless
succession of duets' because this form alone satisfied his
dramatic instinct; to *Traviata* with its glow of romantic
passion; to the splendour and the pathos of *Aïda*; to the
most terrible of tragedies, *Otello*, and the most sparkling
of comedies, *Falstaff*.

The last, indeed, embodies the experience of a lifetime.
An artist's view of life, however rich, of its pleasures and
sorrows, nobilities and futilities, does not constitute a
philosophy. But it has the detachment which philosophers,
who are bound to justify their ways, affect but do not
always possess. The composer, like the poet, needs no
other justification than excellence. In *Falstaff* there is
philosophic detachment, a sense of pity, of finality, of complete harmony; foibles and wits, vanities and love-making
are blended together and have a common factor—human-

ity. It is comedy in which no one is wiser than his fellow. In an odd way it recalls not only Shakespeare's Falstaff but also Shakespeare's rustic philosopher, Jaques, for behind the comedy a more thoughtful spirit broods. The delicacy of the fairy music composes the mind to such thoughts as become night and the silence of a forest. When the uproarious fun of the last fugue is past we feel as if we had seen a mighty ship slipping from its mooring to make her way to unknown seas. The more serious mood is evident even in the idyll of Fenton and Ann Page, for the gentle sweetness of their songs hints that even their love-dream can lead but to an awakening.

To seek in the character of the man traits which might explain his art may be a hopeless venture in the case of most musicians, who often show their muse a countenance very different from that with which they face the world. Verdi, in this respect, was the exception. His life does not explain his genius but, at least, it was not at variance with his practice of the art of music. A conviction of fairness and honesty inspired them both. The instinct which bade him keep a strict account of every commercial transaction made him scrupulous in keeping faith with the public and give his best in all circumstances—sometimes against his better judgement, as when he sought to meet the taste of the Parisians by planning *Don Carlo* on the scale of a Meyerbeerian 'grand' opera. Another trait evident in the man and in the artist was his inborn conservatism which made him suspicious of new-fangled ideas and thus resulted in the carrying out of important reforms in so smooth a way that no one realized at the time either how important or how very much his own they were. Yet another is provided by the simplicity of his mode of life and of his tastes, matching the directness of a style profound in expression but never involved in texture. Most important perhaps is the generosity of a nature always ready to champion the cause of the weak. Unversed in the ways of statesmanship and political expediency he resented bitterly

what he conceived as the betrayal of Italy by France after
the peace of Villafranca (1859), but when France was
beaten in 1870 he would have preferred to share in the
defeat than enjoy the advantages of what seemed to him a
dishonourable neutrality. He chose the heroes and heroines
of his operas in the same spirit. Simon Boccanegra,
Manrico the Troubadour, Violetta, Rigoletto, Don Alvaro
—what a gallery of unfortunates! It may be thought
perhaps that in this choice he was inspired by a romantic
ideal which together with the 'grace of childhood and
dignity of the untaught peasant' showed a new pity and a
new understanding of the poor and lowly. But opera lagged
behind the drama, and when Verdi began to write phan-
toms from the classical or biblical age were still considered
capable of firing a composer's imagination. Verdi's *Nabucco*
was one of four operas of that name produced in the nineteenth century while nine of his contemporaries found
the ideal heroine in Judith. No wonder the censors of the
time suspected Rigoletto to be a revolutionary propagand-
ist and took exception to *Traviata* (long after *La Dame aux
Camélias* had been produced) on both moral and aesthetic
grounds.

Verdi stood well another test to which not a few men—
distinguished and undistinguished—have succumbed: the
test of success. Indeed, he seems to have looked upon
success with distrust. Perhaps he learnt its worth when,
after all the praise that had been bestowed on *Nabucco*, he
found himself without the means of satisfying his landlord
—a trifle which his scruples magnified into a mountain.
Perhaps the loss of his first wife and two children within
a few weeks impressed him with the utter futility of human
hopes and wishes. At any rate the applause of the public,
the eulogies of critics, never affected his development in
the slightest. He was one of the few composers who learnt
early to take critical buffets and rewards with equal thanks.

To assign to him his place amongst famous men is
difficult while his works are still performed by those who

have not the necessary technique or intelligence, who never hesitate to deal arbitrarily with his directions, by singers who turn every high note into an occasion to display their endurance. But most of those who have taken the trouble to clear away from his music the incrustations accumulated during years of licence, and have discovered how many moments there are even in the earlier operas in which everything earthly has been fused away and only the fire of passion remains, will not hesitate to place him amongst the great epic poets of music.

HUGO WOLF
(1860–1903)
By WALTER FORD

ORTY years ago during a visit to Pallanza an Italian friend and musician advised me on my return to London to get the songs of Hugo Wolf, a young composer who was at that time attracting much notice in Vienna, and not to be put off if I found them at first strange and difficult to understand, for they were worth understanding. Not long afterwards I came away from a visit to a shop in Regent Street with Part I of the *Italienisches Liederbuch* (forty-four settings of Italian folksongs, translated into German by Paul Heyse), which had recently appeared, under my arm. It was a happy choice; for, as I learned many years later, Wolf himself had written to a friend that he considered it the most original and artistically complete of all his works. As a preliminary to discussing them with the rest of Wolf's work it will not, I hope, be out of place to cast our eyes for a moment over the history of the Lied before Wolf's name appeared in it. We may be sure that he had studied it deeply, and that when he took a new line of his own it was in no spirit of revolt or antagonism, but because he had new things to say; in much of his work he trod happily and securely in the footsteps of his predecessors.

Beethoven was the first of the great composers to give serious attention to the Lied. Haydn and Mozart had merely toyed with it, as a light diversion for the amateurs of the *salon*, in the intervals between longer and more important works. They produced, it is true, an occasional little masterpiece, but were content for the most part to provide commonplace verses with unpretentious and often indifferent music. That no progress was to be made on these lines was clear to Beethoven, who set the example of choosing for his songs the best poetry he knew, notably Goethe's lyrics and the sacred poems of Gellert. Though he was not one of the world's born song-composers (one would hardly apply the term 'lyrical' to Beethoven), his songs, taken as a whole, were of far deeper significance and importance than anything which had appeared in this field before. The last of them, the noble cycle, *An die ferne Geliebte*, was composed in 1815. He probably felt that his work was complete and that he had given to the Lied a new inspiration and a recognized status.

It is impossible not to find a certain fitness in the date recorded, for 1815 was the year in which Schubert, then eighteen years old, left his father's house in the suburbs of Vienna and came to live in the capital, the year, too, at the end of which he composed *Erlkönig*. For some time to come there was no need for any one else to produce songs but Schubert. Had he written no more than *Erlkönig*, *Gretchen am Spinnrade*, which came a year earlier, and a quantity of other songs already composed, he would still have immortalized his name as the real founder of the Lied, not by theorizing about it, but by creating masterpieces in one type of song after another, as though he drew from an inexhaustible spring. His ideal was an intimate union between German poetry and German music, and he realized it so completely that he brought them, hand in hand, as it were, into every German home, and into thousands of other homes all over the world.

To be compared to Schubert is still the greatest praise that can be given to a composer of songs. His immediate successor was Mendelssohn, whose polished, untroubled, and melodious music, always in perfect taste, appealed so strongly to his own generation that Schubert's songs suffered a temporary eclipse. We find it hard perhaps to realize how this could be; for Mendelssohn in his songs scaled no heights and plumbed no depths. Though most of them look sadly faded now, we must not forget that they came as something quite new to the public for whom they were written, and that half a dozen or more are rightly prized amongst the permanent treasures of art. They are fragrant still with something lovable and gracious which belonged to his personality. It is strange that Mendelssohn with his general culture and literary taste should have troubled to put music to a quantity of second-rate poetry, and that when he resorted to that which was first-rate it made no appreciable difference to his style. It was not a good thing that he found imitators in every country of Europe.

The spirit of song had now moved from Vienna to Leipzig, which was then the most important centre of music in Germany. When Mendelssohn went to live there in 1835 he made friends with Robert Schumann. No one suspected then that this young man of twenty-five (one year younger than Mendelssohn) would in a few years prove to be the most remarkable phenomenon in song since Schubert, and its most inspiring influence. He was thirty-six years old when, without warning, unless his marriage in that year may be regarded as such, he began to compose songs for the first time in his life, producing in that one year about 150, to the exclusion of all other work. These included the Eichendorff *Liederkreis*, the *Dichter-liebe*, and *Frauenliebe und -Leben*. All are full of novelty, in style, in form, in feeling, and in the treatment of words.

Schumann chose these lyrics both because they appealed to his taste as a man of letters, and because like their authors, Eichendorff, Heine, and Chamisso, he was heart and soul a Romanticist. Indeed, any one who would understand what is meant by the Romantic spirit in Germany will find no better or more beautiful expression of it than in the songs of Schumann, especially those named above. We are not surprised, then, to find in his music a very perfect sympathy both with the varying moods which these poems exhibit, with the verbal felicity with which they are expressed, and with the subtle suggestions often lurking behind the words, felt but unexpressed. The result is that in Schumann's songs we meet an intimate and tender treatment of words which was quite new. He was the first song-composer to discover the value of suspensions and syncopations in the voice part for the purpose of underlining words or emphasizing special points of diction. Schubert's straightforward melodies had no need of them. I doubt whether there are a dozen instances in all his 640 songs. Now they have come to be part of the stock-in-trade of composers. We find them everywhere, in season and out of season, so that they have lost the element of surprise and delight which those singers who first met them in Schumann's songs are not likely to have forgotten. In Schumann we find too the first stages of the modern type of song, in which the voice, deprived of an organized melody to sing, declaims the words over a pictorial or illustrative accompaniment, so that the pianist tends to become of equal importance with the singer, as for instance in *Es ist im Flöten und Geigen* from the *Dichterliebe*. In song, then, as in other branches of music, Schumann was not afraid of innovation and experiment.

His influence is felt in every subsequent composer of note. Jensen, whose fresh melodious music has a charm which is quite his own, was admittedly of Schumann's school. His songs, the best of them at least, deserve to be remembered still. Franz, who is obviously indebted both to Schumann and to Mendelssohn, is of less importance. How could other than mild and mediocre songs have come from a composer who said of them with pride that 'apart from the words the music did not pretend to be much in itself'? Cornelius, now strangely neglected, was an original genius of a rare kind; his *Brautlieder* and *Weihnachtslieder* with their beautiful feeling and fine workmanship deserve a place among the classics. His literary sense was not less fine than Schumann's.

Outside, or mostly outside, the Lied, but already beginning to affect its destiny was the new spirit which came into music with Berlioz, Liszt, and Wagner. Aloof from this spirit—indeed in open conflict with it—stood the great figure of Brahms, who in song, as in all the branches of music which he pursued, refused to break with the past, because he knew, and meant to prove, that its resources were not exhausted. To him the past was Schubert. Schubert left legacies to many composers, but Brahms was his heir; for only of Brahms can it be said that his work was the logical fulfilment and completion of the founder's plan. He chose as his main principle that song means a melody for a voice to sing, and is twice a melody when it has the strengthening of a contrapuntal bass. So great was his mastery over the technique of his art that though this principle is felt to-day as a barrier to the freedom of the spirit, it was none to him. His two hundred songs are the sequel and consummation of Schubert's work, yet there is hardly a phrase in them that Schubert himself would have written. In the treatment of words he introduced no innovations.

Brahms died in Vienna on April 3rd, 1897, almost exactly a century after Schubert's birth (January 31st, 1797). Six days before the death of Brahms Wolf composed the last song which he was destined to write. He lived for six years more, but the last five were a death-in-life passed in the confinement of an asylum. His mind was gone. So for the Lied this vital century of its history, which includes the preparatory work of Beethoven, ended as it began in Vienna, with the almost simultaneous completion of the work both of Brahms and Wolf, Brahms the 'last of the die-hards for the classical tradition', Wolf the spokesman of the new age.

A friend said to me the other day, 'How dull it is to read about a man's music, when you have no idea who he was or anything else about him.' Perhaps he is right, so I add this paragraph. Wolf, till the end of his school life, lived with his parents, who were Catholics, at Windischgraz, a small town in south Styria. His father was in the leather trade, which for him was not proving successful, so that, when Hugo at the age of seventeen went to Vienna to study music, he was unable to provide for him as he wished. For more than ten years the youth had hard work to keep body and soul together. He had not Schubert's happy temperament, nor his capacity for making friends to help him through. His health never recovered from the hardships and discomforts of these early years. At the Conservatorium, where he was a student for a year, he learned little except how to play the piano. For his composition he depended on himself and his own studies, which were wide in every direction, classical as well as modern, Italian and French as well as German. He could almost have said like Haydn that he was left so much to himself that he was forced to become original. Later on, from 1884 to 1887, as musical critic of a Viennese society paper, he had every opportunity of hearing music of all sorts. Unfortunately, his ardent defence of the modern school, Berlioz, Liszt, Wagner, Bruckner, and others, and his contemptuous remarks about Brahms, then at the height of his fame and popularity, made him very unpopular with the conservative musicians and music-lovers of Vienna, and added to his difficulties in earning a livelihood. Of all composers he admired Wagner most; but, though without Wagner his genius might have developed on different lines, it is remarkable that there is surprisingly little, even in his earlier songs, that can really be called Wagnerian. In his twenty-ninth year he resolved to cut himself free from the noise, the strain, and the struggle to live which he had endured for twelve miserable years in Vienna, and to seek a spot where he could work in peace. He found it in Perchtoldsdorf, a small village not far from the capital. Here he settled down in 1888, and set to work at once, hoping to realize his cherished dream that 'he was one of the elect'. It was a case of then or never, for he was on the verge of his twenty-ninth year and still an almost unknown composer. Of thirty songs composed before this date and now included in his published works only twelve had been published, but they had hardly attracted any attention.

Some have not yet forgiven Wolf for a foolish and petu-
lant remark which he once made during a discussion upon
Brahms. 'If', he said, 'you have any scrap of liking left
in your mind for Brahms, you are not yet ripe for understanding my work.' That Wolf was prejudiced against
Brahms cannot be held as a good reason for being prejudiced against Wolf. For my own part I have not found
that a lifelong devotion to Brahms has been in the least
disturbed by a steadily growing admiration for Wolf.

Those who come to Wolf for the first time will do well
to leave both favour and prejudice behind, bringing in
their place the patience and determination of the explorer
in a newly discovered land, who wants to find out for himself what it is like, what it contains, and whether it is one
in which he would care to settle down. He will probably
find that much of what he has been told is not in line with
his own experience, and that those who persist in comparing it with lands which they have left are perpetually
looking for things which are not there and missing others
which are under their eyes.

Coleridge once remarked that 'every great and original
writer in proportion as he is great and original, must himself create the taste by which he is to be relished; he must
teach the art by which he is to be seen'. These words lose
none of their value if we substitute 'composer' for 'writer'.
I owe the quotation to Dr. Bradley's illuminating article
upon Wordsworth; and hope that I may be allowed to
add his comments upon it, with the further substitution
of 'Wolf' for 'Wordsworth'. 'There have been greater
composers than Wolf, but none more original. He saw
new things, or saw old things in a new way; the new things
were not private fancies or superficially preceived. If they
had been, he might have won acceptance more quickly,
but they would not have gained a lasting hold.' In other
words it is not his impressions that Wolf has given us, but
his convictions. Let us begin, then, by accepting the forms
which he employs and the idiosyncrasies of his style, and

not waste time in comparing his songs with those composed by earlier masters under different musical conditions, with different resources, and, to some extent, with different ideals.

The table below gives a list of Wolf's songs from 1888 to the end of his working life. I have given 20 as the number of Eichendorff songs because there are 20 in the published volumes, 7 being included which were written earlier. Thus the total result is 200 in nine years, but as four years were lost through two nervous break-downs, when he was unable to compose a single note of music, and one (1895) was given up to his opera *Corregidor*, the nine years may be reduced to four.

Mörike	.	.	.	.	53 songs		1888
Eichendorff	.	.	.	.	20 ,,		1888
Goethe	.	.	.	.	47 ,,		1888–9
Spanisches Liederbuch	.	.	.	34 ,,		1889–90
Keller: *Alte Weisen*	.	.	.	6 ,,		1890
Italienisches Liederbuch. Part I	.	{ 7	(Sept.–Nov.)	1890
				{ 15		(Dec.)	1891
,, ,, Part II	.	22	(Mar.–Apr.)	1896
Michelangelo Sonnets	.	.	.	3		(Mar.)	1897

Moved by Wolf's words quoted at the beginning of this article about the Italian songs, I propose to reverse the orthodox procedure and to consider them first although they were almost the last to be composed. If they are, as he thought, the best, the sooner we make acquaintance with them the better.

We plunge, then, into the Italian Collection. Wolf was referring, I believe, to Part I, but his words may be applied with equal, or even greater truth, to Part II. There are some who say, and others who are ready to believe, that they can trace the signs of the coming trouble to Wolf's brain in these songs. No heed need be paid to them. His brain was never clearer.

Taking the two parts together we find 44 songs, 22 in each, and are at once struck by the fact that only 7 extend

beyond two pages. It looks as if Wolf had come to prize
most of all his gifts the power to compress a wealth of
meaning into a very small space. Though it is exhibited
in notable songs in all his collections, in the one before us
it is the salient feature. At the same time his style has
become simpler and more serenely beautiful than ever
before. This is more markedly the case in Part II, and
may be regarded as a fruitful result of the experience
gained during the preceding year, which was given up to
the composition of his opera *Corregidor*. The songs mentioned in the following paragraph have been chosen, for
the most part, in order to illustrate these points.[1] But
we must first pause for a moment over *Auch kleine Dinge*
(which appeared as No. 1 in the original edition), an exquisitely finished gem in praise of small things and their
power to enchant us: a string of pearls, the fruit of the
olive, and a little rose—'see how small it is and yet how
sweet it smells'. Wolf gives only five bars to his rose, yet,
touched as by a magic wand, it is fragrant still, more than
Schubert's ('Die Rose') which Joachim loved, or sentimental
Spohr's which 'softly bloomed', or even Schumann's, pale
and drooping from the heat ('Meine Rose'). Those who
know *Auch kleine Dinge* will agree that no volume of short
songs could have a more perfect dedication.

Let us start now by linking together two songs, *Und
steht Ihr früh am Morgen auf* (No. 34) and *Gesegnet sei das
Grün* (No. 39), as similar in style and representing Wolf in
his most gracious and melodious mood. In the first we
have a charming picture, seen through a lover's eyes, of a
beautiful girl going to Mass in the early morning. He tells
her that, when she rises from her bed, she frightens the
clouds away and draws the sun to the hills; that angels
haste to bring her shoes and clothes; as she enters the
church, its lamps are lit from her eyes (bells which have
been ringing joyously now cease). She takes the holy

[1] The numbers attached to the songs quoted will show to which
part each belongs; 1–22 indicate Part I, 23–44 Part II.

water, makes the sign of the cross (simple church-like chords suggest the organ, while the voice, until now half-melodious, half-declamatory, drops to mere chanting). She kneels to pray (new music here); the lover exclaims 'Oh, how gracious, how blest thou art! Beauty's crown is thine alone' (the bells are ringing again, stopping for two bars as the last words are sung to a singularly simple but melting phrase). Those who like this song will like *Gesegnet sei das Grün* quite as much. The theme is simple enough, just a girl who means to make herself a green dress, because her lover is dressed in green, because everything looks well in green, because all beautiful fruits ripen from green. As a rule Wolf avoided verses and sentiments like these, choosing those which appealed directly to his dramatic instincts; yet here are two of his loveliest pages, ending with a cadence and a closing symphony of arresting beauty and significance—features which distinguish a great many of these Italian songs. *Sterb' ich, so hüllt in Blumen meine Glieder* (No. 33) (composed on the same day as the last song) provides a perfect example of Wolf's power to produce the deepest impression by the simplest possible means. Just one little phrase, as innocent as though it came from a nursery rhyme, repeated throughout (slightly varied in the second part) over a throbbing syncopated rhythm on a tonic pedal played in bare octaves without variation. An atmosphere of utter peace, tenderness, and beauty pervades this song from beginning to end. It is easy to be misled by the transparent simplicity of *Was für ein Lied soll dir gesungen werden?* (No. 23), a song which belongs to quite a different type, and to pass it over without discovering its worth. It was the last of the Italian songs to be composed. By its side may be placed *Wenn du, mein Liebster, steigst zum Himmel auf* (No. 36), which is in the same style, but far more elaborate and very richly harmonized. The close, at the words 'In Paradies umglänzt von Himmelsfunken', gloriously describes the situation and leads to a fittingly triumphant symphony. Simple in form but full of little subtleties is *Wie viele Zeit verlor ich* (No. 37), in which half-humorously, half-seriously a poor fellow deeply in love complains that he has trifled away so much of his time in loving as to have lost his chance of a seat in Paradise. The subtle discordances in the music are delicious. One more song, of only a page, should certainly not be overlooked, *Heut' Nacht erhob ich mich* (No. 41). It is not quite obvious and may perhaps say little to those who have not tried to sing it; those who have will feel the exquisite delicacy, with which Wolf has touched a very tender lyric.

In the rest of this volume and in the greater part of Part I we have a series of short, highly finished, vivid pictures in which men and women live for a minute before us, one by one, at some dramatic crisis of their lives, lovers for the most part, and in many moods, ecstatic, miserable, angry, jealous, scornful, quarrelling and making quarrels up, serenading and being serenaded, and so forth. Wolf's work in fact is nearly always objective; he had a healthy dislike for the *Ich-poeten*, who use their art in order to exhibit to the world the secrets of their own hearts: he preferred to explore the hearts of others, like Browning in his *Dramatic Lyrics*. Here are some outstanding examples of his powers in this wide field.

Wie soll ich fröhlich sein (No. 31). 'How can I be happy and laugh', cries a heart-broken woman to her lover, 'when you are always cross, and come to see me once in a hundred years? Why come, if it is out of duty? Give me back my heart and go your way. Your folk dislike me. Go and live with them in peace at home. What must be, must.' That there is no real resignation here, the last bitter cry and the crashing discords of the closing symphony make very clear. In *Was soll der Zorn* (No. 32) a woman is portrayed whose passionate heart is consumed with conflicting feelings, horror, reproach, injured innocence, and love. She will die rather than live under her lover's unjust anger and suspicion. 'Take a knife and stab me; if that fails, a sword; if the sword fails, a dagger, and wash away my agony with my blood.' We meet Wolf often in quiet, gracious, or exalted moods; here he strikes hard, every phrase is a thrust that tells, but how tenderly he takes charge of the moving words 'ich bin mir keiner Sünde ja bewusst'! As finely conceived is *Wer rief ich denn* (No. 6), in which another angry woman upbraids her lover with biting scorn: 'Who called you? Who sent you here, if it irks you so? Go back to the girl you love more than me! Go where all your thoughts and feelings are.' But she cannot quite conceal her love; it peeps through here and there. This is no monologue; the faithless one is here, though he cannot speak. Perhaps it is as well, in this case as in the next, *Nein, junger Herr* (No. 7), in which a scapegrace lover is warned, in plain but halfplayful words, that it is not manners to find her company good enough for weekdays and to look for some one else on Sundays. We lose our heart to this girl as she sings her enchanting little tune, which knows how to adapt itself to every change of meaning in the words.

From these dramatic masterpieces we turn to a serenade which has its drama too: *Mein Liebster singt* (No. 20). To the sound of her lover's lute, below her window, playing the fragment of an air that Chopin might have penned, a girl is weeping her heart out in 'tears of blood' while her mother sleeps in bed beside her—a double atmosphere such as Wolf loved. The independence of the voice-part is characteristic. Turn now to No. 44, *O wüsstest du*, and find an equally entrancing serenade, but here the typical serenader sings to his 'falsche Renegatin' of what he has endured for her sake outside in the rain and storm.

Of thirty songs in this collection which I marked as important, the following remain, *Wohl kenn' ich euren Stand* (No. 29); *Du sagst mir, dass ich keine Fürstin sei* (delightfully humorous) (No. 28); *Man sagt mir, deine Mutter wollt' es nicht* (No. 21), quite worthy to join the group of dramatic songs we have left; *Wir haben beide lange Zeit geschwiegen* (No. 19), in which angels from Heaven

bring peace after war to quarrelsome lovers, and a very
seraphic and lovely peace it is; *Nun lass uns Frieden
schliessen* (No. 8), another song on the same subject, with
the lilt of a barcarolle, very finely wrought, in a style for
which in Wolf the only parallel I recall is *Als ich auf dem
Euphrat schiffte* (Goethe, No. 41), *Gesegnet sei* (No. 4);
Und willst du deinen Liebsten sterben sehen (No. 17), a song
of ecstasy; *Der Mond hat eine schwere Klag' erhoben* (No. 7),
of which Mr. Ernest Newman wrote: 'With a mere handful
of notes Wolf manages to say the most gravely beautiful
things, while in the final couple of bars, the music attains
a poignancy of which we would hardly suspect so simple
a phrase to be capable'; *Heb' auf dein blondes Haupt* (No.
18), with its unforgettable final sentence 'dich allein liebt
mein Seele', in which the music seems to enfold the words
as with a lingering caress; two gay songs, *Ein Ständchen
Euch zu bringen* (No. 22) and *Ihr jungen Leute* (No. 16), in
which to the beating of a little drum a girl tells the soldiers
to look after her boy-sweetheart; he has never been to the
wars before, and mustn't sleep in the open air, exposed to
the moon; it would frighten him to death, he's not
accustomed to it; *Dass doch gemalt* (No. 9), with its
beautiful cadence, and lastly, among the humorous songs,
Mein Liebster ist so klein (No. 15), *Mein Liebster hat zum
Tische mich geladen* (No. 25), *Schweig' einmal still* (No. 43),
with a donkey's hee-haw at the end, and *Du denkst mit
einem Fädchen mich zu fangen* (No. 10).

The reader will gather from this long list how varied are
the subjects Wolf chooses and how difficult it is in consequence to summarize his work. He has almost as many
styles as subjects at his command, and these remarks apply
not to the Italian Collection alone but to all. I will leave
it with one reflection, which must be shared by many,
that we have been in an atmosphere which is quite new,
quite different from any which we have associated hitherto
with the German Lied; that Wolf has in these songs shaken
off all the purely German Romantic influences, especially

the powerful influence of Wagner, and exhibits to us not a Wolf who is trying, as it were, to be Italian (speaking for myself I can find little or nothing recognizable as Italian) but a Wolf who has most truly found himself.

This seems a suitable place for some remarks upon a feature in his work to which all who are interested in it are bound to give some thought. For a considerable number of his songs (as will already have been seen) he found that it served his purpose best to build the form upon a single representative or characteristic phrase. He applied, in fact, to song Wagner's principle of the *Leitmotiv*. But more is required of a phrase in which the atmosphere and contents of a whole poem are summed up, than of one which serves as a kind of label attached to a person, an object, or an incident in a drama.

The success of Wolf's scheme depends upon the composer's power to conceive the fitting phrase and then to manipulate it, so that it responds to all the emotional, pictorial, or other suggestions in the poem set. In other words it must be both plastic and expressive. It must also be of sufficient value as music to bear a good deal of repetition. In spite of what can be done by variation in its form, by harmonic changes, by combination with other figures, by using a part of it as a figure by itself, and by modulation or transposition into different keys, it is obviously better suited to songs of small than of large dimensions, for there is a limit to the amount of repetition which a musical phrase can bear. Frequent transposition is a distinct source of danger; if it occurs once too often it becomes suspect as a device or a mannerism, and the spell is broken. On the other hand, the scheme secures unity of design as well as continuity of atmosphere or mood. How far its obvious dangers are avoided every one must decide for himself in each case as it occurs, bearing in mind that in song, as in all music, it is not the form that matters, but the use the composer makes of it. The fact that formal melody is discarded in favour of a declamatory voice-part, which may or may not be melodious, is after all but the modern development, in a small and compact form, of the 'accompanied' recitatives, which are by no means the least interesting feature in the operas and oratorios of the seventeenth and eighteenth centuries. It is, of course, in our day immediately derived from Wagner's music-dramas, and to some extent, as we have seen already, from the songs of Schumann.

*   *   *   *   *   *

Tracing our steps backwards we may pass over the six Keller songs as disappointing and come to the *Spanisches Liederspiel*. This contains thirty-four settings of popular folk-songs, translated into German by Heyse in collaboration with Geibel. Here we breathe an atmosphere widely different from that which we have left behind. It is charged with heavy storms; dark clouds oppress the spirit, and, when the sun shines, it beats with an intenser heat upon a stern, sombre, and passionate race. The change is felt at once in the ten religious songs which form the first volume.[1] It has been well said of them that, 'unlike most German composers Wolf has the power to invest poetry with a piety which hurts and consoles at the same time. There is nothing domestically comfortable about his mysticism' (*Manchester Guardian*). Indeed, some of these songs could be described as terrible in their intensity; *Mühvoll komm' ich und beladen* (No. 7), for instance, in which is depicted the overburdened soul of a woman pleading with hot tears of repentance for the removal of its guilty stains. Wolf does not hesitate to hammer in the effect of the powerful and expressive phrase which dominates the song by remorseless repetition, even to the extent of four or five times in succession. It becomes almost unbearable, as Wolf perhaps intended, the realistic expression of a grief too heavy to be borne, of a soul from which all but one overpowering feeling is excluded. There is no relief. On similar lines is *Nun bin ich dein* (No. 1). Both

----

[1] The references are to the Peters edition.

songs are fully, indeed heavily, harmonized and abound
in poignant discords meant to give pain. They seem to
me to be studies in religious feeling that is worked up to
an abnormal pitch, rather than songs intended to be performed. To a less extent the same may be said of *Wunden
trägst du* (No. 10), for here the tension is relieved by
greater variety in the music, caused by the presence of
two speakers, a woman and her Saviour. Attention may
be called to the singularly expressive passage at the words
'Herr, wer wagt es' and to the changes in the voice part,
when it is repeated in the second and third verses, in accordance with the meaning of the text, and, I may add,
with Wolf's habitual practice in similar cases. If, in spite
of this, we feel that the danger which lurks in much repetition is only partly overcome, this is not true of *Herr, was
trägt* (No. 9), the most impressive and beautiful song in
the volume. It is quite short—only two pages. Again there
are two speakers, a troubled woman and her Saviour; three
questions and three replies; each, as in the last song, with
its own contrasting music, deeply expressive, on the one
side, of anguish rising to agony at the last, and, on the
other, of dignity, pity, and resignation. Here is the strange
little poem. 'What does this ground bear, washed with thy
bitter tears?' 'Thorns, dear heart, for me, sweet flowers
for thee.' 'From such streams will a garden bloom?' 'Yes!
men are binding wreaths therefrom.' 'Whose brow, Lord!
are the wreaths for? Speak!' 'Those of thorns they bind
for me, those of flowers I give to thee.' There is ineffable
beauty in the strange but simple music of these last words
(in answer to 'Speak!'—sung to a note none but Wolf
would have thought of). And the three chords after the
voice has ceased—how direct, how inimitable, how convincingly right they are!

Four songs in this volume are Christmas songs, and in
three of them, Nos. 3, 5, and 6, the musical characteristic
is moving thirds. The same feature will meet us again in
Zum neuen Jahr (Mörike), but nowhere else, I think, in

Wolf. The most attractive of them is *Nun wandre, Maria*, in which Joseph is found encouraging Mary on the weary journey to Bethlehem. 'It is almost over, the cocks are crowing, shelter is near.' The thirds in the right hand never cease their quiet motion, a little up, a little down, while the bass maintains a slow jogging rhythm of its own, to become even at the close of each verse as the travellers come to rest, a true Wolfian touch. *Die ihr schwebet um diese Palmen* (No. 4) is not what it looks like at first, a charming lullaby sung by Mary over her sleeping child to the ceaseless rustling of the wind (or angels' wings?) in the palm-trees. Were it so, Wolf would have given her a more grateful part to sing, instead of the detached and anxious phrases in which she prays that the cold winds may cease to shake the tree tops, for 'My babe is asleep, so tired and with so great a burden of sorrow to bear.' Without this contrast between the voice and the instrumental accompaniment the song, which has little musical variety, would be seriously jeopardized by its length—eight pages—unless we concede to the lullaby, by virtue of its function, the right to be monotonous.

The second and third volumes are full of good songs. A special charm attaches to many of them through the repetition at the end of each verse of a line or a couplet as a kind of refrain. Sometimes it stands also as the first line of the poem as though to proclaim at once its mood and character. Naturally Wolf, a master in musical characterization, has entered with zest into the opportunities thus offered. His refrains never miss fire. Who can hear *In den Schatten meiner Locken* (No. 2) without being haunted for many a day, by its 'Weck' ich ihn nun auf? Ach nein!' or *Seltsam ist Juanas Weise* (No. 3) without the same result from its '"Morgen" spricht sie leise'? To this refrain added piquancy is given at its second and third appearances, for though it keeps its own key of G minor it drops into it deliciously each time from a different chord and key. Both *Auf dem grünen Balkon* (No. 5) and

Wenn du zu den Blumen gehst (No. 6) exhibit Wolf in his most genial and melodious mood. Among his lighter songs none rank higher. In the next, *Wer sein holdes Lieb verloren* (No. 7), he is again at his best, in a vein which always makes him happy, half in fun, half in earnest. A poor lover torments himself in plaintively pathetic tones for having lost his sweetheart. How could he have been so shy or so stupid as not to respond to her very overt advances? He wishes he had never been born.

But of all the songs with refrains none is stronger or more impressive than *Eide, so die Liebe schwur, schwache Bürgen sind sie nur* (No. 10). This opening couplet itself forms the refrain, and is not easily forgotten. The song pulsates in every bar with the cutting accents of derisive scorn for the treachery of lovers' vows. In *Herz verzage nicht geschwind, weil die Weiber Weiber sind* (No. 11) the last hemistich constitutes the refrain. There is a fine irony in this song too, but touched with humour, especially in the refrain at its second entry. Next I will group together *Klinge, klinge, mein pandero* (No. 1) and *Mögen alle bösen Zungen* (No. 13), two songs somewhat similar in their surroundings but dissimilar in mood. Together they afford striking proofs of Wolf's dramatic sincerity and musical versatility. In each we seem to be present at the scene and to understand the central figure of the drama. In the one a girl is playing on her pandero (or lute) a delicious dance for other people to dance to, though her heart is breaking and her thoughts far away. In the other a girl of different stamp, to a lilt of a gayer tune, snaps her fingers as she dances at the malicious tongues of the scandal-mongers, while she sings 'Wer mich liebt, den lieb' ich wieder, und ich lieb' und bin geliebt', and the tongues chatter all the more.

I find much beauty of Wolf's peculiar kind, when he is in a chromatic mood, in *Dereinst, dereinst, Gedanke mein* (No. 22) and *Bedeckt mich mit Blumen* (No. 26), but I have not succeeded so far in finding it in the chromatic

dreariness of *Tief im Herzen trag' ich Pein*, though it is
evidently a song which he felt with his usual intensity,
nor, in spite of very beautiful moments, in *Komm! O Tod*
(No. 24). It is so nearly one of Wolf's masterpieces, but
seems just to fail, perhaps because of its length, perhaps
because the middle section, though the *tempo* quickens,
presents inadequate relief in style to the music of the opening section, which is repeated unchanged in the third and
last. One little rhythmic figure continues from beginning
to end. *Und schläfst du, mein Mädchen* (No. 27) may be
described as jolly; under its pounding and relentless
rhythm no maid could fail to respond to the serenader's
call. In thirty-seven bars one phrase is repeated no less
than seventeen times, in one passage nine times in succession! No one can say that Wolf was not a daring composer.

Let me close with *Alle gingen, Herz, zur Ruh* (No. 21), the
words of which inspired Wolf, as they had already inspired
Schumann (in the duet for soprano and tenor in his
Spanisches Liederspiel), to a song of incomparable beauty.
In Wolf's setting unity of mood is preserved by a
ceaseless throbbing rhythm ♪♪♪ ♩ ♪♪ ♪♪♪ ♩ ♪♪ introduced in a bar of opening symphony, as a single bass
note on the dominant. It is treated now as a middle
part above the bass, now in octaves as the upper part (at
the words 'denn der hoffnungslose Kummer'), against contrasting and clashing octaves in the bass; finally, as the
song nears its climax, at the words 'Und dein Sinnen
schweift in stumme Sorge', there is an outwardly slight but
inwardly momentous change in its movement ♪♪♪ ♩ ♪♪♪
♪♪♪ ♩ ♪♪♪; at the same time the bare octaves give place
to harmonies which increase in richness, significance, and
beauty, till at the words 'Seiner Liebe zu' the climax itself
is reached in one of the most moving passages which Wolf
ever wrote. With the repetition of these words the music

sinks quietly to its perfect cadence; to be followed by four bars of instrumental symphony, in which the opening of the song is most fitly recalled.

*   *   *   *   *

When Wolf published his *Goethe-Lieder* he must have been fully aware that, if they attracted attention, the result for him would be either fame for successful daring or ridicule for presumptuous failure. For among the lyrics which he had chosen were many which the greatest song-composers of the past had made familiar to every lover of music in Germany.

Of all Goethe's lyrics few are better known or present greater difficulties to composers than those which he has attached to the characters of the Harper and Mignon in *Wilhelm Meister*. They are not only among the poetic masterpieces of the world for their literary style and beauty; they are conspicuous also as the noble expressions of strong human emotions. It is worth while to try to understand them before we come to Wolf's settings. The Harper was an oldish man of good birth and education who through a terrible tragedy in his life had nearly lost his reason. To escape from his old surroundings he had adopted the lonely life of a vagrant minstrel, relying on his musical gifts for the supply of his few wants. Mignon had been kidnapped in early childhood by a troupe of itinerant acrobats and taken away from her Italian home. Wilhelm, who succeeded in getting her away from these people, took her to be twelve or thirteen years old. She is throughout the story alluded to frequently as 'the child' or 'one of the children'. Her soul was filled by a burning desire to be brought back to her home in the warm south; to this was added a childlike devotion to Wilhelm as to a beloved father and protector, who would one day fulfil her desire.

The effect upon us of these lyrics, apart from the tragedies behind them, is the more poignant by reason of the restrained and simple language in which they are couched. They seem, too, to drop so naturally into their surroundings that we experience little difficulty in associating them intimately with the persons from whose lips they fall. For all that, Goethe is careful, in the case of more than one song, to let us know that the form in which we have the poem was really Wilhelm's work, after he had heard them sung. This, and other points which surround these famous songs and help us to understand them, will be found in the following extracts from the novel itself:

'Wilhelm was ascending the stairs of an old inn, in a garret of which the Harper had found a lodging, when the sweet tones of a harp met his ears. They were heart-moving, plaintive sounds, accompanied by a mournful, piteous voice . . . a few stanzas, partly sung, partly recited were often repeated and Wilhelm succeeded after listening carefully for a while in making out more or less what follows: *Wer nie sein Brod mit Thränen ass.* Often the old man seemed unable to continue for weeping and only the harp was heard, then the voice joined in again softly in broken tones.'

The second song, *Wer sich der Einsamkeit ergiebt*, was in answer to Wilhelm's request that he should sing again.

The third song, *An die Thüre will ich schleichen*, was overheard by Wilhelm on another occasion:

'He recognised the Harper by its mournful sound, and caught the words without difficulty; they told of the consolations of an unhappy man, who felt that he was on the borders of insanity. Unfortunately Wilhelm could only remember the last stanza.'

With regard to Mignon's *Kennst du das Land*, Wilhelm,

'hearing the tones of a cithern and Mignon's voice, opened his door and asked the child to come in. She then sang him the song in question. Wilhelm was delighted with the expressive melody, but could not understand all the words, which were in Italian, till Mignon repeated and explained them, stanza by stanza. Wilhelm wrote them down and translated them into German; but the childlike innocence of expression vanished as Wilhelm proceeded to put its broken phraseology into order and combine its disjointed parts. The melody had a charm of its own, which was unique.'

Then the child's singing is described:

'She began every verse in a stately and solemn manner, as if she would call attention to something wonderful, as if she had something weighty to declare. In the third line her tones became more hushed and gloomy; "Kennst du es wohl?" was uttered with an air of mystery and deliberation; in "dahin! dahin!" lay an unconquerable yearning; the words "Lass uns ziehn!" she was able so to modify at each repetition that its effect was now urgent in pleading, now forceful in persuasion.'

Her third song, *Heiss mich nicht reden*, occurs some time —months perhaps—later, when Wilhelm was about to depart on a journey. She had asked for the gift of a pearl necklace, which he possessed; as 'he could not refuse to gratify the dear little creature, he gave it her. At the moment of departure she pressed a warm and cordial, though not a tender, kiss upon his lips, as she prayed him to return.' Then is subjoined by the author 'by way of close a little poem, which Mignon had recited once or twice with great expressiveness and which the hurry of so many occurrences had prevented him from inserting before'. How matter-of-fact it all sounds!

The song, *So lasst mich scheinen*, comes a good deal later in the story, and is part of a scene in which Mignon arrayed in a snow-white dress and a pair of golden wings, with a lily in one hand and a basket in the other, brings gifts for two good little twin sisters on their birthday. She took her cithern, seated herself on a high writing-table, and 'sang a little song with touching grace'.

In the case of *Nur wer die Sehnsucht kennt* we read that Wilhelm had 'fallen into a dreamy longing, and as if in harmony with his feelings came the song which just at that time Mignon and the Harper began to sing with much feeling as an informal duet'.

Wolf's treatment of the Harper's songs is undoubtedly of great interest and has received the most enthusiastic praise from some critics, among them Mr. Ernest Newman, who cites them 'as instances of Wolf's literary penetration into the very heart of his poets', adding that 'every critic of discernment has noted the veritably pathological quality, which no other composer has managed to get; over them hangs the cloud of morbidity, the mental gloom of the Harper as Goethe has depicted him'. This is quite true, but it is not the whole truth. The dignity of the man and the respect he inspired are also essential features of his portraiture. No morbidity, no unmanly tears afflict us in the poems. In them the tragic figure emerges as it were sublimated and purified; in the crucible of Goethe's poetry the dross has fallen away. Goethe ennobled the Harper in his verse, as Shakespeare ennobled King Lear. We can contemplate the victims of this grim tragedy as we contemplate King Lear, but not in revolt, not with loathing or depression, but purified, reconciled, uplifted.

Here is music's opportunity. On a small scale a similar one confronted Purcell, and found him equal to it, when he composed his wonderful 'Mad Bess'. Can we say the same of Wolf and the Harper lyrics? If we cannot, the words of Mr. Newman which I have quoted supply the reason.

Pathology and music are dangerous companions, and have proved to be so here, even to some of Wolf's admirers. One of them, a German critic, has written with blunt truth: 'Er [the Harper] steigert sich immer mehr in eine unangenehme Thränenseligkeit.'[1] We have, in fact, in these songs an atmosphere of emotional realism, in which we breathe with difficulty and discomfort; something within us says that it is not right. Goethe, I have heard or read, never wrote his poems while under the sway of the emotion which inspired him. He waited till he was again master of his soul. He has been called the physician of his age. He diagnosed its ills, but was careful to avoid contagion.

It is strange that Wolf, who has presented a realistic picture of the half-crazy harper, seems in *Kennst du das*

[1] i.e. 'He, the Harper, indulges with less and less restraint in the luxury of tears—an unpleasant exhibition.'

Land to have forgotten that Mignon was but a child, singing what can only have been a simple melody, through
which with her beautiful voice and her sensitive southern
temperament she was able to express all that was in her
heart. I cannot associate with her the elaborate and rhapsodical music which Wolf has composed for this poem. Its
atmosphere of luxuriant emotion and cloying sweetness is
not made more acceptable by reminding us of the second
act of *Tristan*. Mignon, it is true, was a precocious child
and emotional beyond her years, but here we have a
Mignon who is frankly impossible: she is not in keeping
with the exquisite and classical beauty of Goethe's poem.
The concluding phrase of her song would be sufficient
itself to bear witness that in this song we have neither
Mignon nor Goethe. Goethe's perfect lyric is still waiting
for its perfect setting. *Nur wer die Sehnsucht kennt*, with
its weary descending chromatics and its persistent reiteration of phrase, is acutely expressive of a heart that is very
sad and has only room for one feeling. The bare octaves
in the right hand, mostly in unison with the voice, continue
throughout the song and enhance its intentional dreariness;
but it is not till the four bars of concluding symphony are
reached that they give place to harmony, with moving
effect. A strange song, which persists in haunting the
memory, whether one likes it or not.

In *So lasst mich scheinen* we have at last the real Wolf.
Before the radiance of this wonderful song, so pure, so
tender, so intense, one neither thinks nor cares whether it
is Goethe or Mignon, nor anything else but just itself. If
the reader will look at the music of the two concluding bars
in each strophe, he will see the extraordinary difference
made by the alteration in the second strophe of a single
note (E♭ to E♮). The surprising effect of the sudden octave-
leap at the conclusion of the cadence (to the dominant of
the original key) is not likely to be missed. The cadence is
unique.

Heiss mich nicht reden, in spite of some phrases that are

both beautiful and touching, especially in the second verse, at the words 'dort kann die Brust in Klagen sich ergiessen', is not convincing; while the final phrase sinks to bathos and a touch of melodrama.

As to the other songs in this group, there is good fooling in the *Spottlied* and a delightful freshness and vivacity in *Singet nicht in Trauertönen*—the song of naughty Philine, who was a member of Wilhelm's theatrical company. In the ballad *Was hör' ich draussen vor dem Thor* we find the old harper forgetting his trouble in the exercise of his art.

The ballads—there are several scattered among his songs —are not the best Wolf. He seems to have relished them as a release from more serious work, and to have let his fancy run riot in a profusion of pictorial illustration, in which no touch escapes his sharp and vigilant eye. Clever, brilliant, and effective they certainly are, but these are not words which rise to the lips in attempting to describe the best kind of music. Indeed, with the ballad in question Wolf was not himself satisfied and thought of removing it from this collection. It seems to be the fact that of all types of song the ballad is the one in which perfect success is hardest to attain. Can we name off-hand even half a dozen that are completely satisfying? The truth is that music is least satisfying when it is most pictorial. Perhaps we have not yet travelled far enough away from the old days, when rich and poor, noble and peasant delighted in nothing so much as a minstrel with good tales to tell and good tunes to sing them to. If a ballad had twelve or twenty verses, they liked it all the better for that. The art of story-telling was then with the minstrel and his melody, helped perhaps by the unpretentious tinkling of lute or harp. The modern singer has every syllable of his declamation carefully arranged for him, while a pianist on a grand piano is equally responsible with himself for the interpretation, for the instrument providing what may be described as a running commentary upon the words.

I have always considered Grieg's *Es war ein alte König*

a model ballad and the best corrective possible, shall we say, to Liszt's *Lorelei*. I am plainly the wrong person to deal with Wolf in this department of his work, so will leave it to others.

If Wolf was overweighted by the problems involved in some of the Wilhelm Meister lyrics, he rose to the height of Goethe's three great poems, *Prometheus, Ganymed*, and *Grenzen der Menschheit* with triumphant ease, and with an entirely different style for each. Nowhere has he given more striking examples of his dramatic and imaginative powers; in the multitude of detail he never loses hold of the main conception, of which the speaker in each song is the impersonation. In the first stands the great figure of the Titan in revolt against Zeus, hurling his taunts, defiance, and denunciation amidst the crashing of thunderbolts. Though the poem is in the form of a monologue, the presence is felt throughout in Wolf's powerful music of a very angry Deity, who is not given a chance of speaking. Only a baritone singer with a voice of exceptional strength and range and declamatory powers of the highest order can do full justice to this great song. On the instrumental side, it demands more than a piano can adequately represent. Wolf accordingly scored it, along with more than a dozen of his other songs, for orchestra. It is, in fact, more in the nature of an operatic scena than a Lied.

In *Ganymed* a very different scene is presented. Intoxicated with the endless beauty of the flowers, the grass, the nightingale's song, Ganymed hears the voice of Spring answering to his love; he cries enraptured 'I come, I come'; the clouds bend to receive him, and he is borne aloft to the bosom of the everloving Father.

Wolf puts us at once into the atmosphere of this fine poem by a gracefully falling and rising diatonic figure, suggestive of a violin, which moves in quavers over the regular beat of the common chord in crochets. This is transplanted, unchanged and without modulation, from the original D major into F♯ major and then B♭—an upward key procession by thirds dear to Wolf, as those need not be told who know *In der Frühe* (No. 24 of the *Mörike-Lieder*). Development of this material completes the first part; in the second syncopation is a salient contrasting feature; the third consists of a repetition of the first, with some important elaboration, beginning and (after an emotional climax at the words *Mir, mir in eurem Schosse*) ending in quiet ecstasy. Within this simple form a wealth of beauty is enshrined.

In *Grenzen der Menschheit* man, reconciled to his fate, eschews soaring ambition. With childlike awe and trust he kisses the hem of the garment of the Everlasting Father. Man should not measure himself with Gods, but keep his feet planted on the solid earth. He is mortal, they are eternal; from them issues an endless stream, wave upon wave, which lifts up and then devours. Each generation is but a link in the chain of man's endless existence.

In Wolf's music the solemn and mysterious chords with which it opens, the more solemn and more mysterious chords with which it closes, and in the middle the stubborn Handelian strength of the slow march in contrast with the fateful rhythm of the irresistibly advancing waves— these, and other points, all combine to make this the most impressive song of a remarkable group. It is *durchcomponiert* on Schubertian lines.

Here they stand, in poetry and in Wolf's music, these three great impersonations: the Rebel, chained to earth, because he hates heaven; the Dreamer, or the Poet, wafted to heaven, because he has no foothold on the earth; the Philosopher accepting the earth, because the Gods have placed him there, but brooding over his fate.

Goethe's *Westöstliche Divan* was founded upon a collection of poems by Hafiz, a Persian poet, of which a German translation had been made. Goethe's work was published in his seventy-first year; as its title indicates, it was Eastern thought interpreted by a Western mind. Each of the twelve parts into which it is divided was named

according to subject—the Singer, the Wine-house, Hafiz,
Love, Zuleika, Parables, and others. Ten of Wolf's songs
were taken from Zuleika, of which *Als ich auf dem Euphrat
schiffte* with its barcarolle accompaniment, is very happily
inspired. *Wie sollt' ich heiter bleiben* and *Wenn ich dein
gedenke* are, if not Wolf at his best, good enough to make
us wonder why he admitted *Komm, Liebchen, komm*. But
how thankful we all should be that he thought of adding
music to a poem from 'The Singer' that seems to call for
it so little!—*Phaenomen*. It requires a word of explanation.
Though Goethe when he wrote it was a septuagenarian,
his heart, as we learn from his biographers, was still inflam-
mable. This helps us to understand the curious inference
drawn in the little poem from the phenomenon of two bows
to be seen in the sky, 'the one brightly coloured, the other
white in the mist, but both heaven's bows'; to which the
poet adds,

> So sollst du, munter Greis, dich nicht betrüben,
> Sind gleich die Haare weiss, doch willst du lieben.

Not perhaps one of the poet's profoundest philosophical
reflections, but certainly a personal experience. No one
but Wolf would have dreamed of setting so strange a mood
to music or found for it such bewitching and mysterious
strains. They do not surrender their secret at once. It is
easy to play the music through, miss it, and pass on, having
also missed the warning 'Very slow'.

In the third volume are many good things. *Genialisches
Treiben* is great fun; the sage that speaks describes
himself, to a realistic accompaniment, as rolling his tub
along like St. Diogenes, 'sometimes in earnest, sometimes
in jest, now it is love and now it is hate, now it is this,
now it is that, now it is nothing and now it is much'.

Blumengruss, of which the piano part recalls, no doubt
intentionally, Schubert's *Geheimes* (*langsam und innig*
stands as a reminder not on that account to hurry the
tempo) is a page of very charming music, with constantly

varied modulations and a grateful part for the singer. A sprightly soprano should find both *Die Spröde* and *Die Bekehrte* quite to her taste, while *Frühling übers Jahr*, which follows, has a Schubertian flavour with its melody, its graceful rhythm, its satisfying harmonies. But the pearl of the volume is *Anakreons Grab*, which with its atmosphere of exquisite tenderness and quietude has made Wolf as many friends as anything he ever wrote. It is quite short—only two pages—and in the simplest form; of its three parts the first and the last have the same music, except in the last bar, and, as usual, changes in the voice part—but how significant they are! Observe that Wolf's instructions are 'Very slowly and restfully', and that the music never rises beyond *mf* throughout, dropping in the lovely little concluding symphony to *ppp*. No composer is so meticulously careful as Wolf in giving the *tempo*, the gradations of tone, and other details which each of his songs requires. It may be of interest to singers to know that, when he was himself at the piano, he played in very strict time. The same has been told of Schubert, when he played his songs and Vogl sang.

*   *   *   *   *   *

The Eichendorff Collection was mostly composed after four months' holiday which Wolf took in the summer of 1888. He had finished all but ten of the fifty-three Mörike songs, but gave up the month of September to Eichendorff. Seven of this poet's lyrics he had set two years before; he now added thirteen, in which it is not difficult to discern that he had enjoyed his holiday, for most of them deal with the open air and the active side of human life—a side of Eichendorff which had not been explored by musicians. Wolf entered into it with uncommon zest. The gem of the collection is *Der Musikant* (No. 2) which is in a small way as fresh and sparkling as anything in Wolf. It is impossible not to love this droll minstrel, who smiles at the hardships of his roving life and at himself for his love of music, but for which he could easily marry and settle down; but 'what would become of his singing then?' He is much more attractive than *Der Freund* (No. 1), a manly, heroic character, in whose company Wolf is somehow not quite at home, or he would never have penned that pompous last page. In *Das Ständchen* he is himself again in the company of an old minstrel, who on a summer night, with the moon peeping over the roofs between the clouds, hears a student with his lute serenading his sweetheart, and recalls his own youthful days before death took his love away. An interesting and pathetic song with its persistent figure in the bass, a haunting melody above it, and the voice adding a third part between. *Der Soldat I* (No. 5) is a lusty fellow of light morals who canters to a rendezvous in the neighbouring *Schloss*. *Der Soldat II* (No. 6) is introduced at once on a galloping horse; swinging his wild sweetheart up behind him, he snatches a kiss with a 'Quick! quick! quick! For Death's at our heels and he comes apace.' This refrain he sings three times as the song ends, but quietly the last time. Death has caught them up. Two pages of great dramatic force with a rhythm which is terrific. There are two other soldiers, of the boastful, swashbuckler type, *Der Schreckenberger* (No. 8), a soldier of fortune who goes off at the end arm-in-arm, as he says, with the fickle dame to a march, not worth much musically, you think, as you play it through—but wait till you have made the acquaintance of Captain Dreadnought! *Der Glücksritter* (No. 10) makes his exit with the same lady and to the same march in an extended form—not improved thereby. For once Wolf might almost be accused of playing to the gallery. It was immediately preceded— a fortnight before, to be exact—by the exquisite *Verschwiegene Liebe* (No. 3), which is steeped in the magic of a summer night, in harmony with a lover's dreams; it may well be placed beside Schumann's *Mondnacht*, which is high enough praise for any song. So perhaps might *Nachtzauber*, though its elaborately woven texture makes it less easy of access. The music of the two stanzas is substantially the same, but with changes both for voice and instrument which are worth noting, as always with Wolf in similar cases. The moving climax is of irresistible beauty. In the last verse, after the line 'Komm', o komm' zum stillen Grund', the word 'komm' is heard twice again, as the song dies away in almost silent ecstasy. Wolf, it may be observed, had no pedantic scruples about this kind of word-repetition. These Eichendorff volumes have plenty of it.

Seemanns Abschied (No. 17) depicts a blustering, fiery sailor, who describes the unpleasant things in store for the girl who jilts him, and for the lazy soldiers on land, sergeants, cavalry men, and musketeers, while he will be revelling in the glorious dangers of the sea. A marine pendant to the soldiers of fortune. He is provided like them with a noisy march. Wolf is again in high spirits. He relishes too the would-be hero of *Lieber alles* (No. 11) and the mixture of humour and pathos in *Der verzweifelte Liebhaber* (No. 14), with whom, poor fellow, everything has gone wrong, learning is no good, his coat is in rags, his lute won't sound, his girl can't bear him. What a lot of things he would like to do to get rid of it all, and find content at last! As with other songs in this collection, the music is on the lines originated by Schumann, that is, the voice part consists of a series of melodic phrases strung together quite charmingly, but not constituting a formal melody. Wolf, we know, admired Schumann more than Schubert, and in setting Eichendorff it is quite likely that he purposely made no secret of his admiration. I think Schumann would have relished the touch of pedantry and formality which is kept up all through *Der Scholar* (No. 13) by a mournful *continuo* in the old style. More directly in Schumann's vein and style is *Die Nacht* (No. 19), composed eight years earlier (1880) but introduced into the Eichendorff volumes, along with six more of his earlier songs, of which the best are the two *Soldat*s already mentioned, the love-sick, laughing, scornful *Zigeunerin* (No. 7) and the *Waldmädchen* (No. 20), dancing, leaping, and flying, a flame, a roe, a bird, till she skips out of sight.

In this little medley of songs there may not be a great deal of Wolf's finest work, but it represents in the less serious numbers a vein which is decidedly entertaining and spontaneous, and deserves more attention from lovers of Wolf than it has perhaps received.

*   *   *   *   *   *

The Mörike-Lieder to which we have come at last were the first fruits of Wolf's real life as a composer. They represent the largest, in some ways the freshest, and certainly the best known and the most popular of all his collections. There are more songs in it composed on traditional melodic lines, and more that are sure to appeal to the generality of the public that attends vocal recitals. There is the less reason to dwell upon them here. No fresh praise is required for such deserved favourites as *Verborgenheit*, *Der Gärtner*, *Begegnung*, *Das verlassene Mägdlein*, *Ein Stündlein wohl vor Tag*, *Auf eine Wanderung*, *In der Frühe*, and *Er ist's*. I propose therefore to attend chiefly to the interesting group of ten songs which he had still to set when he returned from his summer holiday and the Eichendorff interlude.

The first nine took him only six days, the last, *Auf eine Christblume (II)*, following a fortnight later. Among them are *Der Feuerreiter* the longest, the most thrilling, the most imaginative of all his ballads, which he recast later into the form of a cantata for solo, chorus, and orchestra, and *Gesang Weylas*, unlike in style to any other of Wolf's songs and apparently one of the most popular; but it may be surmised that some at least of its popularity is due to the fact that it is the easiest of them all both to sing and to play, and has besides a vocally irresistible and effective final phrase, with a strong resemblance to the climactic phrase in the deservedly popular *Verborgenheit*.

Two other songs, *Neue Liebe* and *An die Geliebte*, may be grouped alongside the two *Peregrinas*, which were composed earlier, as characteristic of Wolf when he was most under the influence of Wagner, and led by it into that dangerous sweetness which is the snare of Wagnerian chromaticism. Whether we find it acceptable or not, it may be said emphatically that Wolf, however chromatic he may be in these moods, is always characteristically Wolf, not diluted Wagner. It must also be said that he had completely outgrown it when he wrote his Spanish and Italian songs.

The remaining five songs are religious. Of these *Schlafendes Jesuskind* is of such transparent and innocent loveliness as to give it a place beside three of Wolf's earlier and best loved songs in this collection: *Gebet*, *Auf ein altes Bild*, and *Auf eine Christblume* (*I*). *Karwoche* should be with them too, though its beauty is of a different and more elaborate kind, easily recognizable as akin in style to some of the best of the Italian songs, though the hand that drew it was not then quite so sure. In *Zum neuen Jahr* the rhythm, different from that of the words, is felt as hindering their rejoicing swing. Nor is the melody striking enough to compensate for the loss. Neither this song nor *Auf eine Christblume* (*II*), for a different reason, which the reader who turns to it will perceive, is as interesting as the rest of this group, of which only one more remains to be mentioned—*Wo find' ich Trost*, a song composed on a large scale and with much elaboration, foreshadowing the treatment of the same theme, a soul in anguish for its sins, in some of the Spanish songs, but the anguish here melts into blissful rapture and thankfulness, as it contemplates the divine love which 'hing am Kreuz und büsste mein Verschulden bis es in ein Meer von Gnade sank'—a moving passage (with a Lohengrin flavour) which in the stern Spanish songs could scarcely find a place. Wolf's religious songs stand quite alone in German music. The atmosphere which we breathe in them is that of southern Catholicism and the age-long associations which have gathered round it, not that of the Protestantism of the North. They suffer from being scattered among the many volumes of his songs. If they were collected into one volume, the total impression, upon some people at least, would be profound, even overwhelming.

Humorous songs figure in these as in other volumes: *Abschied, Zur Warnung, Selbstgeständnis,* and a ballad, *Storchenbotschaft.* Now in the half-humorous, half-serious touches which flicker over, or permeate, not a few of his songs, Wolf is delicious, but in some of the songs which can be labelled humorous the difficulty, which never troubled Mozart, of being amusing and writing good music at the same time is not quite overcome. Nor do I feel at home in the riotous and tempestuous moods of the drinking songs, or in some of the passionate love songs. Wolf once said of Brahms, forgetting perhaps *Meine Liebe ist grün,* that 'he could not exult'; it is true he could not with Wolf's impetuosity, but with all my admiration for Wolf, it is when he exults most, or at least when he is most exuberant, that I like him least. Again, I must observe that there is none of all this in the Italian songs.

*   *   *   *   *   *

There is so much confusion of thought on the subject of words in song that in an essay upon Wolf, whose individual way of handling words has rightly been eulogized by all his critics, some discussion seems imperative. What we need is a point of view which will guide us safely, whose songs soever we may be examining. It is futile to waste time in picking out examples of so-called false accentuation; they abound in the songs of all the great composers (in Schubert's *Erlkönig* and in Wolf's *Prometheus,* to name two songs at random). I say 'so-called', because it is essential to distinguish false from unusual accentuation. What is false from the point of view of the spoken word, or what looks wrong on paper, may be not only appropriate but stimulating when properly sung. One instance must suffice as typical of many which might be cited. In a collection of German articles on Wolf a writer complains that Schubert

S

in the opening words of *Das Wirthshaus*, 'Auf einem
Todtenacker', has made the poet impress upon us that
there was only one churchyard, not two churchyards, and,
secondly, that he maltreated 'Todtenacker' by accenting
the component part of the compound. (In English it would
mean that we had to sing '*Churchyard*' instead of '*Church*-
yard'.) Now the writer in question probably argued in this
way, either because he saw that each of the offending
syllables falls upon the first beat of the bar and therefore
must have the chief accent (which is by no means always
true), or because in listening to a performance of the song
he was made conscious of the faults which he described.
In that case the fault was committed not by Schubert but
by an incompetent and unintelligent singer. It should be
noted also that *Das Wirthshaus* is marked *sehr langsam*, and
that in this *tempo* the syllabic values of speech are *ipso
facto* changed and in places even obliterated, the short un-
accented syllables assuming equal status with their longer
brethren. It is only when music adopts the same pace as
speech that we can expect anything like a reproduction of
the spoken word. An exact reproduction it can never be,
for the accents of music are more rigorous, more emphatic
than those of speech; and if, as often happens, the musical
rhythm is borrowed from the verses, it maintains a strict-
ness of time which, if transferred back to speech, is felt at
once as preposterous. Again, if the spoken word is taken
as the standard for composers, it follows that all dwelling
upon syllables and all ornamentation, even the simple
appoggiatura, must be ruled out. So the man of theory,
who says that the best songs are those which can be sung
as they are spoken, is forced to include in it the principle
of 'one syllable—one note'. He usually adds, too, 'No
repetition of words'. But we know from George Mere-
dith that 'there is nothing like a theory to make a fool of
a wise man'. The truth may now be stated. Words in
music are not judged by the standards of poetry any more
than words in poetry are judged by the standards of prose.

We talk about poetic licence; we have a right to talk about musical licence too.

It is usually in the name of literature that musical licence receives castigation, some of it, it is true, deserved—when bad phrasing or accentuation makes nonsense of the words —but most of it not, for the reason given above—the failure to distinguish between accents which are false and accents which are unusual. The odd thing is that we are easily moved to wrath by small syllabic disturbances, but accept with equanimity liberties taken with poetry which from a literary standpoint are much more serious and quite as common—the substitution, for instance, of a musical for a poetic rhythm, as in Schubert's *Trockne Blumen* or Wolf's *Zum neuen Jahr*—two parallel cases. More striking are cases where metres are disregarded, which have exceptional literary importance—Sapphics, for instance, in Beethoven's *Adelaïde* and in Brahms's *Sapphische Ode*, or the Asclepiads (dear to those who know Horace's *O fons Bandusiae*) in Brahms's *Mainacht*. In another type of song, usually described as *durchcomponiert*, it is the stanza-form that goes to the wall, as in Liszt's *Lorelei* and hundreds of other songs. We need not pursue the subject farther; enough has been said to justify the statement that we can look for no more than a partial satisfaction of our literary taste when we leave our study arm-chairs for stalls at a vocal recital. Here we listen to poetry with other ears, and for a different kind of gratification. The way is now cleared for the introduction of an illuminating passage about words from a paper on Virgil prepared for the British Academy by Mr. J. W. Mackail:

'It is in the manipulation of speech, as well as in the handling of human life, that Virgil takes rank as a master mind. His sensitiveness to language is unique, more especially the way in which he perpetually, it might almost be said of every line of the *Aeneid*, gives words and phrases a new colour by variation, sometimes obvious, sometimes so delicate as to escape notice, of the normal or classical diction. Language always remains with him a fluid medium, and *he handles words so as to make them different*' (the italics are mine).

We have now to realize that what poetry does for normal speech, or prose, music in its own way does for poetry. It makes it different. It shows us what words might be in a world where men did not speak but sang. Song is just such a world, and we discover that much which is contrary to our use and experience here is there both natural and enchanting; as when, for instance, Wolf leads a word or a syllable on to a higher note when our instincts, musical or literary, expect it to go down! And his busy syncopations —what are they but musical devices (they have no counterpart in speech) employed in order to give a new piquancy, a new value, to words? They are right in the place which Wolf has prepared for them, and we exclaim, 'We have never heard them like that before.'

We are mistaken, then, if we think it is mere verbal felicity, or skilful reproduction in musical notation of the spoken word, that we admire in Wolf. Other musicians with literary tastes can display that power as well as he, and yet produce results as dull as ditch-water. Though music and poetry join hands in song, they do not form a partnership on equal terms, for in a musical composition music must predominate. It is because this is not recognized that so many modern songs are useless. They create the impression that composers are so scrupulously deferential towards the texts of poetry that they cannot, or dare not, write freely in their own beautiful language of music.

This is not true of Wolf. All the songs which have been praised in this essay were chosen in the first instance for their value or their interest as music; but it will appear, I think, that they might equally well have been chosen to illustrate his masterly handling of words, and to emphasize the fact that in this handling the music in which the words are set is the most significant part. If that failed, nothing else would be of any use.

It must be obvious that in all that has been written here

I have thought chiefly of singers as my readers. In what follows I have no others in my mind.

We make a great mistake if we judge Wolf's songs simply by playing them through on the piano, even when the vocal part is included. They must be sung. Wolf, like Schubert, sang much in his boyhood, and in after years, though he had not much voice, he was able to show his friends effectively how he meant his songs to go. He knew then quite well what he was doing in making unusual demands upon the patience and the voices of his singers; but he is always, or nearly always, their friend. They will find, in compensation for their trouble, some intimate secrets, some inward joys, which are reserved for them alone, but this condition is attached—that in every song they should know the poem as well as he knew it himself, and be able, like himself, to read or declaim it to their friends. One can hear him saying to them, before he sang, 'Listen to this; it will explain my music, and my music is worth explaining'. Good singing, even when allied with musical intelligence and a perfect ear, is not enough. With these gifts the singer may surmount with ease all the difficulties in the vocal line—some of Wolf's intervals have been called impossible to sing—yet it may sound wrong. To sound right it must be *felt* right; and the singer who feels them right will often discover that the passages which look worst at first become in the end a sheer joy to sing.

But this is not all. Though a singer needs all that is implied in the terms diction and declamation, and cannot acquire it without prolonged study, he should not feel that he is thereby excused from an equally prolonged and serious study of his own special art; for to declaim well and sing indifferently is a negation of that art, as fatal to a loyal presentation of Wolf's songs as of any one else's. For his vocal line is not a line of declamation added to the instrumental score but part and parcel of his musical scheme; words and music were conceived together in the composer's brain and should be honoured equally.

One thing more. It has already been mentioned that the point of view in the majority of Wolf's songs is dramatic. In them the singer impersonates a character, but there is no stage, and there must be no stage effects. The operatic singer, on the contrary, plays his part in brilliant surroundings and must of necessity be brilliant too, both in voice and in style; he must display his gifts; he must be sure of making his effects. We naturally speak of his work as a performance. The singer of *Lieder* should dislike this word, for he must appear not so much to be performing to an audience as speaking to his friends; he must create something of the atmosphere of a home, though he stands on the platform of a public hall. This is what is meant when the character of the *Lied* is spoken of as 'intimate'. Something of the kind was implied by Joachim when he congratulated a young performer in these words, 'Ah! I see you understand the effect of non-effect.'

Who of us, I would ask in conclusion, that without haste and without prejudice has travelled through the volumes containing Wolf's songs has not been conscious, when he lays them down, of a rare and great experience? What does it matter if he finds him sometimes disappointing, sometimes irritating, sometimes dull, sometimes extravagant? Wolf with his temperament would not have been human if in so large an output it were otherwise. There can be no successes without failures. Surveying his work as a whole, I find in it a beauty that is new and precious, an intense sincerity, a glowing life, a vivid imagination, a desperate determination to depict real people, real passions, real scenes. Very few of his songs can be passed by as merely pretty, or as composed just for the purpose of making music with nothing vital to say. In the bewildering diversity of the subjects which he has treated and of the characters which figure in them, we cannot but marvel at the wide range of his sympathies and his rare knowledge of human nature in its joys and its sorrows, its laughter and its tears, its love and its hate, its strength and its weakness its faith and its despair, its adventures and its peace. He has music for them all, and behind and through this music we feel the beating of a very sensitive and understanding heart. It is this more than his intellectual and literary qualities that makes the great moments of his best songs strike so hard and linger so long in the memory. They bear the stamp which only genius can set upon its work, different in every example, but unmistakable.

Beethoven, Schubert, Brahms, and Wolf have all found their last resting-place in the same cemetery in Vienna.

PRINTED IN
GREAT BRITAIN
AT THE
UNIVERSITY PRESS
OXFORD
BY
JOHN JOHNSON
PRINTER
TO THE
UNIVERSITY